Word of Mouse

THE NEW AGE OF NETWORKED MEDIA

Jim Banister

AGATE

CHICAGO

Printed in Canada.

Library of Congress Cataloging-in-Publication Data

Banister, Jim.
    Word of mouse : the new age of networked media / by Jim Banister.
        p.   cm.
    Includes index.
    ISBN 0-9724562-6-0 (hardcover)
    1. Information society. 2. Digital media—Social aspects. I. Title.

HM851.B36   2004
303.48'33—dc22

                                                            2004009163

10   9   8   7   6   5   4   3   2   1

Agate books are available in bulk at discount prices.
For more information, go to agatepublishing.com

TABLE OF CONTENTS

DEDICATION

For my mom and dad—
cliché, but deserved. You guys rock.

ACKNOWLEDGMENTS—AND A NOTE ON "MEDIA"

Thanks to the many brilliant minds I've worked encountered over the last ten years while straddling the ever-more-blurred line between mainstream media and "new" media. There are many others far too numerous to be exhaustively inclusive, but I must thank a few special folks with whom I've worked, or who have had a significant impact on my efforts when it came to the content or completion of this manuscript: Toby Coppel, Maria Wilhelm, Oliver Eberle, Brad Scherick, Michael Dowling, Jon Medved, Harry Medved, Hassan Miah, Scott Jarus, John Geirland, Peter Clemente, Liz Dubelman, Dr. Leonard Shlain, Greg Thagard, Anthony Stonefield, Shane Dewing, Robert Tercek, Linda Keeler, Lisa Crane, Rob Kenneally, Randy Blotky, Chris Barr, Jim Kinsella, Bob McNeal, Rob Burgess, Steven Koltai, Rich Zahradnik, Lou Dobbs, Scott Teissler, Norman Pearlstine, Bruce Probst, Craig Forman, Eric Pulier, Michael Dunn, Mika Salmi, Thomas Hoegh, Steven McKenna, John Roberts, Lisa Eisenpresser, Tony Rogers, Robert Gonzales, Todd Steinman, Todd Papaioannou, Bill Kovacs, Stephen Roloff, Mark Federman, and Derrick de Kerckhove. Many thanks for sharing your thoughts, insights, and time. I'm quite certain there are others I'm forgetting. I'll have to thank you in person.

I must single out my erstwhile partners-in-crime during my amazing tour of duty at Time Warner: Jim Moloshok and Jeff Weiner. Your intelligent, critical, and fraternal repartee was the white board on which many of the concepts in this book were formed or evolved. And a special nod to Terry Semel, a man of unimpeachable integrity. It's more than likely this book would never have come to fruition were it not for you.

Doug Seibold, president of Agate, you're the hardest-workin' man in the book biz. My gratitude for showing me how to mold raw ideas into enjoyable and educational prose. Also, kudos to the unsinkable Agent Jayne Rockmill. Where you get that pathological optimism is beyond me. There's an infomercial idea in there somewhere.

I'd especially like to thank Lorne Lanning and Drew Henry, perpetually willing sounding boards and great friends. You guys embody the entire spectrum of reasons one might ask the perennial question, "Who ya gonna call?" For solving problems, bouncing around ideas, sharing a river, or celebrating successes, you guys are on the top of the list. I must also give a fond thanks to Mark and Susan Torrance. I cherish those special bits of guidance and affection you've provided, and you have my eternal gratitude for the incredible environment you've created and shared. Those visits helped more than you know.

Finally, I'd like to thank Jim, the Elder, whose steady, humanistic outlook, boundless intelligence, and innate creativity rooted me in a security upon which I found the confidence to take risks; and Sara Lee, the One and Only, whose innate optimism, aesthetic brilliance, cleverness and unwavering love were the lens through which I saw that anything is possible, including this book. And you've given me four wonderful brothers with whom I enthusiastically and gratefully share life.

Regarding the use of the term "media" throughout this book: I found myself resisting the idea that I should always treat it uniformly as either a singular or plural entity. In cases where it felt like I was referring to something clearly plural (multiple "mediums"), I opted for the plural verb form (e.g., "media are"); in cases where it felt like I was referring to something more general or more amorphous, I used the singular verb form ("media is") that's become so common (and, I understand, so controversial—among copyeditors, at least) when referring to "media" as an overarching entity in contemporary life. I have tried, with the guidance of my editors, to follow my gut on this issue through the course of this book, using the term in the way that felt most appropriate in each particular case, and attempting to be as consistent as possible about it.

Jim Banister
May, 2004

Learning from the Past

The proliferation of electricity throughout the twentieth century provided the foundation for whole new realms of invention—from the washing machine to the telephone to the space shuttle to the internet. Understanding the historical period that saw the emergence of harnessed electricity is instructive in understanding how media and media technology are agents of change in our society today. Electricity and the internet (and the larger scope of media changes represented by the internet's emergence) are both examples of phenomena that were little appreciated or understood by the majority of the populace—or businesspeople—in their early development, but which had the power to transform not only how business was and is still done, but also how people speak (in terms of the popular lexicon) and even behave.

In 1831, British physicist Michael Faraday discovered the principles for harnessing electromotive force—that is, how to generate electricity by purposely moving charges from one place to another. Queen Isabella II of Spain once asked Faraday, "What possible use can be found for electricity?" Faraday replied, "Of what use is a newborn baby?" What use, indeed. But it was almost another fifty years before Edison was credited with creating the first commercially viable incandescent lamp (1879) and the first electrical distribution system for lighting and power (1881), among his other legendary electricity-based inventions. "Commercially viable" is the operative phrase. Not only did the technology itself have to be economical to build and operate, but systems had to be put in place that could meter the usage of something as amorphous and ephemeral as electricity. This was no small task, but the taste for what electricity could do was too savory for either the public or entrepreneurs to ignore.

Edison's pioneering commercial enterprises were based on the principles of "Direct Current" (or DC). This is the same type of electricity that flows from batteries, and it's generally fine for operating household devices like phonographs, televisions, telephones, or lamps. To this day, though, DC power is subject to inherent physical limitations; all materials have a built-in resistance to the flow of DC electricity. Conductive materials (like copper) have relatively low resistance, while insulating materials (like rubber) have very high resistance. Even over highly conductive materials, DC power can only travel relatively short distances without creating high levels of heat that can literally burn up the very wires over which it travels. It's relatively expensive to move DC power over long distances. It requires an abundance of geographically dispersed power generators, batteries and prohibitively thick, cumbersome cables. Even so, in the very early days of electricity's emergence into a useful technology, the lure and promise proved too strong, and those that could afford it swallowed the bitter pill of the uneconomical DC-power transmission solution.

It was another fifteen years after Edison's first commercial lamp before the eccentric genius Nikola Tesla teamed up with George Westinghouse to create the world's first "Alternating Current" (AC) power-generating station at Niagara Falls. Without going into the specifics of how AC power works, it has the notable characteristic of being able to circumvent the resistance inherent in conductors and travel economically over very long distances. Despite Edison's loud and public maligning of AC—not surprising, since it ultimately resulted in the downfall of his monopoly on the provision of electricity—the Tesla system of power production and distribution lowered the actual "electrical resistance" in the infrastructure necessary to move power from one place to another, and simultaneously lowered the "economic resistance" in the marketplace to widespread adoption of electrical systems and the products that needed it to operate. Indeed, with improvements in capacity and efficiency, the AC power format is the technological platform on which all of modern society still rests more than a century later.

As the use of electricity spread, new terms appeared in our language. Terms like "AC/DC," "generator," "transformer," "induction," "electrocution," "blackout" and dozens of others became necessary additions to the popular lexicon to help explain new dynamics upon which the changed world operated; and many terms already common to the English dictionary took on whole new meanings—terms like "power," "current," "grid," and "wire." Electricity was new, it was sexy, and it fueled the imagination of the public, as well as of entrepreneurs looking to make a buck off that public. Even so-called experts didn't know all the possible applications of electricity. Many (notably Edison himself) didn't really know how electricity worked, only that it did. The patent office was a busy place while would-be industrialists competed to devise the next radio, phonograph, or lightbulb. Look in the Sears catalog circa 1900 and you'll find outlandish devices like the "Electric Cod Piece"—guaranteed to cure gout, consumption or even impotence. As long as it had the term "electric" attached to it, a new product had a good shot at success. But the general public's ignorance of the true nature and applications of electricity was exploited. And not just the general public: astute businessmen actually invested in the manufacture, marketing, and distribution of monstrosities like the electric cod piece. But many of those investments weren't based so much on the nature of electricity as they were on the nature of *markets*. Bankers and businessmen aren't philosophers or scientists. They aren't in search of truth or innovation or altruism or creativity (except in new ways to make a buck). They are in search of profit. Trends in the marketplace provide fertile ground for those profits, and trends fueled by emotion, however irrational, are often the most fertile. Finance is an abstraction of commerce, and the movement of figures on paper is easily removed from the realities of the movement of goods and services that actually touch customers. It didn't matter whether an electric cod piece worked or not; to an investor or banker, it only mattered that people would buy it in large enough quantities over a long enough time period such that profits, or the stock value of the company that produced it, would go up as a result. Such is the nature of finance.

Irrespective of some of the more liberal interpretations of what electricity could or could not do, and the opportunistic bent of bankers and financiers, the value of electricity as a basis for useful (if not revolutionary) inventions remained sound. Through trial and error, applications were found that could sustain themselves as ongoing enterprises—telephones, radio, television, household appliances, etc. Even so, these items were always at risk of obsolescence. Using the same foundation of the electrical grid—the ever-expanding distributed system for delivery of electricity—products and services got better. Companies and products that didn't keep pace with the advances in employment of electricity were left behind. Edison's DC power was left behind by Westinghouse's AC power, the telegraph was replaced by the more articulate telephone, and the CD player unseated the phonograph.

The internet today is as misunderstood as electricity was in its infant years. In 1995, no one knew what would or would not work on the web. Many would argue that no one knows even today, several years and hundreds of billions of invested dollars later. To make matters worse, the internet was born with a genetic defect. The system was never designed for commercial use. Utilities like water, electricity, gas, and telephone were designed from inception to be metered, allowing for usage to be charged (and even then, it's often done badly). Not so the internet, which was conceived as a government-subsidized medium, not a commercial venue. As I explain in the following pages, its nature is far removed from anything we've seen before, and long-term, viable commercialization of the internet requires new and different way of thinking—thinking that will also benefit nonprofit endeavors.

But that didn't matter in the early years of the internet. Mass emotion can fuel markets, which for the savvy financier means boom time. Pyramid schemes are those where the first ones in (and subsequently out) get rich, and the millions of folks who end up holding up the peak of the pyramid get crushed. Similar mass-scale examples of legal fleecing include the mass exodus to the promise of the New World in the eighteenth century, the California Gold Rush of the nineteenth century, and the electricity-fueled Age of Invention of the early twentieth century. During all of these periods, clever financiers made a bundle off of emotion-ridden hopefuls. The internet-fueled 1990s boom was no different. In fact, it could be argued that the dot-bomb bust of the past few years was more widespread than that suffered by the relatively few who had the courage and stamina to weather the tribulations of eighteenth-century exploration, or the pains of nineteenth-century land and mineral lotteries. Never has it been easier for the everyman to participate in public markets. This meant a windfall to contemporary financiers and venture capitalists who could quickly pawn off their relatively inexpensive investments on a voracious public appetite for sexy, well-marketed shell games at emotion-fueled prices.

I'm disappointed in the eager ignorance of a public that was unwilling to recognize, and eventually admit, that the party had to end, and angry with the irresponsible financiers who tainted a fundamentally sound and singularly incredible invention such as the internet. It remains so, in the haze of a lingering public hangover; and we remain confused. Those VCs and bankers who told us what would work turned out mostly to be no better than snake-oil salesmen who were long gone after we awakened with burnt trust and impotent retirement portfolios. Our ignorance of the nature of the internet has not been diminished, and our trust in public markets and financial pundits is all but gone. All we know is we are *still* using the internet, more of us and in more ways than ever before. Still, both commercial and noncommercial entities continue to approach the internet the way Edison used electricity, with a DC-like linear, conventional-wisdom philosophy more akin to how we use television, radio, and other traditional media. Many employ old techniques and outdated dynamics that are not appropriate to this fundamentally different medium. Pushing these outdated methodologies onto the internet has, not surprisingly, met with great resistance, and resulted in many spectacular failures. A few offerings like the once-promising-but-now-also-ran Napster and the still-flourishing eBay tapped into lower-resistance "AC" modes of the internet. But these are only the tip of an iceberg of huge, real, and inevitable promise.

As it turns out, the internet is the latest relative in a family called "networked media." The resoundingly successful telegraph and telephone are its early ancestors, and interactive television, mobile and fixed wireless, broadband internet, and dozens of other means of networking the world promise to be its progeny. Networked media lower the barriers to interaction between people, businesses, and this thing I will call "programming," the stuff—content, services, applications—that flows through networked media.

In his book *Superdistribution: Objects as Property on the Electronic Frontier,* Brad Cox touches on this concept with respect to the distribution of software applications. A pioneer of object-oriented programming, an approach to software programming that touts a swappable, modular, plug'n'play approach to creating software, Cox correctly identifies a kind of superconductive distribution possible over networked media like the internet. He dubbed this dynamic "superdistribution" and offered it as a solution to allow software to flow freely without resistance from copy protection or piracy, accounted for via a "charge-as-you-play" commerce model. This is certainly the right track.

Electricity is a resource that many of us employ on a daily basis without really understanding, or needing to understand, its physical properties. Similarly, "network" and "media," like electricity, are terms frequently used with little appreciation of their actual meaning, especially when we need to extend it to encompass new territory. In the following pages, I attend to that deficiency, attempting to foster greater understanding of media as a science and art; I try to offer a roadmap to those interested in how to employ networked media (whether existing or nascent) in ways that are native, self-sustaining, and profitable (if that is the aim).

Of course, this book ultimately asks more questions than it definitively answers, but my aim is to frame the field of study using empirical resources and personal experiences that have proven accurate on numerous occasions—numerous enough to compel me to share it with you, and sorely test my own communication abilities.

CHAPTER 1

Misunderstanding Media

If you can keep your head when all about you are losing theirs,
[then] yours is the Earth and everything that's in it.
—RUDYARD KIPLING

On April 12, 1996, I was in Sunnyvale, California for a meeting with the folks at a small company called ISI. This was a somewhat bootleg organization run by Bill Foss, an early Netscape employee who was still on that company's payroll. This was a cause of frequent consternation to some of his fellow Netscape employees. You see, ISI was operating the website infrastructure, servers, bandwidth, etc.—called "hosting"—for Netscape, Yahoo!, and half a dozen other upstart companies that hadn't planned for the rapidly rising demand for their web wares. Not surprisingly, there were executives at Netscape who thought Fosse had a conflict of interest in making money off both companies, but he had been effectively inoculated by Jim Clark, founder of Netscape. It was Bill who made the original introduction between Clark and Marc Andreessen, what forensic historians will forever consider the spark of collaboration that ignited an eventual worldwide craze. Moreover, the handful of ISI engineers was fulfilling a critical need that Netscape hadn't anticipated.

Bill and I had known each other from our earlier days in computer graphics, and we were reunited during an investigation I'd undertaken on behalf of Warner Bros., for which I then worked—an effort to figure out how to develop an internet web-hosting business that wouldn't crash and could scale with demand. Warner Bros. website traffic was piddly compared to what Bill and his pirate-hosting companions were experiencing. As Netscape was the highest-trafficked website in the world at the time, it was way ahead of anyone else in terms of understanding scalability and reliability issues. Surprisingly, few people had anticipated the hardware and software demands of rapidly scaling user-base and usage, which was becoming painfully evident to those trying to offer reliable web services. The small group working under Bill held a huge advantage over the eventual competition that would emerge in the form of Exodus, Akamai, Level 3, Worldcom, and others, in that they were serving the two biggest websites in the world at the time, Netscape and Yahoo! In all, at one time early in its life, ISI was serving the needs of a huge majority of *all* traffic pinging its way across the internet, a not-so-surprising fact given that virtually all of the websites of any significance were then originating from Silicon Valley-based companies. (While connected as a whole to the internet, AOL and CompuServe had shunned the IP and HTTP protocols of the internet and instead chosen early on to adopt their own proprietary network infrastructure, client software, and browser technology.)

So there we were on a hot Sunnyvale day at ISI, where the background music to our meeting was the frequent and aperiodic pinging of the computer in ISI's small but well-appointed conference room. Each ping was a one-point rise in stock of a little company of which I'd only recently become conscious—Yahoo! had gone public that very day. It took a couple of years for me to catch on to what had actually been happening that morning, so focused was I on the well-being of my corporate masters. My hosts all had friends-and-family shares of Yahoo! and were distracted by the computer pinging, as it registered tens of thousands of dollars in additional wealth with every point the stock rose. Yahoo! was a company with little revenue and lots of promise, but it was pinging every ISI person in that room to a higher level of riches by the moment.

I must be honest. At the time, I didn't nearly comprehend the significance of Yahoo!'s IPO and others like it that followed swiftly after. I was (mostly) happily ensconced in the seductive embrace of Hollywood and its trappings. I must have understood the ramifications at some level, though, because the point of that meeting was to brainstorm a way to convince Time Warner to outsource to ISI the hosting of all of its rapidly growing web traffic, garnered from its Pathfinder, CNN, HBO, and Warner Bros. websites, in return for a 22 percent ownership stake in ISI. Time Warner passed on the investment opportunity. The worth of that (and many other) passed deals was worth many tens of millions of paper dollars just a few years later.

Who would have known? In 1995 or 1996, one could have shed a coveted executive position at any Fortune 500 company for a *secretarial* position at Excite, Lycos, Broadcast.com, Sonic Foundry, eBay, Akamai, or any of dozens of other internet-era companies, and made far more money. Time Warner could have simply outsourced its hosting needs to ISI—using dollars Time Warner was already spending internally for the same service—and it would have earned tens and possibly hundreds of millions of dollars in value through ownership in ISI, a value fated to grow exponentially for the short few years necessary for Time Warner to liquidate its ownership. Of course, we knew something was up. We "new media" executives at Time Warner were excited about the possibilities of the internet and its sibling technologies. The founders of Time Inc.'s Pathfinder service were true visionaries, seeing clearly the intrinsic possibilities offered by the new medium. CNN quickly became one of the top-trafficked websites in the world, recognized for its cleverness and innovation in extending news to new media. And Warner Bros. Online was profitable in its second year of operation, frequently recognized for its innovation, and consistently one of the top-ten news information and entertainment websites in the world. We were all focused on diligently building businesses and exploring how this new thing called the internet could and should be used to complement traditional media. We were looking for the root value in this thing called the internet; eventually, however, we found we were hunting in the jungle while the real quarry was in the canopy. The true game was not in building businesses, it was in building hype.

The Madness of Crowds and the Foxy Few

In April 1994, Jim Clark and Marc Andreessen started Netscape Communications Corporation, with Clark investing $4,000,000 of his own money. In September 1994, the venture capital firm Kleiner Perkins Caufield & Byers provided Netscape with a second round of financing and John Doerr, general partner of Kleiner Perkins, joined the Netscape board. Kleiner Perkins is arguably one of the most powerful venture capital firms in the world and a principal investor in some of the most successful and innovative companies of the latter half of the twentieth century, including Intuit, Electronic Arts, Genentech, Handspring, Lotus Development, LSI Logic, Macromedia, Zagat, and such internet notables as Amazon.com, Travelocity, FreeMarkets, and Google. Netscape used its initial infusions of capital to develop its first product, released in the last quarter of 1994. But extensive product development costs, combined with initial sales and marketing outlays, meant that by spring 1995, the company needed new sources of cash. A consortium of five companies—three major media companies (Times Mirror, Hearst, and Knight Ridder) with TCI and Adobe—joined to acquire 11 percent of Netscape's stock for around $17.5 million.

During the first two quarters of 1995, the company and its products became increasingly well known, and Netscape was widely mentioned in both the trade and general press. By June 23, 1995, Netscape was ready to announce that it was filing for an initial public offering (IPO). Through its underwriter, Morgan Stanley, Netscape planned to offer 3,500,000 shares of common stock, having initially estimated a value somewhere between $12 and $14 per share. On August 9, 1995, the day of the IPO, the offering had swelled to 5,000,000 shares offered (4,250,000 in the United States and Canada and 750,000 elsewhere) at $28 per share, so oversubscribed was the offering. They were effectively selling a relatively small percentage of their company—nearly 10 percent—to the public for almost $140,000,000.

In the firm's prospectus, Netscape quoted a net loss of over $4 million. Despite never having declared a profit in its short operating history, the stock was immediately the subject of intense speculation.

Most now believe that the spectacular, sudden rise in Netscape's share price was fueled by the media's interest in the internet, the overall bullishness in the market for technology stocks, the positive results of similar public offerings, and the flowering of strategic commitment to the internet from such large firms as AT&T, Microsoft, and IBM. Nobody knows the real and definitive reasons, and everyone has their theories, but on the day of Netscape's IPO, the stock opened to the *true public* at $71, so high was the demand of the powerful institutional traders who dominated trading at the opening. Their appetite for the stock more than doubled its price before any ma-and-pa stock investors could get a hand in. It went as high as $74.75, but ultimately settled to a $58.25 close on the first day, confounding many pundits who had predicted that the stock could rise at most as high as $40. At the end of trading that day, the company had a market capitalization of more than $1 billion. Instantly, Clark's shares were valued at more than $500 million, Jim

Barksdale's (the new CEO) at more than $240 million, and Andreessen's at more than $50 million. Commenting on the firm's initial success in the capital market, Clark himself attributed it to "a fair amount of luck, good timing, and instinctive faith that this was a good market. And a few things done right, too. It's always a combination of all those things: timing, luck, and good execution."

Perhaps. But I'd venture to say it was mostly a result of plain old good marketing—and not of their product, but of their promise. They had a gold-bond management team, one of the top venture capitalist companies in the world, and a powerful investment banking firm behind them. Netscape and its powerful cabal of financial wizards spun a tantalizing story about a not-well-understood technology that required inordinate faith in the unknown. They were selling a religion more than a company.

In its IPO prospectus, Netscape admitted, "As of June 30, 1995, the Company had accumulated deficit of $12.8 million. Although the Company has experienced revenue growth in recent periods, such growth rates will not be sustainable and are not indicative of future operating results." Despite this warning, they were able to sell less than 10 percent of their company for hundreds of millions of dollars, releasing a relatively small portion of their stock to the public to ensure that demand for the shares exceeded supply. Thus, the price of a Netscape share ownership had increased more than 100,000-fold since the company was founded a little more than a year earlier.

Initial public offerings aren't new. Any public company—from IBM to Microsoft, from Coca-Cola to Nike—has gone through the process. Netscape had a sound business idea with great core promise. It was the poster child for a new technology (and a fundamentally new form of media) whose emergence still reverberates throughout the world. But its financial handlers were perhaps too good at selling the promise. Its IPO ignited a firestorm of opportunism the likes of which had not been seen for many years, and many firms with far more diaphanous business plans followed quickly in its footsteps. For every Netscape—a sound business plan with elephantine hype—there were dozens of companies with half-baked and twice-hyped ideas ready to draft behind the tremendous bow shock Netscape created on the financial markets.

VCs are closely tied to the fate of a company. They are generally deeply involved with the startup and operations of the new companies in which they invest. Even so, VCs are ultimately in the business of making money, not products or services. Underwriters and bankers are yet another step further removed from companies than VCs. Financial institutions like these are committed only to their ability to fashion and sell "financial instruments"—bonds, IPOs, commodities, and the like; they make money whether a company/person is buying or selling. They often care little about what is being sold, only that it *can* be sold and that they get their cut. For every $28 share of Netscape sold to the public that day in 1994, Morgan Stanley received $1.96, amounting to a tidy $9.8 million for its coffers. All for ensuring Netscape's IPO was fully subscribed. That doesn't count the commissions their in-house brokers commanded for over $200-plus million in "value" created between the stock's first-day opening ($28) and first-day high ($71), which ended up almost entirely in the hands of their favored institutional investors.

Broadcast.com, an audio/video streaming company with revenues of $19 million and net loss of $15.6 million, went public at $18 per share and shot to $74 on its opening, closing that day only slightly lower at almost $63 per share. iVillage, an online community site aimed at women, had net losses of almost $46 million the year prior to its public offering, yet was able to go public at a price of $24. The share price increased to $95 on the company's first day of trading; by the end of the day, its shares had edged down to close at $80.13, a staggering 233 percent increase, giving the company a market valuation of $1.86 billion. Akamai, the internet infrastructure company, went public starting at $26 a share. By the end of the day, investors had bid the price up to $145 a share. A month later the stock was selling at $327 a share. The investment banks behind these IPOs, of course, scored fees similar in percentage to those Morgan Stanley realized in taking Netscape public.

This was easy pickin's. In 1996 alone, according to the VentureOne Corporation, some 260 venture-backed high-tech companies nationwide went public, raising nearly $12 billion, more than double the number of IPOs in 1991 and more than triple the $3.9 billion they raised. In 1999 alone, at the height of the lunacy, a staggering $36 billion of public and private money was pumped into Net companies in 4,000 rounds of funding. What the hell was going on? Supply and demand, great marketing, and a healthy dose of herd behavior. The public had been stampeded into an irrational, frenzied, get-rich-quick scheme perpetrated by investment bankers and venture capitalists. They were brilliantly selling a load of codswallop, and taking weighty commissions on every shipment.

The Dot Con

Martin Smith, the producer of the PBS *Frontline* documentary "Dot Con," presented potent evidence of premeditated larceny at work in the financial industry's cultivation of the dot-com bubble, or at the very least a conscious conspiracy to fleece the public. Smith and his colleagues assembled data that claimed, "...many of the initial public offerings (IPOs) were manipulated by venture capitalist firms, investment banks, and big investors to pocket billions of dollars at the expense of smaller investors." The documentary presented virtually irrefutable evidence that the "con" was not a one-time event, but a pattern of behavior on the part of investment banks and venture capital firms, repeated hundreds of times in the late 1990s and the year 2000. It went as follows. First, an investment bank, collaborating with a venture capital firm that had provided initial funding to an internet start-up, urged the young company to go public quickly, long before it would have otherwise sought to do so. Even significant beneficiaries of the scheme, many of whom had passion and hope for the longevity of their creations, sometimes lamented these premature public offerings. Said Brian NeSmith, CEO of CacheFlow (whose stock went from $24 to $126 at IPO): "Going public at that time [was like] raising a first or a second round of venture capital. There [were] a lot of unproven elements.... I [hadn't] proven that we [could] be profitable. I [hadn't] proven that I [could] really grow the revenue. I [didn't] have all of the members of the management team. The product may even have [had] some technology issues that we [had] to validate.

Ignorance was bliss for bankers. There wasn't a person on the planet who knew what the distilled value of the internet and related technologies would eventually be; but as long as they could parlay that permeating ignorance into marketing the long-on-promise/short-on-history stocks they represented to even more ignorant investors, it was a boon they couldn't afford to pass up, regardless of the ethical implications. After the Netscape IPO, whose share price climbed from its IPO price of $28 to a high of $165 only five months later, all the big investment banks saw an opportunity for a windfall. Huge profits were reaped in the "pop" alone—that initial jump in stock price after the opening. If someone could actually get hold of the stock, they were virtually assured a grotesque profit by simply flipping the in-demand stock shortly after the IPO's opening.

David Siminoff, a money manager at Capital Group, which oversees the American Funds, one of the largest mutual funds in the world, noted, "In a four-year period, I saw over 500 IPOs. We probably owned 200 or 250 of them for 10 minutes.... [A]t eight or ten dollars a share, you thought, OK, I can understand how this can compound to 20 percent a year if they hit their targets, but when the first print of the IPO was 95 dollars, it was very easy to sell."

If one were fortunate enough to get a lowly 10,000 shares of Netscape at its opening price, an astute investor could have flipped it hours later for a profit of as much as $430,000. Not bad for a few hours' work. That same process with shares in Broadcast.com would have grossed a healthy $560,000. In iVillage, a tantalizing $700,000. And in Akamai, a whopping $1.2 million. Should that 10,000-share investor have had the foresight or luck to hold onto the Akamai stock for a mere month, they would have walked away with more than $3 million in gross profit. The numbers were too staggering to pass up, and anyone who could get into the game did. To aid in the "pop," VCs and bankers would keep the "float"—the percentage of overall stock released to the public—sufficiently low, much lower than the public's voracious demand, ensuring that any insiders who wanted to sell their shares had a ready-and-waiting market.

These stock prices didn't reflect the value of the company, or any prediction of future earnings. The stock itself, and its evanescent "buzz," was the commodity. As long as starry-eyed individual and institutional investors could be convinced that a stock was attractive, investment banks and insiders benefited. Smith and his documentarians found that, not infrequently, in exchange for being allowed in on the IPO, clients kicked back money to the investment banks by paying commissions far in excess of going rates. In this way, the banks and their favored clients effectively split the proceeds of the IPO.

But the financial industry's unscrupulous behavior didn't end at initial public offerings. In a 1999 *Forbes* article, Suzie Amer detailed more of these excesses. When Broadcast.com was eventually sold to Yahoo! for

$4.5 billion (a transaction rumored to have been negotiated in a mere two weeks), investment banker Morgan Stanley charged Broadcast.com an estimated $8 to $10 million. Another famous Yahoo! transaction—its $3.7 billion merger with web community site GeoCities—was negotiated in less than two months, mostly over the Christmas holidays, with bankers completing due diligence in just two days. Goldman Sachs's fee was $23 million for representing GeoCities. Thomas Weisel Partners charged Yahoo! an estimated $4 million (for a consultation only).

In 1998 alone, Morgan Stanley worked on twenty-eight high-tech merger and acquisition deals at a total value of $59 billion. With fees in the .5 percent to 3 percent range, that works out to a minimum of $300 million in fees to Morgan Stanley. Even though the mergers and acquisitions of the day were typically stock-only—paper transactions that swapped one stock for another—the investment banking firms almost always took their entire fees in cash, from monies that came out of the companies' original IPOs or private investments.

When banking institutions make tens of millions of dollars on transactions entailing the offering of a company's stock to the public, merging two companies, or aiding the acquisition by one of another, it's easy to see how they delude themselves into believing they are "adding value" or performing a righteous service; but in fact, they tend to place themselves above the intrinsic value or lack of value in the companies or markets in which they swim. They were placing *their* business ahead the welfare of the businesses—and general industry—they were rabidly encouraging to IPO, sell, buy, merge, or acquire. They don't consider the larger financial or industry ecology; they focus on the kill—the deal, the fee, the profit.

Again, opportunistic financial markets are not a new thing. As long as there have been financial markets, there have been periods of hype-driven hysteria perpetrated by those in the know, working the supply-and-demand dynamic to their advantage. "Tulipmania" famously swept Europe in the 1600s; the Mississippi Scheme of the early eighteenth century made a few well-connected Frenchmen ridiculously wealthy (and ruined dozens more for every one of them); speculation in the railroads and several gold and land rushes dominated the financial landscapes of the nineteenth century; and the inflated promises of electricity and the automobile left a trail of razed fortunes. But in each case, there was a core of value at the center of the madness. If the essence of an invention or commodity has intrinsic value, the core always flowers into a substantive part of our economic and technological landscape, albeit typically at its own natural pace, not that selfishly predicted by financial predators.

Yes, the financial community is innovative, but only in its cleverness at making a buck off a buck. It creates new "financial instruments" at a whim, and it is only in retrospect that the FTC, the SEC, or other regulatory bodies implement new laws to rein in any unethical excesses perpetrated in the effort to profit from genuine value-added businesses. It's the nature of financial markets to become increasingly abstracted from any real product or service. The financial industry claims it creates value by creating wealth. But as we've seen in the seamy, scandal-driven revelations that have dominated the business news over the past few years, the vast majority of that wealth stays in the hands of a few, while the less-sophisticated, less-connected general public is often exploited.

In the case of the internet, greed and avarice tainted a dynamic new medium and its related technologies that, sans financial frenzy, would have grown into a normal, healthy, well-contemplated, and market-vetted childhood. Instead, our perceptions of the internet were traumatized, delaying our clearer understanding of its ultimate impact on individuals, enterprises, and the world.

Some claim there is a bright side to the events of the late 1990s. J. Bradford DeLong, professor of economics and University of California-Berkeley, takes the position that investment frenzies like the internet boom are ultimately good for the population as a whole. He told *Wired* in 2003, "In four years, the craze sucked up $600 billion worth of purchasing power. On the flip side, public markets paid for a build-out of network infrastructure, and burn rates pushed the envelope of the culture at large. Even Andy Grove said in the pages of *Wired*, 'The dotcoms threw themselves on the bonfire, but they created a bigger flame as a result.' So while the Intels, Dells, and Oracles might be shells of their former market-cap selves, huge amounts of useful stuff found its way to consumers."

As DeLong has it, the egregious behavior of financial institutions is essentially acceptable, as it precipitated a saturating build-out of needed infrastructure. But his assumption erroneously assumes we needed that infrastructure to emerge in one massive flood, ultimately with side effects that poisoned the economy for several years. Chemotherapy—a massive dose of chemicals that poison the body, gambling the immune system can outlast cancer cells—is still one common treatment for cancer, but I suspect some day the medical community will look back and classify it as a near-medieval practice, alongside bloodletting and leeching.

The bubble had a similar poisoning effect on the economy, but that's where the analogy ends. The economy wasn't sick. It didn't need a massive influx of overhyped investment—it needed long, sustained, visionary investment in a set of technologies whose time had come. The cost of the bubble was unnecessarily high. If capital markets and investors had stuck to their traditional metrics of success—profits in five-to-seven-year time frames—entrepreneurs would not be frozen out of funding circles as they are now, and, to this day, would be steadily growing companies and developing innovative new products and services.

There were three main undesirable side effects to the blitzkrieg of build-out: as in all bubbles, the true nature and value at the core of the bubble was obscured by the frenzy surrounding it; the market was wounded, causing a wane in the tide of investment and leaving some pretty good ideas high and dry; and the only companies that can afford to continue innovating are those that have large capital reserves or the assets to draw on credit instruments—that is, traditional companies with the least to gain from innovation got a leg up to squash threatening innovation, or to pick up intrinsically valuable technologies or companies for a song.

Whether the late-1990s build-out was optimal, though, DeLong's argument is obviously true—an infrastructure does now exist on which we can build. However, control of that "useful stuff" is now out of the hands of those entrepreneurs and visionaries who thought them up in the first place, and typically under the paws of a shortlist of megacompanies. During the downturn in public perceptions of internet-related technologies and companies as viable investments, major institutions with a vested interest in perpetuating their traditional dominance—often those that most resisted the onset of these paradigm-busting technologies in the first place—have gained more control over technologies and consumer behavior within the now permanently changed media landscape. Arguably, it's a survival of the fittest dynamic at work, but that's too broad a stroke. By what criteria have the dot-com companies that survived the dot-bomb flourished? By what criteria have the other companies that have picked over the wreckage of fallen dot-commers, sweeping up juicy tidbits of valuable technologies, intellectual properties, or customer bases, been deserving of this windfall? Are they the strongest? The smartest? If so, at what exactly? Certainly not innovation.

Furthermore, a potent argument can be made that at the still-galloping pace of technical advancement occurring worldwide, North America will soon be eclipsed by regions of the world only now mobilizing their own modern telecommunications infrastructure. Regions like China, India, and much of Europe have also benefited from the egregious expenditures laid out so early in the life of wired and wireless technology. Those regions are likely to leapfrog the U.S. in innovation and implementation, going directly to "version 2.0" networks; this is where the U.S. might have evolved naturally, but now we haven't the money—or the collective stomach—to invest. Much of the future innovation and productivity gains will appear overseas and not in the Olduvai Gorge of networked-media life—the United States.

Rehashing the dot-com bubble and subsequent dot-bomb burst, even at this remove, can be painful to think about and painful to read. However, it's essential to separate the fictions and realities of that so-recently-passed era. The whole cycle was wrought more by the hype and manipulation of financial capital markets than it was by anything intrinsic and specific to the internet, or media technology in general, and it was catalyzed by a general change in the economy. *Ignorance of the true essence* of the emerging digital technology milieu—its real limitations and real possibilities—inflated market caps, just as it later deflated market caps and desiccated investment pools. The financial frenzy obscured and temporarily damaged the essence of a world-changing development and stunted our understanding of its core significance. The internet even contributed to its own troubles by making it increasingly easy for the average person to trade on the stock market, fueling the bubble's rapid expansion.

Nevertheless, it's now increasingly clear there was (and is) *something* there at the core of all the hype. There really was some gold at the heart of the gold rush, some land and mineral resources at the heart of the Mississippi Scheme, and electricity ultimately did create the foundation of modern civilization, once understood and applied in grounded truths.

New Media: Noun or Adjective?

For thousands of years, mankind used only a few kinds of media—gestural, verbal, scriptural (written words), and pictorial (images). The first is the oldest and most primitive form of communicating thoughts or ideas. It involves our sense of touch and bodily movement—gestures—adapted for the highly developed visual systems of our ancestral hominids. Regarding the second—spoken language—scientists disagree on exactly when structured verbal exchanges developed in our ancestors, though we know it was somewhere between 50,000 and 1,000,000 years ago. Regardless, the vast variety of spoken language is still the predominant medium of human interaction around the world.

Scriptural and pictorial media have been around for thousands of years, but it was only recently—in the last few hundred years—that the consumption of text and graphic media left the realm of the privileged literate few and made its way to the masses. Today, the majority of the world is literate to one degree or another, and the written word and graphic or photographic images have splintered into many forms—newspapers, magazines, pamphlets, brochures, even television and the internet incorporate popular lexicon and pictorials liberally within their content. In fact, the internet was fueled directly by explorations into *hyper*text—the technology of "activating" words in electronic documents such that they link directly to other documents, which was the underlying technological essence of the internet boom's first beneficiary: Netscape, whose browser was nothing more than a hypertext interpreter.

But hypertext, and the internet in general, are only two of a litany of media technology innovations witnessed in the last century or two. The photograph, phonograph, telegraph, radio, television, and many others—all were invented in the last 150 years. Text and hand-fashioned imagery had dominated for thousands of years (and in many ways still do), yet in a fraction of that span dozens of new technologies appeared for the creation, manipulation, and distribution of text, sound, images, moving images, and information of all kinds.

In the last thirty years alone, we got the CD-ROM, game consoles, arcade games, DVD, personal data assistants (PDAs), mobile phones, and many others. They are all digital, and they all tend to be lumped into the catchall category commonly referred to as "new media," a term applied liberally over the last couple of decades. The moniker was slapped onto any technology created for the delivery of a media experience that did not immediately fit into one of the (now) traditional industry categories of publishing, television, film, or radio. We didn't use the term when radio appeared over a hundred years ago, even given its stark differences from newspapers. Nor did we apply the term when television made its way onto the world stage and (many thought then) threatened to replace radio. However, the sudden increase in digital computing of the last few decades begat an explosion of new media technologies over the same period. The playing field of media is no longer simple.

"New media" is not an industry; it is a process—and, absent the artifices perpetrated by financial markets, one that quickens to match the accelerating cycles of technological innovation. It is also independent of any one media (e.g. the internet) or economic event. Media technology and its use by humans for communication, entertainment, and commerce are now going beyond the roles in which we were accustomed to seeing them. We are entering the age of *metamedia*—beyond the medium—where we transcend the devices through which we interact with media and engage each other in new ways, many of which were not possible before. The internet is still special in this context. It has already touched millions of lives and is changing the face of media, business, and the world forever. However, it should never have been treated as a separate industry; *new media is just media.* The internet just happens to represent a special inflection point that acts as an evolutionary catalyst to business and society at large. It represents a class of media that functions on a different set of dynamic principles than media that have come before. The fact the internet turns out to be special shouldn't surprise those who use it on a daily basis. What might surprise many is that the internet represents the adolescent development stage of a specific lineage of media—*networked media.*

Networked media first emerged more than 150 years ago with the telegraph; it encompasses any media whose endpoints can connect to each other in myriad point-to-point combinations. The telegraph represented the infancy of networked media, and the telephone its childhood; the internet represents its adolescence, and networked media is fast emerging into adulthood via the emergent global infrastructure that now links together telephones, computers, PDAs, mobile phones, wireless appliances and, soon, televisions, household appliances, and, eventually, cybernetically altered humans. The maturation of networked media is a by-product of the onset of the Age of Networks, the age into which we now pass—a time in science, technology, and society where connectedness and holistic considerations of the world in which we live assume primacy, a stark departure from the millennia-old reductionist approach to the understanding the world around us. Our comprehension of media and media technologies in the context of networking will affect us profoundly, as profoundly as the understanding of networks is affecting work in biology, genetics, astronomy, quantum mechanics, and many other fields of human study.

Just as the ability to record language and numerals on parchment changed the role of biological memory in recording human affairs, every new medium—from photography to motion pictures to television—has been accommodated by an evolution in how we see ourselves and relate each other. Similarly, the internet—a networked medium—has transformed the face of media, business, and communication since its appearance only a scant few years ago. But sound explanations of why it has effected such a profound change have been lacking, and methodologies are virtually nonexistent as to how to wield the technology in predictable, responsible, and (as we should have always realized, but seemed quick to ignore) profitable fashion. Of course, something doesn't need to be profitable to have value—decreasing costs, increasing productivity, or enabling new society-enriching behaviors are often more important uses of new technologies than mining new revenue streams. The internet is the most visible representative of the broader class of networked media—an even more pervasive concept and one that is taking human social and cognitive evolution to a new level of complexity. We have not even begun to grapple with the implications of this phenomenon, just as electro-magnetism pioneers like Benjamin Franklin and Michael Faraday could not foresee the far-reaching uses of electricity.

What will become clear is that networked media is transforming the "consumer" from a passive recipient on a supply chain into a multi-faceted *humanode*—the human endpoint, or node, in this über-network. We are no longer just "consumers," but also producers, marketers, distributors, and vendors of programming and products, unrestricted by geographical or physical limitations. We are no longer just passive vessels into which media, advertising, and information can be slopped. Again, we have yet to grasp the opportunities for business, personal expression, and social interaction that this development makes pos-sible. Networked media is also driving changes in literacy to match the capabilities of these technologies. Never before have young people been fluent in so wide a variety of media, technologies, and programming—a development I call *symphonic literacy*.

This book's aim is to bring order, strategy, and system to a domain often characterized by murky thinking, when thought is given to it at all. Networked media is now mature enough to act as a sustainable foundation for the emergence of whole new forms of human interac-tion and invention easily as profound as that which sprang from the foundation laid by the spread of the electric utility at the cusp of the twentieth century.

So why is there still a vague odor of trepidation hanging over the internet? The ubiquitous proliferation and increased usage of the web continues unabated. With notable exceptions like eBay and Yahoo!, there remains a taint to "internet" businesses, when every one of those people who hold that opinion publicly or privately is likely using the internet more today than they were pre-bubble burst. Securing an investment for any business that uses the word "internet" as anything but an ancillary aspect of its business plan continues to be problematic. It's an injustice, albeit an understandable one given the pervasive ignorance surrounding the medium, and the severity of the dot-bomb penalty so many suffered for allowing that ignorance to persist. It's time to provide foundational guidelines for how to evaluate and employ both past and coming changes to the media landscape.

CHAPTER 2

The Dot Calm

An invasion of armies can be resisted, but not an idea
whose time has come.

—VICTOR HUGO

On frequent mornings, I'll grab my laptop and head down to my favorite local café in Brentwood, California, order my soy latte, and retire to my preferred spot on the patio. I plop down, crank up my computer, and go to work. If I need to do a bit of research, order a book off Amazon.com for reference, or fire off an investigative email, I don't wait until I get home. I fire up my browser and do my business right there. The proprietors of the Coral Tree Café have joined legions of other physical establishments in offering internet access to their patrons. They have chosen the most progressive route—wireless internet, a capability increasingly integrated into modern PCs, and which can be retrofitted to many older models. And they offer it free as a customer service. The Coral Tree is not alone. In 2003, throughout select markets and expected to roll out soon across North America, mighty McDonald's began offering internet access. Taking a more commercial bent, McDonald's provided customers with access for a nominal fee.

Wireless access to the web via PCs, smart phones, and handheld devices is accelerating the already healthy growth in wired-internet access, where the cost of building or retrofitting terrestrial infrastructures—wires—to accommodate broadband is the gating factor for more widespread adoption. Even so, by early 2004 more than 20 million U.S. homes had broadband internet, and millions more were in line to get theirs when the infrastructure could accommodate them. Smaller nations like Canada and South Korea, which can be rigged for infrastructure much more easily than the massively populous U.S., have broadband penetration percentages twice as high as that for the U.S.

E-commerce is flourishing on this foundation of ever-more-ubiquitous connectivity. According to *Barron's,* U.S. online sales for travel jumped from $8.6 billion in the first half of 2001 to $19.7 billion two years later. Ticketmaster, the leading broker of event tickets, now sells more than 50 percent of its inventory online, up from less than 2 percent in 1997. In 2003, according to *Business Week,* eBay saw more than 30 million people buy and sell over $20 billion in merchandise. These are not omens of a declining or troubled industry.

The dot-com craze has passed. So has the worst of its succeeding antithesis—the "Dot Bomb," the "Tech Wreck," the "Stock Defrock," the "Park-it Market," the "Summit Plummet." Still, a bizarre radiation of mistrust and ignorance lingers around the internet, affecting not so much the public, as usage and purchasing numbers show, but investors and the commercial sector. Fortunately, the levels of toxicity seem to have dropped low enough for financial markets, various industry sectors, and ever-hopeful entrepreneurs to emerge from their dot-bomb shelters to find a more sober media and technology landscape. The relative calm provides an opportunity—and a responsibility—to reflect, to analyze, and to reconstitute our understanding of the internet and related media and technologies. Time is proving the internet's intrinsic value—a worth that never evaporated no matter how low the NASDAQ sunk. Now it can grow healthily.

Today, the internet is used by more people in more ways than ever before. Tens of millions have laptops and handheld computers. Commercially, worldwide revenues in the web services are expected to go from about $1 billion in 2001 to more than $12 billion in 2006. In the wireless sector, sibling to the internet, revenues of wireless networks are projected to go from $1.5 billion to more than $3 billion in the same period. Sales of smart phones and related services, which combine internet capabilities and traditional mobile technologies (like voice), are on a trajectory to increase from less than $1 billion to more than $15 billion, according to *Business Week.* That doesn't sound like a blighted internet landscape, does it?

In fact, it sounds like a robust and flourishing industry landscape, and it's nothing compared to what will come. It is the dot-calm before a storm of innovation and growth the likes of which will make the industrial revolution, and its succeeding technologies of electricity and internal combustion, seem pedestrian. At the end of 2003, a mere 13 percent of the world's population was on the web using all manner of personal or business computers, net-connected cell phones, and internet cafés. The continuing emergence of ever-more-diversified networked devices—smart phones, appliances, game consoles—combined with the inevitable demand from other modernizing countries and cultures ensures that a massive chunk of the unconnected 87 percent of the world's population includes many potential customers. Yet, in 2003, just 15 percent of venture capital went into early-stage tech-oriented companies, compared to 35 percent in 1995. It's not surprising. VCs didn't know what they didn't know back in the heady days, and now they do (know what they don't know). That is, without guiding principles and reliable metrics, they're reluctant to take risks in irrationally bad markets. The clever ones knew that all things come in cycles: the dawn of the twenty-first century was a tough period in which to engender enthusiasm for any business that rested heavily on the internet, no matter how good the idea. Thus, at the end of 2003 more than $70 billion in ready-and-waiting investment funds sat on the sidelines. Tom Curley, former publisher of *USA Today,* drawing on his previous job developing one of the web's largest news sites, observed to *CBS Marketwatch* that now that the bubble has burst, "...people are trying to integrate [the internet] into business strategies. This is a far better time for the Net, and people's investments in the Net make a lot more sense."

"The bubble burst took the internet from 'figure' to 'ground'," explains Mark Federman of the McLuhan Program at the University of Toronto. In the parlance of Marshall McLuhan, "figure" describes the visible, noticeable nature of a dynamic or event, and "ground" relates to the inner nature of what is hidden by extraneous circumstantial noise—the façade of figure. In the case of the internet, "figure" was the frenzied race to make money off of money—the bubble—which obscured the intrinsic nature of the web and related technologies. "True effects start to come out in the ground state," adds Federman.

Carlota Perez, a research fellow at SPRU—Science and Technology Policy Research—at the University of Sussex in England, is equally optimistic, though she's somewhat more quantitatively oriented. In her *Technological Revolutions and Financial Capital,* she asserts that bubbles, of which there have been several major ones in the last few hundred years, don't mark the end of a revolution. Invariably, they set the stage for the longest periods of growth—the true economic golden ages lasting decades after the crash, and frequently much longer than that. Such was the case with the prosperity that evolved out of the widespread adoption of electricity and the growth of the auto industry. Perez exhumed five ages of modern techno-economic history and autopsied them. What she found in each case—the Industrial Revolution (c. 1771), the Age of Steam and Railways (c. 1829), the Age of Steel and Electricity (c. 1875), the Age of Oil and Automobile (c. 1908), and the Age of Information and Telecommunications (c. 1971)—were four distinct phases in each techno-revolutionary cycle—irruption, frenzy, synergy, and maturity.

The irruption phase inaugurates the surge. A big bang of paradigm-shifting technology occurs, inflaming the imagination of young entrepreneurs and attracting the often stagnant caches of cash controlled by the industries and wealth-holders from the old paradigm. Perez asserts that the big bang for the most recent technological surge was the birth of the microchip in the early 1970s, and it certainly qualifies. While the internet and World Wide Web are inextricably dependent on the microchip, they qualify for their own big bang status, and most definitely had the most to do with the most recent irruption—the birth of modern networked media.

The frenzy phase soon follows. In this phase, financial capital reigns and its immediate interests overrule the operation of the whole system, decoupling the paper economy from the real one. It is a time of speculation, corruption, and unashamed (even widely celebrated) love of wealth. Brilliant successes in casino-like scenarios make the wielders of financial capital believe themselves capable of generating wealth by their own actions, almost as though they'd invented magic rules for a new sort of economy. The general behavior of the economy is increasingly geared to favoring the multiplication of financial capital, which in turn moves further from its role as patient supporter of real wealth creation. Increasingly, the notion of "fundamentals," the root metric of financiers and market makers in other times, is swept aside as price/earnings ratios diverge from any grounding in reality. Sound familiar? It's a period of what Susan Strange has called "casino capitalism," and the "house" is financial capital—VCs, bankers, financiers—while the patrons are the public.

Then comes the crash, the rapid deflation of the frenzy bubble, the inflection or turning point. It's inevitable, as paper values by this time have diverged so far from real values that they can no longer support their own weight. The re-leveling of the economic landscape can take some time. The crash of 1929, the bubble-pop of the frenzy that followed the ages of the automobile, electricity, and mass production, led directly to the Great Depression. Perez asserts that "...the length of the recession will depend on the social and political capacity to establish and channel the institutional changes that will restore confidence and will put the accent on real wealth creation"; eventually, a period of synergy emerges where "confident optimism of company expansion replaces the arrogant self-complacency of cunning speculation."

This is the phase we are entering with networked media. In September of 2003, AOL—now simply a division of Time Warner instead of its parent, and a company that at one time, according to *eMarketer,* commanded more than 30 percent of all online advertising—apologized to the marketplace. According to Frank Barnako at *CBS Marketwatch,* the top advertising executive at the company claimed he was "sorry for the 'arrogance' shown by its salespeople; sorry for overpromising and underdelivering for clients." With new management blood in place, AOL's leaders were "bullish about current opportunities." In doing so, they were acknowledging behavior typical of frenzied times and the need for humbler attitudes towards their business and their customers. The postmerger company wrote down almost $100 billion in inflated values and expectations, the bulk of which was linked directly to the AOL-related portions of the business.

Perez's synergy phase demands a "return to the primacy of the real economy" where growth is generally seen as "firmly rooted in real production." Furthermore, the sectors that provide the foundation for this phase include:

1. *Core industries of the paradigm shift that are still advancing and expanding* In the case of the internet, these are represented mainly by the survivors—Amazon, Yahoo!, Google, eBay—who relied on size, momentum, or sound business practice to endure the downturn, and continue to pull the paradigm forward and expand it.

2. *Increasing the infrastructure's coverage and services* While the actual physical wiring of the planet has slowed significantly, the amount of long-haul infrastructure built out during the boom was staggering. It chiefly took the form of metropolitan, cross-country, and inter-country optical fiber—much of which remains "unlit," lying dormant in the ground or at the bottom of the sea, waiting for monetizable demand to justify its activation. However, even during the boom, the wiring of the "last mile"—individual homes, apartments, office buildings—remained a barrier to connecting the majority of the population. By most estimates, DSL (digital subscriber line), the method by which many broadband users connect to the internet, is available to less than one-third of the U.S. population, and can't be made more available without major upgrades to local phone company wiring infrastructure—an expensive proposition. Fortunately, wireless technologies now promise to bridge the limitations of terrestrial wiring schemes.

3. *The whole of the old economy being modernized and rejuvenated* The adoption of networked media to increase productivity will be addressed later in this chapter.

4. *A group of new industries and services that supplement existing industry and bind the entire economy within the fabric of the new paradigm* Hundreds of powerful technologies, methodologies and businesses that observe the native laws of networked media can and will flourish.

This synergy phase is the time to invest, but a long-term view must be maintained. Think of the age of networked media as a time when truly sound businesses will flourish, and from which unpredictable innovations, products, programming, and enterprises will emerge, able to flourish when rooted in realistic, informed ascription to the capabilities and limitations of the technologies and marketplace.

The final phase of Perez's model, maturity, is typified by a flattening of growth and a relatively stable foundation from which a new techno-revolution can sprout. It will be some time—decades, probably—before the age of networked media reaches that stage of its life. For now, let us focus on the realities of the phase in which we find ourselves.

The Four Horsemen

Yahoo!, eBay, Amazon.com, and InterActiveCorp stand out as standard-bearers of network-based content, community, and commerce. They serve as good general indicators of the health of consumer-oriented internet businesses. Though they all took their hits during the bubble-burst, for the most part, they continue to flourish. They are representative of an industry grounded in the realities of a postfrenzy economic trough, but which remains optimistic about its future. As a rule, these companies *get* networked media, and their successes or failures now rest more on tractable business practices rather than moody public markets.

Yahoo!, the quintessential web brand and perennial must-buy for anyone advertising online, has staged an admirable transformation since the turn of the millennium. When advertisers began pulling back, Yahoo! was largely a one-trick pony. Advertising-based revenues at the time represented more than 90 percent of its overall revenue, about half of that, according to Jim Hu and Scott Ard on News.com, coming from "pure-play" internet companies whose over-the-top marketing budgets were rapidly evaporating.

In the palmy late 1990s, "... [Yahoo! was] used to sitting by the phone and taking orders [from advertisers]," said one executive close to the company. "Then, the phone stopped ringing." Yahoo! possessed an arrogance shared by its competitor across the country, AOL, which with Yahoo! once commanded more than 50 percent of the overall online ad market. Yahoo! had to wean itself off of its dependence on dot-com advertisers, commit to serving advertisers from traditional industries, and start working harder for its money. That was a problem. It had too many millionaires, gorged on monies gleaned from the heyday, and too little talent. Most of its employees knew little about the internet, virtually nothing about the media business, and even less about advertising—their one and only cash crop. On one occasion of outrageous hubris, Yahoo! ad-sales staffers called on a major Hollywood studio, touting the power of Yahoo! in promoting the studio's film fare. The Yahoo! executives presented a business case full of holes that demonstrated a willful lack of comprehension of the feature-film marketing business. When the studio executives turned them down and the film in question went on to perform less than desirably, the same Yahoo! executives took out a full-page ad in the Hollywood trades claiming the film would have done better if it had been advertised on Yahoo!. Of course, no good can come from publicly dressing down a client, potential or otherwise. This kind of audacity was rampant during the boom, and combined with the media coverage devoted to the instant millionaires being minted daily, it made traditional industries resentful.

During the boom, the perennial division-wars inside Time Warner (a favorite if involuntary sport within most such megacompanies) were intensified. Throughout its fiefdoms—Time, Inc., CNN, HBO, and Warner Bros.—Time Warner had an array of talented people who understood both new and traditional media, and had sound ideas on how to evolve the two together. Jerry Levin, then chairman and CEO, had neither the political clout nor the inclination to dictate a holistic internal internet strategy to his myriad divisions, a flaw that ultimately led to the disastrous AOL merger. Though it could be argued the divisions were relatively civil to each other regarding new media strategy, there was little true synergy or leverage employed, a sad state for the largest media company in the world. My Warner Bros. colleagues and I would often privately observe of a failed attempt at synergy or cooperation between Time Warner divisions, "Do you think Yahoo! Finance competes with Yahoo! Sports like this?!" Well, in fact, they did. Hindsight proved that our fantasy image of Yahoo! (and other companies leading the internet charge) as a cooperative, egalitarian vessel of commerce with all oars pulling in unison was a phantom, even as their market caps were then soaring to ludicrous heights. Yahoo! didn't (and still doesn't) escape the turf wars typical of any commercial institution of size. Nor do they "know it all" or walk on hallowed ground. They rode a wave, exploited momentum, and kept their warts and deficiencies well-hidden. When the bubble burst, and the company actually had to become clever and responsible, it had to abdicate the arrogant, best-known-brand-on-the-web mentality for which it was renowned. It's the tough times that vet management talent. Yahoo!'s ad-sales people have either become real ad-sales people, instead of a phone bank of order-takers, or been let go.

One Yahoo! insider who came aboard postbust summed it up: "There was a lot of low-hanging fruit." These were simple changes to the business that helped it monetize existing assets—primarily Yahoo!'s gargantuan user base and traffic. Some of that juicy fruit came in the form of paid search. Prior to Terry Semel's arrival as CEO, Yahoo! did not offer sponsored search—a highly targeted form of advertising where companies pay to have their URLs pop up alongside results from searches on keywords that relate to their brand, which has become a billion-dollar-a-year (and growing) business. In 2003, Yahoo! still attributed almost 70 percent of its overall revenue to advertising, but that revenue base is much more solid, and tempered by a growing diversification into fee- and subscription-based services.

Any institution of size will invariably have internal politics, bastions of ignorance, and some degree of midlevel management mediocrity—and Yahoo! is no exception. Still, under Semel's stewardship, Yahoo! has evolved from a company with the right pedigree of VCs and bankers (when such was requisite to success during the frenzied boom times), a lucky group of people with impeccable timing, and a relatively laissez-faire business, into a cleverly run, hardworking enterprise that's maximizing its assets, diversifying its brand, and raising revenues and profits.

On the other hand, eBay needed no such savior. From early on, CEO Meg Whitman skillfully managed the growth of the company, transiting the Y2K bust with nary a blip. Here's a true exemplar: eBay (as I will demonstrate in later chapters) was born genetically superior to virtually all of the other businesses birthed by the internet, and it was reared adroitly by its savvy management. In 2002, while other web companies were struggling, eBay's profits rocketed 176 percent, to $250 million, on net sales of $1.2 billion (from transaction fees on $15 billion in goods moved through the eBay economy). A year earlier, in 2001, when other companies were dourly downplaying their future performance to manage plunging expectations, *Business Week* reported that Whitman forecast eBay would grow to $3 billion in net sales by 2005. This figure was derided at the time, but barring catastrophe, it seems she'll make that easily.

On the other side of North America, Barry Diller maintains from his New York headquarters that he dislikes mission statements—but admitted in very mission-statement-like fashion that the goal of his Inter-ActiveCorp is "to be the largest and most profitable e-commerce company in the world," according to *Barron's*. Bold words, but he is off to a helluva start and has achieved a strong position from which to achieve that goal. In 2003, according to MediaMetrix, his company had 7 percent of the U.S. interactive-transaction market with a reserve of $1.2 billion in cash, and anticipated new tracts of fertile, untilled marketplace in his future. U.S. online travel sales went from $8.6 billion in 2001 to $19.7

billion in 2003, and Forrester Research predicts it will double in the ensuing five years. By early 2004, airlines derived a mere 17 percent, hotels 10 percent, and rental-car agencies 12 percent of their leisure-travel revenue online. That's a lot of potential upside for online travel sites like InterActiveCorp's market-leading Expedia.com. Ticketmaster, another Diller subsidiary, was doing less than 2 percent of its business online when he bought it in 1997; now it gets almost 50 percent of its sales through the web, a clear indicator that moving ticket sales online makes it both cheaper to operate and more convenient to use.

All evidence considered, Diller seems to maintain a brutally practical model for his businesses, one that has less to do with the artificial tides of stock prices than with simply ensuring that incoming revenue exceeds outgoing expense. While he has gained significant personal wealth from his stock ownership in InterActiveCorp, that appears incidental to his building his e-commerce conglomerate into a sound and significant real business. He attributes his e-commerce epiphany to a long-ago visit to home shopping television channel QVC. In an oft-repeated story, on Diller's first visit to that network, he watched monitors displaying readouts of buyer activity side by side with what was being offered on television. Bar graphs of sales volumes rose and fell in waves, measuring mass consumer behavior in real time. It sounds to me that this showed Diller the emerging dynamics of networked media—millions of people collectively connected by technology to some purpose, which in this case was buying behavior. He eventually bought QVC's rival Home Shopping Network, which in 2003 accounted for some 40 percent of InterActivCorp's revenue. This quintessential mix of television and telephone was a precursor to the power of internet-enabled e-commerce; as hybrids of linear and networked media, companies like Home Shopping Network and QVC still add to the e-commerce pie, though in ever-shrinking proportions.

Diller's belief in the future of the internet is so strong, in 1999 he even tried to buy the web portal Lycos for an inflated $6 billion. He failed—a loss that some called lucky (certainly he might agree, given it ended up being one of the worst-hit web properties in the bust). Diller lost the deal because he wouldn't budge from his offer of a mere 2 percent over Lycos's market cap at the time, an already extravagant price derived from the risible "market cap per click" metric that permeated pre-bomb business. Diller was a lot more than lucky. By all appearances, he knew the emperor had no clothes. I can only imagine that it pained him even to offer the $6 billion for a website that defied his practical business sensibilities and, at the time, was trading at the unjustifiably Olympian multiples of the day. Diller's turned out to be a rare approach to engaging in internet-based business: sticking to fundamentals and cross-pollinating with related non-internet business. He married commercial pragmatism with long-term vision in a mixture that has inarguably worked. Today, InterActiveCorp continues to be one of the few prime movers in e-commerce.

The other company that qualifies for this elite group is the ubiquitous Amazon.com. In eight years, Amazon.com's sales went from $500,000 (1995) to over $5 billion (2003). The company has gathered 35 million active customers and its U.S. sales account for approximately 4 percent of total U.S. online retail sales. In the process, it has built one of the most recognizable brands in the world. In 2003, it was rewarded with the highest-ever American Customer Satisfaction Index (ACSI) services score. This satisfaction resulted in its customers advance-ordering some 1.3 million copies of *Harry Potter and the Order of the Phoenix*—clear indication that Amazon.com is the first stop for many online shoppers.

So far, Amazon has run faster and farther than competitors, benefited most by its dogged commitment to custom technology invented and deployed by Amazon.com itself. All told, Amazon has invested $1.1 billion in its technology platform so far—an investment that CEO Jeff Bezos claims is the company's "best spent money," and the culmination of which is a proprietary architecture that gives Amazon control of every aspect of customer experience from design to service. Without a doubt one of the very few behemoths of online retailing, Amazon still has chosen an inherently perilous path. E-commerce is arguably the most easily commoditized form of programming in networked media, and Amazon's competitors are catching up.

Forrester Research's usability experts conducted reviews of five leading online retail sites in 2003, and Amazon came in fourth with a score of 19 out of 50—impressive in that it's well above the retail average of 3.1, but lagging behind Lands' End, L.L. Bean, and Wal-Mart, the last of which is making bold moves to extend its bricks-and-mortar dominance into networked media. eBay's gross sales outpace Amazon.com's almost four to one. Though most of that revenue is auction-based commerce, eBay has made moves into traditional retail and intends to tap into the potential shopping needs of its own tens of millions of regular customers who pledge allegiance to the online auctioneer every month with their products and cash. Froogle, Google's budding retailing portal, could spell the biggest trouble for Amazon and other big online retailers. Through a combination of retailer-supplied links and crawler-based results, Froogle users can search for products across the web; those who know how good Google search technology is know the implications. Its search expertise and large retail customer base could ultimately add up to the easiest way for consumers to find products online—from any site, with the best price and terms—especially if Google's current partnership with Amazon helps it to better understand online shopping behavior.

Even the revitalized portals of Yahoo!, AOL, and MSN still attract between 10 and 40 million more unique monthly visitors than Amazon. Though they are more likely to be general web surfers and not the committed "shoppers" that frequent Amazon's virtual doors, the portals are increasingly efficient at converting their visitors to shoppers. They too have their eyes on increasing their retail sales revenues. Amazon's long-term role in online commerce will depend on how it rides the overall evolution of networked media. Ultimately, like all commercial networked media enterprises, it will have to rely on how its specific qualities, technologies, and services—like its brand, customer service, and programmatic differentiators (e.g., its patented "1-Click" checkout technology)—distinguish it from its networked media competitors. All in all, but particularly as a brand and a shaping force in networked media, Amazon.com is here to stay for the foreseeable future.

The four horsemen are simply a few of the most visible examples of real, sustainable, flourishing, web-centric businesses. There are dozens of smaller company examples, but in general the game has changed from a focus on increasing stock prices to increasing margins. However, it is inevitable Wall Street will continue to put unhealthy pressure on companies in every sector, including the internet, to adopt a shortsighted focus on raising stock prices rather than achieving longer-term innovation and growth. It's an unfortunate reality, but one that should be resisted. While companies large and small showing solid performance and sound promise are bringing some internet- and tech-oriented stocks back into favor, there's still a risk that institutional investors (which overwhelmingly drive stock market trends) may inadvertently fall back into spurring their stocks to precipitous heights (and may already be doing so).

For the long-term health of commercial networked media, the urge to "churn" stocks in pursuit of short-term profit must be abandoned and a more farsighted view must be adopted. Such a perspective is essential to promoting further innovation and profit-making opportunities.

For some net-centric companies, and for corporations in general, it seems, the risks created by aggressive stock trading may be lessened by stable management and large shareholders. An analysis by *Barron's* and Bernstein Research showed that the top fifty companies as measured by percentage ownership by blockholders—individuals or institutions controlling blocks of more than 5 percent of a company's stock—tended to have historically more stable stock prices and generally outperform companies whose stocks are primarily owned by individual investors, outpacing the S&P 500 by as many as six percentage points. More than 60 percent of eBay is owned by blockholders; founder Pierre Omidyar still holds an 18 percent-plus ownership stake in the company and a board seat. A similar percentage of Yahoo! stock is controlled by block-holders, and the percentages are even higher when one examines the float—the number of shares available to the actual public. Institutions own 79 percent of publicly traded eBay shares, 69 percent of Yahoo! and a whopping 88 percent of Amazon; individuals own the rest. It seems that as long as blockholders don't sell, it bodes well for a company's stock performance.

Largely, though, stock price has become less of a concern for these companies. While coping with volatile stock prices is still a priority of their management, internet companies know now to keep attention focused on growth, profitability, and continued innovation. The stock market will do what it does, but what matters most today is that companies are generating real profits, or on a predictable road to doing so, based on a deeper understanding of the native dynamics of the web and web programming. These companies understand they must market their products and services instead of their stock.

A Congenital Defect and the Free-to-Fee Phenomenon

Even though the promise of the internet was artificially exuberant, and the subsequent bust unnecessarily harsh, the internet was actually genetically flawed. It was born without the ability to monetize transactions or transport, or easily measure usage. This fact, well documented and often lamented, delayed the web's emergence as a mature for-profit medium.

For the first five or six years of the web's commercial life, very few business plans were based around charging consumers for content. In earlier days, only internet service providers (ISPs)—gateways to the vast new world of the web like AOL, Earthlink, AT&T, and dozens of others—benefited from the monthly access fees paid by internet users. The net's nascent years were marked by competition for eyeballs (unduplicated reach) and traffic (at first the ubiquitous and ultimately misleading "hits," to the more reliable page views or page impressions). Monetizing those metrics was less important than increasing their scale. This mindset so dominated the embryonic internet years that there was little incentive for the marketplace—notably the ISPs, the backbone companies (those providing the long-haul internet wires and fiber), the PC manufacturers, the browser software companies (notably Netscape and Microsoft), and other major industry players—to push for a pervading measurement and monetizing system. So, like other media outlets before it, most internet sites relied on monetizing the traffic their sites generated using the mainstay revenue generator for radio, television, and print—advertising. Never mind that even the more mature cable industry couldn't make it with advertising as its only source of income. In fact, cable networks at the time garnered well under 50 percent of their revenue from advertising; the rest of the cable networks' income came from sharing a portion of subscriber revenues from the cable system operators—the television analog to ISPs. But ISPs weren't about to pass along any of their subscriber fees to internet content companies; the ISPs were struggling to make a profit with what they were charging consumers just for internet access. Internet content and service companies were on their own, and they were a one-crop (advertising) economy, with vague dreams about some day being able to charge consumers for their service or content.

The situation was compounded by the unbelievable pressure generated by competitors offering the same content or services free. Since there was plenty of money backing a multitude of companies offering essentially the same things—news, web portals, search, chat—to create a competitive landscape, the race was for eyeballs. The money would come later. At least that was the prevailing mindset. If one site wanted to charge, it was a virtual certainty the consumer could find another website offering essentially the same thing for free.

Then there was the issue of how consumers would pay for activity online. From the beginning, the public openly expressed its fear of using credit cards online, even though for decades those same consumers thought nothing of reeling out card numbers over the phone, or handing a credit card to a waiter in a restaurant. Web credit card usage was demonstrably less risky than those offline uses (not to mention that consumers are not responsible for legitimate fraud, online or offline). More importantly, people living outside the United States are much less likely to own a credit card, a primarily North American construct. Europeans and Asians, for example, are more likely to own a debit card, if anything. By now, of course, wherever credit and debit cards are used, they're also being used on the internet with impunity. The 2003 holiday season saw 23 percent of shoppers' total budgets spent online (up from 15 percent in 2001). In total, shoppers spent $8.5 billion online in November 2003 alone, according to research from Goldman Sachs, Harris, and Nielsen that was publicized in *USA Today*. However, the vast majority of those billions are spent on hard goods—books from Amazon.com, cars auctioned off of eBay, videos rented from Netflix, gift baskets from Simply Classic, and the myriad of other physical goods available from thousands of other e-commerce sites. But another type of potential e-commerce remains mostly untapped. Credit cards are only viable for purchases of $3-$5 or more. Credit card companies charge vendors around 3 or 4 percent for the service, and it is generally agreed that the floor for those fees is around 25 cents. That is, regardless of the purchase price, a vendor will pay a minimum of 25 cents or so to the credit card company to process the transaction. On low-price goods and services—between a few cents and a few dollars, commonly referred to as microtransactions—that processing fee could wipe out a vendor's profits.

Microtransactions are not a new thing. Anyone buying a newspaper, stamp, or candy bar, or feeding a parking meter, or playing an arcade game, or contributing to the welfare of a street person is engaging in microtransaction. A significant percentage of the gross national product comprises products or transactions of less than $5. It's no stretch to assume that the 300 million people in the U.S. alone make, on average, at least one purchase of less than $5 every day—that's almost $1.5 billion dollars a day in small transactions, or $548 billion per year, and the actual number is probably far higher. While some of these purchases don't and may never translate to the web, some have and many will; other types of microtransactions are emerging that only media like the internet or mobile phones can accommodate—for small bits of information or entertainment, or simple services. The web simply wasn't prepared to capitalize on that huge portion of our existing buying habits, nor have web programming and services been constructed in a way to take advantage of microtransactions. Imagine being able to drop ten cents for a comic or commentary from your favorite satirist, a quarter for a bit of specialized search, or a couple bucks for a chunk of research for a report. "Every bit of content has value," says Vin Crosbie, microtransaction pundit. "A price can be set for even the most commoditized of content. As electricity never became 'too cheap to meter,'" information's value will never be too cheap to measure, no matter how wired the home or office"—or car or airplane or fill-in-the-blank.

A significant percentage of online companies "would sell content they're currently giving away if they had a viable micropayment system," asserted Avivah Litan, an analyst at Gartner Research who specializes in internet commerce. According to Forrester Research, the market for music downloads will go from $16 million in 2003 to $3 billion in 2008. And a Strategy Analytics report stated in 2003 that mobile-gaming revenues could top $7 billion by 2008. "The market is ready" for micropayments, said Ron Rivest in late 2003. Rivest is cofounder of Peppercoin, one of the leaders in the emerging pack of micropayment-solution technologies. Before 2004, "it was 'will people pay?' Now it's 'how will they pay?'" observed Ian Price, CEO of British Telecommunications' Click & Buy division, which uses micropayments to sell articles, games, and other web content, in *Technology Review*.

An obvious workaround employs "block buying" techniques, many of which are in place and working. These entail buying blocks of credit that can be used in dribs and drabs for microtransaction-level purchases. Prepay systems like eBay's PayPal can do this, but it requires pretransferring larger sums of funds from a credit card or checking account and some onerous security hoops through which to jump. Most sites and services simply bet on or require a certain level of usage (like a restaurant or store has a minimum for credit card purchases). While Apple's iTunes sells individual songs for ninety-nine cents, Apple consolidates purchases into individual charges of up to $20. It would follow that Apple has statistics that indicate its users don't buy one song, but instead buy many songs over weeks. Apple has thoroughly thought through these payment dynamics. The company offer iTunes gift certificates, prepaid cards, and even "iTunes allowances" that provide parents a way to let their children buy music online safely and legally through their own iTunes accounts, stocked with refillable credit purchased with the parents' credit cards, which the children can then use as they wish.

Mobile wireless didn't suffer from the same defect as the early internet or the existing internet. While the wireless networks are proprietary, and technologically based on a different set of protocols than those employed by the internet, they have the notable advantage of intrinsic metering and billing systems. Wireless operators routinely measure and bill for small transactions—minutes of voice usage, ring tones, downloaded games, text messaging. And more people worldwide, it turns out, own a mobile phone than a credit card or debit card. In 2002, it is estimated that some 103 billion SMS (text) messages were sent worldwide, generating upwards of $11 billion for mobile-network operators. Most came from interpersonal messaging, but 20 percent of those revenues were from news alerts and marketing and commercial messages. Mobile phones are a brilliant mechanism for wrangling microtransactions: stand in front of a vending machine, send a text message to the number on the machine, and have a soda pop fall out, charged to your phone account. Use the same mechanism to pay for parking, bus or train fare, or a newspaper. The wildly popular *Pop Idol* TV show in the United Kingdom (original of *American Idol* and other incarnations worldwide) was the first to generate tens of millions dollars in votes from viewers via mobile calls and text messages. However, this global mobile-phone-as-microtransaction-device proposition is not without problems. It requires mobile-phone companies to become creditors. This is a role they're quite willing to take on for phone calls, text messages, and even mobile internet access, over which they have some level of control; but unlike international mobile phone operators, the U.S. carriers have proven less aggressive about opening up their billing systems to third-party content and service companies. It is inevitable, however, and unlikely that mobile phone providers will pass up the first-in-line direct consumer relationship they can forge outside their core competencies of mobile voice and data services. By making the mobile phone the ultimate micropayment device, mobile-phone providers could become the equivalent of a cable company, phone company, credit card company, telemarketing company, and internet service provider all rolled into one—an enviable consumer relationship by any measure.

But other forces are also at work to ensure that microtransactions take the internet and related networked media to amazing new heights. First, the internet bubble-burst forced networked media companies to find real revenue streams for their programming. Second, there is no way consumers will stop using the internet, as they're using it more every day and for more things. Consumers are hooked on web content and convenience, and the companies offering them have been forced to put up tollgates to charge for it. It's already happening. According to Jupiter Research, revenue from paid content worldwide is expected to increase by 20 percent per year, from $2 billion in 2003 to $5.8 billion in 2006.

Even with the inevitable spread of microtransaction metering and billing infrastructure, many entrenched content and service companies will have a difficult time pricing their content. According to Vin Crosbie, "The problem most online publishers face nowadays [is] they want to charge more than their content is realistically worth." An entirely different mindset must apply for creating content and offering services in a networked world enabled with microtransaction capability. The traditional basic units of content or service were typically defined by the economics of physical goods—it's the same cost to manufacture and ship one CD with two songs as it is one with twelve songs, for example, so it's infinitely more profitable to sell and ship a twelve-song CD for $15.99 with a $0.50 manufacturing cost than a single-song CD for $1.00 with the same manufacturing cost. Now there are economical ways for individuals or companies to sell one song instead of an album, one article instead of a whole magazine, one bit of research instead of whole research report. Some would argue that the "aggregation model" is what helps these companies make money—but as soon as consumers really understand that there is an alternative to taking what they don't want to pay for with what they do want to pay for, that model will change forever.

The Second Act

Not all metrics of success or progress in networked media are tied to revenue or overt commerce.

At some level, all companies are media companies; that is, they are fundamentally dependent on media—text, graphics, photography, telephone, and communications—for their operation. Historically, the introduction of new media technologies has created efficiencies in those operations. If enterprises don't adopt new technologies, they risk losing the advantage to those that do. "Everybody has had access to the same technology," advised Bill Gates in *Business Week*. "The fact is that some companies have taken technology and used it more effectively than others. And the ones that don't use the technologies effectively fall behind." Telephones, copiers, printers, desktop publishing, videotape—all have contributed to speeding up cycles of communication, improving that communication's clarity and effectiveness, and/or creating direct cost savings. Those cost savings and increases in efficiency are collectively considered a measure of productivity. In these respects, the web is no different than its predecessor media. Even in what's been a weak economy, network-based technologies are delivering staggering productivity gains. It's a secondary effect of the bubble, delayed by the years needed to integrate new technologies into existing institutions and to teach people how to use them to create efficiencies.

There are five big reasons why the internet's emergence will continue to yield positive productivity effects in the marketplace. Derived from work by Timothy J. Mullaney and Peter Coy published in *Business Week,* they are:

1. *Latecomers joining the party* Industries that lagged in productivity growth in the 1990s, such as government and health care, are now getting serious about tech investments and deep, committed adoption of web-based methodologies. For example, in the U.S., the federal Office of Management and Budget now espouses dozens of new programs aimed at cost-savings efficiencies, e.g., upgrading the online tax filing system used by the Internal Revenue Service, which saves them $1 per return for every online filing. They're gearing up to accept more than 100 million returns in 2007, up from 40 million in 2002.

2. *Networking supply chains* A huge cost savings is expected to come from a retail industry project to standardize and maintain e-catalogs of the products retailers sell. The project is called UCCnet, and it's coordinated by the Uniform Code Council (UCC) trade group, the organization that administers the little bar codes

we see on virtually every consumer good. It sets the stage for what the UCC expects to be a decade-long surge that ultimately could save stores and consumer-goods manufacturers tens of billions of dollars a year.

UCCnet will be responsible for maintaining manufacturers' product catalogs in a centralized database and distributing them to retailers. If done properly, it is expected to virtually wipe out the "bad data" problem experienced by most retailers, where stores order products they don't really need and manufacturers ship wrong products or product versions. UCCnet promises to bridge the profit-compromising chasm between retailer and manufacturer and help eradicate the wholesalers-retailers version of piracy: shrinkage.

3. *Productivity lag* When enterprises buy technologies, productivity doesn't jump right away; it takes time for the technology to be assimilated enough to affect the metabolism of the institution. A recent study by researchers at MIT and the University of Pennsylvania concludes that the biggest gains from technology investments come five to seven years later. "There's a big learning curve," said James Q. Crowe, CEO of Level 3 Communications Inc., to *Business Week*. "We're still working with investments we made years ago."

4. *Weak economic conditions* Productivity is more important in lame economies than strong ones. To survive a downturn, most commercial enterprises have to wring productivity gains out of infrastructure in which they've already invested. They have to be clever, and those wiles often involve technology. Mighty Intel, which has invested billions of dollars in chip manufacturing technology, is seeing a flattening of the traditional PC market as consumers display an increasing satisfaction with the superfast chip-based PCs they already have, instead of opting for the superduper-fast chips Intel continues to develop. Intel is retooling a good chunk of its manufacturing infrastructure in a heavy bet on the rapidly expanding markets for chips in mobile phones, handheld computers, and networking gear—which is expected to be a $45 billion-a-year market before much longer, versus the $25 billion annual market for PC and server chips.

5. *Collaboration and telecommuting technologies coming of age* The continued proliferation of web-based and real-time communication technologies like instant messaging, wireless SMS, and even email, is increasing productivity and steadily speeding commerce and communications. For example, the airline JetBlue was one of the first to commit heavily to a technology called "voice over IP," which lets corporate data networks handle phone traffic using internet protocols. This allows the company's "reservationists" to take calls from their home, essentially instituting a virtual call center for reservations. The airline's call-center attrition rate is now just 5 percent versus the industrywide 30 percent, and JetBlue now has more than 700 reservationists working from home using web-based telephonic tools. This saves in the cost of providing workspace to those employees and boosts their moral. Said JetBlue CEO David Neeleman, "They're a happier, more motivated, more loyal workforce." Technologies like these also contributed to JetBlue's industry-leading profit margins in 2003.

Sector	Projected size in 2007	2007 cost savings	Examples of where savings will come from
Manufacturing	$1.6 trillion	$56 billion	Online sales and pushing e-biz deeper into their operations
Financial Services	$1.1 trillion	$44 billion	Web-based paperwork automation
Retail	$1.0 trillion	$21 billion	Industrywide initiative to synchronize and correct data via the web
Health Care	$630 billion	$12 billion	Federal rules to streamline paperwork took effect October 2003
Federal Government	270 billion	$7 billion	White House is pushing web into every major department.
Education	$370 billion	$1 billion	Distance learning and self-directed study over the net.

Figure 2.1. Networking Technology Significantly Increases Productivity. Cost savings are measured in comparison to what it would have cost those industries if they had not instituted networked-based systems. (Source: Economy.com, Inc., Business Week)

A sizeable chunk of the money spent during the tech boom was devoted to networking and web-based systems, and that technology has found its way into industries and companies whose primary products or services are not rooted in networked media. Those industry sectors that were a bit slow on the uptake in adopting web-based technologies are now starting to reap the benefits.

The Webs We Weave

If you pay attention to the press, particularly what it has to say about scientific research and technological developments, you'll begin noticing more and more the words network, web, complexity, connectivity, online and others terms that relate to the pervading tide of networking. We've entered a new era that will eclipse the frenzy of the 1990s tech boom, steeped as it was in ignorance and greed. Now common sense and observed, empirical evidence are coming to the fore, as Perez has written, as we search "for coherence through the widespread application of the now established paradigm"—networks—"as the logic of both production and consumption." That is, networks are pervading everything.

Go to any Starbucks coffee house and you're likely to see people with some manner of electrical device—laptop or mobile phone or PDA charger or other electricity-dependent consumer product—plugged into the wall, using electricity that spins the Starbucks power-usage meter a few notches. This electricity is supplied free to the Starbucks customer. There's no need for a pre-paid electricity card, or to open a special account with a joint venture between Starbucks and the local electricity utility; there's no special Starbucks-only plug configuration. Rather, there's perhaps only the vague intimation that those customers should actually buy a coffee, tea or muffin—patronize the establishment in some fashion—before monopolizing one of their chairs and tables and tapping into their localized electric grid. Yet for internet access, Starbucks charges even more than McDonald's—up to $6 an hour, the price of two lattes. And not too many are buying. Demand for this service, as reported in *Wired,* averages fewer than two customers per day per store. Starbucks claimed it was just trying to cover its costs, but a good chunk of those costs were for a billing system and the customer support necessary to deal with client complaints when the billing system burped. It's unlikely Starbucks and McDonald's will be charging for internet access for long, though, as free is becoming the norm. Go to any one of the 600 franchises of Schlotzsky's Deli across North America and you'll get online for free. The Texas-based sandwich chain lets anyone sign up and use its network for free, and advises its franchise owners to beam wi-fi signals through the walls into nearby hotels, parks, and college dorms, a marketing beacon to regular patrons and potential new customers alike. Starwood Hotels, which includes the W Hotel and Westin chains, has mandated that all of its properties have wireless access. No nook or cranny of its properties—from rooms to lobbies to restaurants—will be exempted from the blanket of wireless web access available to their clientele.

Mirroring my beloved Coral Tree Café, scores of small businesses are boarding the free-access train. They see it as a competitive advantage, or simply a cost of doing business. Says Jamis MacNiven, owner of the iconic roadside restaurant Buck's in Woodside, California: "Charging for online usage would be like charging for salt and pepper." Or electricity. Wireless internet access is destined to become ubiquitous, and free, in retail establishments. It will be harder to find electrical plugs to recharge batteries—a technology woefully lagging behind the devices that require them—than it will be to get online.

But networking goes beyond the infrastructure being rolled out to support people wanting to check email, research homework, book travel, or buy products—i.e., everyday web surfing. Wireless networks are becoming increasingly sophisticated, leapfrogging the logistical and economical limitations inherent in terrestrial cabling and the bandwidth issues of all-seeing satellites, and enabling access to an ever-widening worldwide web from almost anywhere. Sophisticated computer-enabled networks of sensors are emerging for all sorts of future applications—from swarming nanobots that could be deployed as forward scouts in military applications or to monitor (and eventually cure) medical conditions from inside the human body, to all manner of products being tagged with two-way digital smart tags to track them through the supply chain, report back to the manufacturer after purchase, and even track the product through its entire lifecycle. Paul Saffo, director of the Institute for the Future, noted in *Time* magazine, "Wireless, web, and sensors are a very potent combination. With an entire global-positioning system on a chip just bigger than the head of a pin, we can give geographic awareness to everything. We're getting close to putting GPS inside any arbitrary object, like keys. If you lose your keys, you could just access the web and ask where they are."

For an example of the efficiency this technology creates, consider the lowly parking meter. The Australian company Reino has created a "smart meter" that can be networked. Parkers can pay their tithing by coin, credit card, or even using their mobile phones. To pay by phone, dial the toll-free number on the meter and punch in the meter number and how much time you want. Done. The meter will even send a text message to your phone when time is running out, giving you an opportunity to text back, upping the time on the meter and charging you automatically. Parking officials can log onto a website to monitor the real-time performance of all the smart meters in the city—like a running tally of the day's receipts—and even change parking rates at the touch of a button. The unkindest cut is that smart meters can alert a miles-away officer that a meter has run into violation and, once the officer is on the scene, wirelessly send a preformatted ticket to the officer's handheld for printing.

The spreading networked infrastructure is already host to all manner of activity, but it still represents only a glimmer of what's to come. Microchips came about sixty years after the commercial harnessing of electricity. What will sixty years of networking technology reap? While many gun-shy corporations continue to resist tech expenditures or direct adoption of the web into their existing operating methodologies, users of modern networked media are making it a bigger and bigger part of their daily lives: "making dates on Match.com, downloading music from the Net, instant messaging, sending photos on their PCs, and building a grassroots model of economic exchange at eBay," as *Business Week* observed. This networked technology is growing into a massive, pubescent creature: uncomfortable with its new size but still expanding, awkward but demanding to be understood, appreciated, and respected for its new heft.

Like teenagers, though, networked media like the internet don't yet know their full and final potential. To begin with, all technologies are on a march to becoming digital, and all digital technologies are fated to be networked in one way or another. That the internet and related technologies are permeating culture, business, government, education, and virtually every other aspect of civilized society is hardly arguable;

but we still don't have a holistic understanding of this entity. While media networks are dependent on these new technologies, ultimately the technologies are incidental. Any network is ultimately a medium, an in-between, the space between here and there. Media networks are designed for a purpose—to carry programming, for which a new, truly networked-sensible understanding is needed.

"Innovation is all over the place," observed Rael Dornfest, O'Reilly & Associates programmer and technology maven, in *Business Week*. "It's coming from all corners. It's coming from the citizen engineers. It's coming from the research labs. It's coming from the logical progression of things. And it's coming from those brilliant people who are either burnt out, or are out of jobs, or who are rebuilding after the bubble burst. There's no one place to look for it."

For long enough, too many have used the tech bubble and subsequent bust as an excuse to horde huge capital reserves that could otherwise be funding this continued innovation. Too many have been lackadaisical about better understanding how networked media are so profoundly affecting our entire society—or, worse yet, exploiting the public's relative ignorance of media like the internet in self-serving propaganda warfare. It's time to do it right—time to arm ourselves with a fuller comprehension of the dynamics of our new networked world, and develop both a sound philosophy to guide our efforts and a manageable framework in which to operate.

So where do we go next? How do we pierce the resistance, prune the obscuring spin, and drive off the pall of misperception that continues to shroud networked media and its related media technologies? The first step is to provide context and perspective, and develop a common set of truths, rules, and dynamics, starting with our basic concept of "media."

CHAPTER 3

Understanding Media

You can learn how to be you in time. It's easy.
—JOHN LENNON

In 1964, Marshall McLuhan published *Understanding Media: The Extensions of Man*. It was a seminal work, yet it took years for it to be truly understood and appreciated. In it, McLuhan set forth a framework for understanding how media—mostly mass media like print, radio, television, and film—affect human cognition and social evolution. It's most famous tenet is that the "medium is the message," a principle which asserted that the mode of media delivery (alphanumeric symbols on paper, video on television, audio over radio) affected cognition easily as much, or more, than the content of the message. That is, watching a film on a fifty-foot screen engaged human sensual and intellectual faculties differently than, say, listening to the soundtrack of that same film via CD. This may seem obvious today, but the main thrust of McLuhan's postulate seemed to be that as new modes of technology are developed to engage human beings in information, education, or entertainment—or allow human beings to engage in communication with each other—human cognition evolves and social structures are affected as a result. The human race changes as media technology changes.

Interestingly, even though the term has become such an entrenched part of the world's lexicon, McLuhan stopped short of producing specific, fine-grained definitions of different kinds of "media." The incredible changes to media technology over the forty years since McLuhan wrote his seminal work require us to break it down to its elemental meaning and then try to rebuild it with fresh understanding.

The term medium can be confusing. Let's start with the elemental: "medium" can be used as an adjective or a noun. In the former context, many associate the word with a description of how some like their meat cooked, but the literal meaning of the word is "middle," and therein lays the definition we need. The noun "medium" refers to that space between up and down, hot and cold, overcooked and undercooked, here and there, publisher and reader, filmmaker and audience, or you and me. It is that 'in-between,' the middle; a medium relates to the middle-ground—figuratively or literally—between an origin and a destination, and carriage of something across it or through it. In other words, a medium is the means by which information or materials are moved from one place to another.

In this context, are MP3 players, cassettes, CDs, and vinyl LPs the "medium," or is the intrinsic audio—that is, the sounds—contained on them, or which pass through them, the underlying medium of each? Are television, videotape or DVD the "medium" or is video—moving pictures and sound—the underlying medium of them all?

The keepers of the flame at the McLuhan Program at the University of Toronto explain this as "nested" media. That is, the content of one medium is yet another medium (e.g. the medium of DVD carries the medium of film). It's a nifty thought and one way to slice the investigative pie, but the approach creates a house-of-cards definition for treating the actual employment of media. It also conflicts somewhat with McLuhan's own "the medium is the message." McLuhan himself differentiated between the two, pointing out that the medium—that which carries the content—affects human cognition as profoundly as the content itself. With this, I agree. However, the message—that is, content or, more appropriately, programming—is the only one of the two that most individuals or institutions have control over. On a day-to-day basis, people don't manipulate the medium, they manipulate the message.

With this in mind, what can be done to classify media in a constructive fashion? Your voice cannot be heard unless you have a voice box that vibrates molecules in the natural medium of air that carries your utterances to another's ears. Without it (as in outer space), sound is absent. That same natural medium—air—provides the means for birds and airplanes to fly using aerodynamic principles. Similarly, a boat sails or a fish swims through the natural medium of water. Taking the concept further, a Mother's Day card could not arrive without the transportation media—truck and airplanes—used by the delivery service carrying the communication medium of ink on paper. A feature film could not be seen by distant audiences without trucking and airline services (transportation media) and the communication medium of film.

There are two "parental" categories of media:

Natural Media

A natural medium is any medium that exists regardless of the direct actions of humans, and can be engaged by human senses or through devices built to extend human senses. There are two subcategories of this type of media—inorganic (solid, liquid, gas, ether) and organic (genetic, touch, gestural, vocal, smell, taste).

The former category refers to the most basic structure of the universe and borders on the philosophical. It is the material making up the infrastructure of our world and beyond. As far as we know, it exists with or without plant and animal life, and through it sound, smell, matter, light, and other electromagnetic phenomena move whether humans, plants, or animals detect them or not. But of course fish move through the medium of water (liquid), birds fly in the medium of air (gas), and some insects and mammals burrow in the medium of the earth itself (solid), the same medium upon which (most of us) humans move from one place to another.

The latter category comprises those media used by living things to communicate and interact. It is a chimpanzee conveying affection through a grooming touch; pollen wafting on a random breeze to ultimately seed the offspring of a distant plant; the sophisticated plumage of a male peacock displayed to attract the affections of a female; and the first bits of sound uttered by early hominids on their way to building a sophisticated language. These are media adapted by life-forms from inorganic media to ensure survival.

Manufactured Media

As humans evolved, we created our own technology. Naturally, many of these technologies arose from continued strivings to increase our odds of survival. Any medium invented by the human mind and fashioned by human hands is considered manufactured media, and manufactured media include two main classes: transportation media and communication media. Transportation media include any medium that enables movement of physical atoms from one place to another. Communication media refers to any media that moves memes—information patterns held in human or computer memory—or ideas from one place to another.

The category of manufactured communication media is defined by three characteristics:

- They are man-made
- They employ analog or digital technologies to store or transmit information in native or encoded form
- They employ either natural media, transportation media, or both for delivery from originator to recipient, transmitter to receiver, creator to consumer, and often back again.

This book is primarily concerned with the phylum of manufactured media and the class of communication media. That is, except where specifically called out otherwise, the term media will mean manufactured communication media.

So let's try to answer the questions posed earlier. "Audio" itself is not a medium. It is the physical principal through which sound is emitted from a source, travels through a physical medium (air, water, the neighbors' wall), and reaches our ears, where it is interpreted by our physical and mental cognitive processes. But radio, CDs or vinyl are media—that is, manufactured communication media. They are the carriers of the source information that will ultimately be reconstructed for our ears and mind to consume. Similarly, video is not a medium (it is a physical process, as well); but videotape, television, and the internet are media. If we stick to our definition—medium as a means of carriage or distribution—the answer will always be easy. MP3 players, CDs, videotape, DVDs, and even radio and television are all media. In that context, audio and video are technologies that enable those media to do their job: that is, to carry information—often referred to as content (a misnomer, about which more below)—from one place to another.

To better refine our understanding of media, let's momentarily detour into the realm of the philosophical as it relates to human cognition, and ask a more fundamental set of questions: why do we need media? And how does it relate to our concepts of the real and the virtual?

The Great Wall of Media

Media are intrinsic to human interaction and communication. Without media, our thoughts, ideas, even our relating of past experiences or imaginings of hopeful futures, would be locked inside our heads with no means to communicate them to others or record them for posterity.

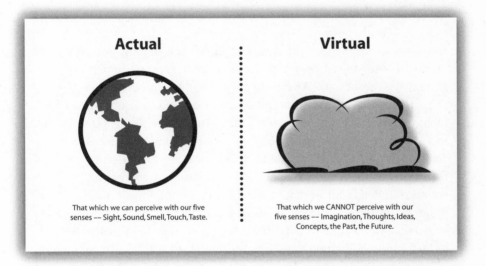

Figure 3.1. Actual Reality v. Virtual Reality

Our modern concept of "virtual reality" is decades old, dating to the early days of computer-generated imagery and science fiction, but its basis is ancient. We've always dealt with a "virtual" reality any time we dreamt, read a book, or been on the receiving end of a story from a storyteller. But what does it mean to be "virtual?" The conceit of any story, whether the story is told by book, television, film, is virtual, right? But the images and sounds carried from that virtual world—text, audio, moving pictures—are actual, that is, perceivable through our senses.

This raises slippery, koan-like questions. If a child is born without the ability to see, hear, touch, taste, or smell, what is real and what is actual to that child? Without the ability to interact through sensory perception, and thus isolated from other humans and from all evidence of anything external to her inner world, she would be trapped inside her mind, but free to imagine or dream anything that would translate directly as her "reality." Or consider an adult woman who falls into a coma and loses all sensory apparatus after having lived decades of life with her full capacities. A coma usually describes a deep unconscious state where the sufferer cannot respond to sensory stimuli (though it's possible for a coma patient to still sense the stimuli). The scenario I'm outlining is a complete blockage of sensory stimuli—like a spinal block for all senses. A person suffering from this imagined affliction would exist only in the virtual.

As far as science knows today, it is our senses, and our ability to process those senses into a worldview, that gives us our perception of reality—the actual. Anything beyond that which can be directly sensed, then, is virtual—that which can't be touched, tasted, smelled, seen, or heard. The "in-between" the actual and the virtual is media. In fact, there is a growing body of thought that our senses actually create what we perceive as reality. That is, there exist deeper levels of reality so abstract that our minds have natural barriers reining us into a realm of understanding that maintains our sanity. Physicists like David Bohm assert that the real universe is a fluxing and crisscrossing morass of energy waves in infinitely diverse frequencies—from beyond-super-high-frequency gamma rays (one millionth of a billionth of a meter in wavelength) to super-low-frequency radio waves (kilometer-long wavelengths) and beyond. Quoted in Michael Talbot's *The Holographic Universe,* Bohm calls that infinite confluence of energy "the implicate order," a much deeper and truer level of reality than we as humans can perceive, and describes the explicate order as that superficial manifestation of those energies rendered perceptible by our five senses. Even the kabbalah, a form of ancient Jewish mysticism, speaks of the 1 percent universe and 99 percent universe. The metaphorical 1 percent is the level of reality in which we live, breathe, work, and play, and where our limited thought processes are entrenched; the 99 percent is the true reality—the realm of "the light," an allegory for the life-force, infinite truth, or God, and a term which is, not surprisingly, a perfect parallel to Bohm's description of the infinite electromagnetic energy pervading the universe at all levels, most of which we humans cannot perceive.

Whatever our personal beliefs, most of us understand that a natural barrier separates the actual and virtual worlds, the "seen" and the "unseen," the pure imagination and the sensory incarnation. This barrier separates ideas from product or programming, concepts from physical form, and thoughts from action. The human mind is naturally tapped into virtual reality—we have absolutely no limits on our ability to dream, conceive, and imagine, whether we apply it to art or to developing a business plan. But there is a prodigious barrier to the expression and incarnation of those thoughts in forms we can share with others. This virtuactual barrier is the Great Wall of Media (See Figure 3.2). Bridging this middle ground between imagination and manifestation is the very essence of a practical definition of media. The ability to manifest the virtual (ideas and concepts) into the actual (viewable, touchable, hearable, taste-able, smell-able physical incarnations) is accomplished by punching holes in the wall to allow others to experience what we wish to communicate.

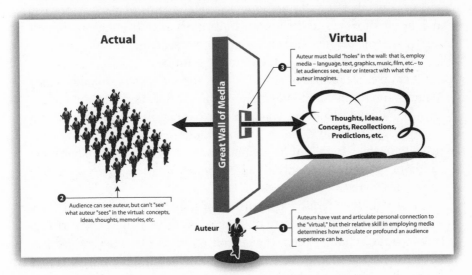

Figure 3.2. The Great Wall of Media is the "virtuactual" barrier we transcend to relate ideas, thoughts, experience, and imagination to others.

Language was one of the first pinhole punctures in the wall. Language provided a means to impart what was inside one person's head and communicate it to another. Written language was a slightly larger portal, and it provided a method to communicate concepts to large groups of people living in the writer's own generation and beyond. Reading patterns of ink on paper is an actual experience, but the concepts represented are virtual. And reading still demands an effort on the part of readers to use their personal link to the virtual—employing their own imaginations—to visualize what the writer attempted to communicate. Watching television, a movie, or video is also an actual experience, but the story being viewed takes place in a virtual reality, unless it's live, but even then it might be as "virtual" to the viewer as watching fiction. Live footage from military action in the Middle East might be actually occurring, but for someone at home who has never been to war, or visited the Middle East, it's as virtual as any bit of fantasy television they might watch.

Even the contents of a prerecorded live event (or a "history" program or book) are virtual. This may seem nonintuitive. The past is as virtual as the future. Imagining the future is an act of tapping into virtual reality, since the future isn't "real"; similarly, as soon as a moment of reality comes into the actual and passes, it returns to the virtual. History is only as "real" as our efforts to preserve accurate records of what happened, and we all know that perceptions of history change from person to person. As Orwell wrote, "He who controls the present, controls the past; and he who controls the past, controls the future."

Of course, recordings of actual events are not always complete. They require tapping into the imagination—the virtual—to fill in the blanks, even if the reader/watcher was present. We had video and eyewitness accounts of President Kennedy's assassination, yet we still debate what really happened. Details of the "actual" event vary from person to person or group to group. The only thing everyone seems to agree on is that he was murdered.

Even with the interpretive nature of most media, the movie and video screen have become very articulate portals for viewing virtual reality from within actual reality. The screen requires that viewers use less of their personal link to the virtual in contemplating the concepts presented. But movie and video screens are far from perfect. All media are doorways of varied articulation through the virtuactual barrier, and varied levels of effort are required by the consumers of that media. That effort depends on both the capabilities of the media technology and the talents of those employing those capabilities (writer, filmmaker, musician, et cetera).

As different media evolve and proliferate, the barrier between the virtual and the actual becomes more and more perforated. We barely notice it. Today we can "actualize the virtual" through incredible media inventions like special effects, ride films, game consoles, simulators, and virtual-reality apparatus. These media technologies allow us to communicate ever-more fantastic concepts and entertain at an unprecedented level. Similarly, we can "virtualize the actual." The model on the cover of any popular fashion magazine is a derivative of the real woman—a virtual representation of the real thing. Notwithstanding photography's natural actualization characteristics—capturing an instant in time, for example, on film—the retouching, computer graphics, and other digital manipulation tools are used to shape, tone, and mold the model's image into an idealized, virtual version of the real human. In a related vein, a conference call doesn't require the physical presence of the participants. The conference call is a virtualization of a meeting that would normally require the actual presence of all participants. Blanketing a game player's sense of sight and sound using a computer display and speakers—and some day, goggles and headphones—abstracts the player from reality and transports the actual person to virtual reality. Connect that player to thousands or millions of other players within the same virtual environment and you have the next step in the evolution of the dynamic of a conference call—massively multiplayer games, a very popular form of entertainment today.

As more electronic devices become connected, the ability to bridge distance, time, and the worlds of the virtual and actual gets easier and easier. Where all media perforate the wall, networked media is catalyzing and accelerating that perforation in ways heretofore unseen. Soon, they will make that Great Wall of Media translucent, if not transparent.

Brian Aldiss's story "Supertoys Last All Summer Long," on which Steven Spielberg based the movie *AI*, takes place in a world where over-population is rampant, genetically engineered tapeworms keep us slim, windows turn into computer monitors, mail is all electronic, and teddy bears have rudimentary locomotive and language skills. David, the young protagonist, ponders life with his companion robot bear: "Teddy, you know what I was thinking? How do you tell what are real things from what aren't real things?" The bear shuffled its alternatives: "Real things are good." Later in the story, we learn that the boy is simply a more advanced model of the same technology that enables the bear. The android boy and his bear overhear their owners talking about how they've won the parenthood lottery run each year by the Minister of Population, and so they will be having a real child. The final words of the story are potent: David asks, "Teddy—I suppose Mummy and Daddy are real, aren't they?" And Teddy replies, "You ask such silly questions, David. Nobody knows what 'real' really means."

We Interrupt This Program...

Television networks refer to their shows as programs and those executives responsible for choosing those programs as programmers. The pamphlet handed out at a Broadway musical is called a program. Any baseball aficionado has heard the familiar call to "get yer program!" at the ballpark, a reference to the printed guides sold to fans who wish for more intimate details on the teams, the competitors, and other data relevant to that day's contest.

The term has been used for centuries to connote a plan of proceedings, or actual proceedings themselves, for any gathering of people for the purpose of entertainment, politics, or business. It's evolved somewhat with the advent of new types of media—shows for radio and television were respectively referred to as radio programs and television programs. Computer scientists appropriated the term to describe a collection of instructions understandable by a computer to execute a specific series of instructions. Ask a computer science professional what programming is, and she might say, "the Linux operating system on my computer." Ask an executive at CBS what programming is, and he might offer *Survivor* as an example. Even genetic engineers borrowed from the computer scientists, employing the term to describe the information coded in DNA (now generally recognized to be a kind of biological computer); psychologists similarly adopted the term from computer science in the context of behavior modification, drawing largely unsubstantiated parallels between computers and the human brain.

For any media, programming is the collective and proper term to be used to describe the whole of the constituent elements of audio/visual stimuli collated to create a media experience. Voice, music, movement (dancing or acting), environmental effects (lights, smoke), and graphically sculptured sets combine to form the programming we experience at the theater. Voice, sound effects, and/or music are the singular programming elements contained in audio media like radio, CD audio, or audiotape. Text is frequently the only programming element contained in a book, though it's sometimes accompanied by graphics and/or photographs. Programming is the stuff that flows over the air, through cables, down the wires; is imprinted on the paper, the discs and tapes; or is digitally combined to form the web pages on a computer.

Sometimes, certain industries have different catchphrases for programming, different words with essentially the same meaning. For example, the publishing industry often uses the term "editorial." But even editorial is simply a combination of text, graphics, and photography, all three of which are elements of the broader, and equally misused, catch-all term "content." In a *Wired* magazine interview in April 2003, Barry Diller rhetorically asked, "What is content?," before answering in the following manner: "Content is that which resides between two sides or four sides [I assume he meant of a page or screen]. But in internet terms, when you talk about content, what you're really talking about are goods and services—the selling of goods or the dissemination of services. That's what interactivity is." He's right, and he's wrong. The definition of content shouldn't change from medium to medium, a requisite to which he alludes in conforming the term to encompass networked media. In fact, commercial transactions, the "interactivity" to which Diller mostly refers, are a kind of content unto themselves. It's called commerce, an equal partner to content. The terms editorial, content, or commerce alone are insufficient to describe the "message" carried within any media. While content is indeed a critical element of all programming, with many sub-elements, and commerce is indeed a critical component of interactive or networked media programming, they are still ultimately a subset of the full definition of programming.

A broader and more useful definition of programming would include four main constituent elements:

- *content*—those media elements actually consumed by the senses (e.g. text, graphics, animation)
- *community*—anything that connects individuals to a programmer or to each other

- *commerce*—anything for which individuals, institutions, or enter-prises pay or provide some value in exchange.
- *code*—any programming element that is interpreted by the media device to execute some function of the device.

Like primary colors, these "four C's" can be taken separately or com-bined in myriad ways to form any type of programming for any media.

The Medium of Business
(or, All Companies Are Media Companies)

The means through which we carry out commerce have evolved with technology, and throughout history the well-being of commerce has relied on media. There's some evidence that the earliest known examples of writing found on Mesopotamian ceramic shards dating back more than 5,000 years were records of products and transactions. From those roots grew the modern day oracle of business recording, computer da-tabases, the absence or destruction of which would plunge markets back to the Dark Ages. Furthermore, what contemporary business believes it could survive in the cacophony of media messages without its own ad-vertising, endorsement, or product placement in print, television, radio, and now the internet? How can any sizeable company hope to compete on any substantial scale via word of mouth alone (though many have started that way)?

And what about internal communication? The medium of ink on paper is as essential today to a company's healthy operation as it was for the fictional Ebenezer Scrooge—though today's computers, inkjet printers, and turbocharged photocopiers make the production of that ink on paper slightly less onerous. Early promoters of office automa-tion mistakenly identified the computer as a replacement for paper, but of course the proliferation of computing technology drove the use of paper up, not down! Regardless, in today's commercial landscape, the use of ink on paper is not enough anymore. Most if not all enterprises have adopted media technologies like photography, the vu-graph (used in overhead projectors), videotape, and the multimedia-capable com-puter. Historically, the use of these somewhat more sophisticated media was relegated to corporate divisions or company representatives that dealt with external communications (like marketing and advertising), or specialized "media services" groups within the corporation to help make slides, vu-graphs, or graphics for reports and presentations. But even that has changed. No modern company functions without applied multimedia used in all aspects of its business, internal or external, and sophisticated digital media tools are in the hands of every employee.

Then there are the industries that earn their revenue by monetizing media. For commercial media companies, media is their work product. Television networks, movie studios, book and magazine publishers, and newspapers all create, package, distribute and/or sell specific incarnations of media. However, the bulk of commerce does not boast media as its work product. Most of commerce is involved in the sale or rental of products or services unrelated to media.

Or are they? How would financial markets have worked without pen and ink, and later without the telegraph-enabled ticker tapes, and still later without computers? How would the airline companies draft plans for their ever-more-complex flying machines? Or book reservations on them after they were built and in the hands of an airline? While media is certainly vital to personal expression and the not-for-profit institutional activities of government or education, it is the most critical aspect of any commercial endeavor. Understanding media—its efficient and economical usage in the value chain, its effect on human cognition (employee or customer), its effective employment through marketing and sales in informing customers of product features and prices, its ability to give voice to the customer—is essential to business success. Of this there should be no doubt.

Not surprisingly, however, most company executives or employees know little about media. There wasn't really a need when ink on paper was still the predominant form of communication. But digital technology has changed all that, causing an explosion in media form and function that has infiltrated commerce faster than business people have been able to develop a true understanding of what it is and how it works. Computing technology and its attendant multimedia inventions—e.g., digital pre-press, printing technology, presentation software like PowerPoint, digital video editing—have affected commerce and communications deeply. It was the evolution of the internet, however (and its sibling, networked media), that has done the most to illustrate the lack of media savvy that still hampers business today.

This ignorance is tantamount to the automobile business not recognizing the intrinsic importance of the rubber and petroleum industries, or the housing business ignoring the timber industry. The rubber, timber and petroleum industries produce products that are directly incorporated into or used with cars and houses; but short of warning labels, instruction manuals, and warranties, media isn't typically incorporated directly into the products. Even so, media is vitally important to the supply chain of all of these kinds of companies. Overall, it is easily more important to every step in the design, manufacturing, distribution, marketing, and sales of a product than any other aspect of those processes—save for the human workers themselves, or constituent elements of the product itself. But as yet there exists no guidebook through the panoply of media and media technology.

Let's continue trying to build that guide by providing some ideas about how to further organize media.

CHAPTER 4

Organizing Media

To know the world, one must construct it.
—CESARE PAVESE

Remember learning high-school biology and the taxonomy of all living things? After the terror of that recollection wears off, recall that "taxonomy" is the classification of organisms in an ordered system that indicates natural relationships. Carolus Linnaeus published just such a system of organization in his *Systema naturae* in 1735, which established the modern scientific classification system for plants and animals. Before this system was put into use, there was no uniform method of naming organisms, which caused confusion in the scientific community. Although the specifics of the Linnaean classifications have been revised many times, the idea of an orderly, international naming system was a key to the birth of modern biology. This taxonomy guided biologists in making comparisons, looking for new creatures, and asking about the origins and transformations of life.

Biological taxonomies exhaustively categorize life according to a tree-structure of categories that include kingdom, phylum, subphylum, class, subclass, infraclass, order, family, genus, and species. For example, humans are of the kingdom *animalia,* phylum *chordata,* subphylum *vertebrata,* class *mammalia,* order primates, family *hominidae,* genus *homo,* and species *sapiens.* It's no wonder scientists call us all *Homo sapiens* for short.

The demand for classification systems arises in any field of study as diversity and complexity increases. Developing a taxonomy can be a productive step in the process of understanding and explaining what we know or experience by organizing perceptions into categories. Of course, a taxonomy inherently diminishes the complexity and richness of whatever is being categorized, as it is a reductive technique designed to make it easier to consider the parts in the context of a whole. Nonetheless,

Linnaeus's biological taxonomy, for example, has helped thousands of biologists, botanists and anthropologists in their research and studies, all in an effort to provide a clearer understanding of the world in which we live. At this moment in the evolution of science and society, we have no other generally acceptable methodology of organization without fragmented classification. It is necessary for rigorous treatment of any subject or the function of any complex organism. Enterprises organize by position, and thus classify their employees by such. Governments, militaries, insect colonies and pack animals do similarly. It is intrinsic to organizational theory. Though holistic approaches are perhaps more important to understanding and exploiting any complex phenomena, much can still be learned by atomizing a subject into its component parts. Virtually all fields of study have organizational systems similar to that started by Linnaeus for biology: chemistry has the periodic table, physics has the electromagnetic spectrum (among other metrics), library science has the Library of Congress classification, and geology has the geologic time scale.

So why is there not yet a definitive organizational (and thus classi-fication) system for media? For starters, during most of human history, media technology and morphology changed very, very slowly. Variants were scarce or nonexistent. Superseded only by the media of sound and speech, lexical media (reading and writing) appeared some 5,000 years ago and dominated the nonverbal media landscape (along with hand-drawn pictorials) until the nineteenth century. But written language and imagery wasn't mass-produced until the fifteenth century. Photography didn't appear until the mid-nineteenth century, to be followed (rela-tively) swiftly by film in the early twentieth century and television in the 1930s and 1940s. Then, the explosion of technological development in the latter half of the twentieth century caused myriad different types of media to appear within a very short span of time. Magnetic tape emerged in the 1960s, cable television was commercially born in the 1970s, the personal computer in the 1980s, DVD and the World Wide Web in the 1990s. Audiotape, videotape, iPods, cellphones, video games, and dozens of other media that vary subtly or profoundly from that which came before—all emerged in recent years.

It's past time for us to classify all media and describe their intrin-sic differentiating characteristics. Such a classification is essential to achieving a better understanding of media and to expediting a specific investigation into networked media.

A Taxonomy for Media

Classifying media "life forms" can help us understand their respective unique properties, the native dynamics of each medium, and the relationship between different media.

The taxonomy of life (biosystematics)—which has been growing steadily since Linnaeus introduced it in the eighteenth century—is vastly more elaborate and multifarious than a taxonomy for media, or mediasystematics. The goal here is not necessarily to provide a comprehensive taxonomy, but to show that media forms are diverse enough to benefit from the effort to create one, and to create a useful comparative framework. First, we assign each of the two overarching media parentages introduced in the last chapter—natural media and manufactured media—to a phylum.

Of course, the media of most interest here are in phylum manufactured, but it's worth spending a little time investigating phylum natural—those media provided by God or evolution or both, depending on your philosophical bent. Within natural media, there are two classes—inorganic and organic. Inorganic media exist whether or not mankind, or any other life form, exists. They are the physical media composed of the basic building blocks of the universe. They don't imply life, nor do they imply sentience (self-awareness). I must assume the orders of gas, liquid, and solid are self-evident, but will point out they are all mezzo-physical manifestations. That is, they assume a physics that we experience on our everyday level of existence, and don't necessarily hold on the micro- or macro-scales, beyond what our direct senses tell us is "reality."

Phylum	Natural									
Class	Inorganic				Organic (Communication)					
Order	Solid	Liquid	Gas	Etheric	Visual (Sight)	Aural (Sound)	Physical (Touch)	Olfactory (Smell)	Taste	Electro-chemical (DNA, etc.)

Figure 4.1. Media Phylum: Natural

The media phylum natural, class inorganic, order etheric, in particular, is a swindling attempt at tying off that thread, whose pulling would invariably and irretrievably unravel this discussion into the philosophical, metaphysical, and quantum mechanical. At some level, we accept that a wall is indeed solid (without some serious applied force) and can serve as a medium for sound to pass through or a termite to chew. We must also grant that there are likely forms of media that exist and function purely on a microcosmic or macrocosmic scale. For now, let's just aggregate those dynamics into this etheric catch-all.

The media phylum natural, class organic should be familiar to us all, as they exist specifically to serve the basic biological needs (and, in the case of man, wants) of living things. They are essentially mapped to sensory perception, but in the broadest definition of the term. That is, media within the phylum natural and class organic are fundamentally communication media.

Our senses are electrochemically based mechanisms, so we could justifiably classify all organic natural media as electrochemical. (All communications media rely on our sensory apparatus, but organic natural media assume direct organism-to-organism interaction without the aid of artificial technologies.) But the five main mechanisms as they evolved in humans are so specialized, and so intrinsic to human perception of reality, they deserve special (if brief) treatment as separate media.

Natural organic visual media evolved to match the sense of sight possessed by many animals, which allows them to detect energy within specific parts of the electromagnetic spectrum. We have no evidence that plants possess any visual sense as we commonly accept it (though plants often evolve to accommodate the visual sense of animals), but there are many examples of organic visual media from the animal kingdom: the mating rituals of many species incorporate elaborate gestures—"mating dances"—meant for the eyes of potential mates; insect colonies appear to use elaborate patterns of movement to communicate information to other colony members; and countless varieties of fish, fowl, insects, and mammals use sophisticated colorings and markings to either fool predators or lure victims.

Natural organic aural media combine inorganic media—solids, gases, liquids—with the apparatus developed in living things to detect sonic vibrations traveling through those inorganic media. The use of this medium requires at least an auditory sense, but is often accompanied by a vocal apparatus. Other animals, like bats and dolphins, create sound and use a sophisticated biological apparatus called echo-location, which classifies as an aural medium, to "see" off what those sounds bounce off. Humans have a highly developed ability to create and detect sound which, along with sophisticated brains, has led to the evolution of sophisticated language. Primitive utterances—grunts, squeaks, barks, and growls—are aural media, but structured speech—language—because it was designed by mankind, falls into the realm of manufactured media, about which more below.

Natural organic olfactory media involve animals' ability to identify and classify things by detecting free-floating molecules using specialized sensory apparatus and processing the information with their brains. Smell depends on sensory receptors that respond to airborne chemicals. In humans, these chemoreceptors are located in the olfactory epithelium, a patch of tissue about the size of a postage stamp located high in the nasal cavity. Even sperm possess odor receptors that enable them to swim towards certain chemicals. Many mammals even have a separate system for detecting pheromones—specialized airborne scent molecules emitted and detected by animals to elicit mating behaviors. Pheromones classify as a species of olfactory media.

Natural organic physical media refer to flora's and fauna's ability to detect physical contact with other organisms. Venus flytrap is a plant that can sense and entrap insects upon touch. The tentacles of sea anemones recoil upon contact with anything other than food. Cats purr when we stroke them; dogs pedal a back foot when we scratch them just right. Chimpanzees express affection through the act of intimate grooming. Human beings convey profound meaning through a silent hug or passionate kiss.

Natural organic taste media are similar (and physiologically closely related) to olfactory media in that they involve specialized apparatus evolved on certain animals. Humans detect taste with receptor cells clustered in taste buds. Each taste bud has a pore that opens out to the surface of the tongue, enabling molecules and ions taken into the mouth to reach the receptor cells inside. The primary taste sensations appear to have evolved as chemical differentiations that best served mankind in its survival and evolution.

Natural organic electrochemical media can be somewhat misleading. Taste is a chemical and neurological function, as is smell; in fact, all our senses encompass electrochemical dynamics one way or another. But they are classified separately here as highly specialized electrochemical processes intrinsic to human perception, and thus orders in their own right. Electrochemical media encompass transfers of chemicals from one organism (or sub-organism) to another that implies information transfer. DNA is the most profound electrochemical medium—a molecule containing the blueprint to life. But cell-to-cell communication and other autonomous sub-organism dynamics are also included in this class and order.

The collective phyla of natural organic media essentially amount to our senses, the ultimate arbiters of our perception of reality. Phyla manufactured are those media created by man. The differences between class transportation and class communications were introduced in Chapter 3. To restate: class transportation are those technologies invented by humans to move physical materials from one place to another, and which employ phylum natural, class inorganic—water, air, earth—to do so. Airplanes and helicopters are transportation media of order aero. Boats, barges, ships, and submarines are of the order aquatic. And so forth.

Phylum	Manufactured					
Class	Transportation				Communications	
Order	Aquatic	Terran	Aero	Astro	Static	Dynamic

Figure 4.2. Media Phylum: Manufactured

Communications Media: Static versus Dynamic

Now we're getting to the meat. Phylum manufactured, class communications can be bifurcated into two orders of media: static and dynamic. Order static traditionally encompasses well-established manufactured communications media families like print, paint, photography, and sculpture. Modern printing technology has climbed to incredible heights. Even sculpting/modeling has taken great leaps in speed, efficiency, and productivity with the advent of technologies like computer graphics and stereo lithography. The end result—the content, if you will—remains the same: symbols on paper or another static surface, or a physical three-dimensional object of sorts created to convey some meaning.

Order	Static		
Family	Iconic	Scriptural	Glyphic
Genus	Paint, Photography, etc.	Books, Periodicals, etc.	Sculpture, Architecture, etc.

Figure 4.3. Phylum: Manufactured, Class: Communications, Order: Static

Many derivative or parody works of art have riffed on Michelangelo's *David,* Botticelli's *Venus,* or even Bartholdi's *Statue of Liberty,* but the artists did not intend them to be changeable. The works were created to be unique visions captured in paint or stone or metal, subject only to the change in the physical materials in which they were solidified. Similarly, Plato's *Republic,* Homer's *Iliad,* Newton's *Principia mathematica,* or Dante's *Inferno* were all intended as immutable works whose intrinsic ideas could be (and were) built on by later writers, but whose textual content was meant to be etched in ink and paper for all time.

Dynamic media can capture an auteur's meaning or vision in similar ways, but they are different from static communications media in that they convey works—for entertainment or to impart information—that are meant to transpire over some period of time. Gesture is the original dynamic medium, and spoken language followed it; live theater became their natural combination, as did so many classic incarnations of dynamic media—stories told around primitive campfires, Greek tragedies performed in the round or in amphitheaters, ancient and bloody encounters in the Roman Coliseum, Shakespeare's prolific works for the stage, modern Broadway shows, live music or even live sporting events. Any situation where performers engage an audience is dynamic media. Today, radio, television, and film are arguably the most recognizable modern incarnations of dynamic media, but the order also includes LP records, CD/DVD, games, animation, the telephone, and the internet.

Order	Dynamic			
Family	Spatial	Linear	Interactive	Networked
Genus	Mobiles, time-dependent architecture, toys, etc.	Film, television, radio, video, oratory, live theater, etc.	CD/DVD, pay-per-view, conversation, interactive theater, etc.	Telegraph, ham radio, telephone, Internet, mobile wireless, etc.

Figure 4.4. Phylum: Manufactured, Class: Communications, Order: Dynamic

Dynamic media provide a canvas for auteurs to produce time-varying works designed to be frozen in their original form for all time (or as long as the physical media on which they're recorded survive)—e.g., films, television programs, radio shows—or to create media or works of programming where the audience or users experience change by design, different each time the audience or users participate—e.g., electronic games, interactive theatre, or even simple channel-surfing.

Of the four types of dynamic media, I will focus on linear, interactive, and networked, as they are most subject to the effects of advances in digital and networking technologies. The landslide of innovation around these three families of media has revealed more of the über-nature of media and the more accurate definition of programming that will become increasingly important as we delve more deeply into this subject.

Linear Media

Linear media is characterized by two main features:

- *A one-directional flow of programming* Programming—the "message"—from a single individual (e.g., an orator), or a small group of individuals (e.g., a high school play), or enterprises (e.g., a promotional video), or institutions that make media their business (e.g., centralized sources of linear media product such as television networks and movie studios) that flows to an audience only enabled to consume, passively viewing or hearing.

- *Programming that lacks the elements of community, commerce, and code* Creators or programmers of linear media are limited in their palette of creative elements to content only. Television, video, radio, film, and much theater are linear media.

For example, the television show *Friends* was a product of the production company Bright-Kauffman-Crane, financed and distributed by Warner Bros., and licensed to NBC, which "retailed" it via broadcast. NBC spent millions of dollars blanketing the marketplace to let potential audiences know when and where it could be viewed. If you wanted to see it, you had to sit in front of a TV set on Thursday night while the only thing coming through the box was audio and video content.

By the design of the producers and distributors (and the limitations of the medium of conventional television), the audience couldn't change the content; nor could they change the flow of the content (other than changing the channel). Besides the people you watched it with in your own home—and statistics show that more than half of television audiences watch shows alone—you had no contact with other fans of the show while you were watching it. No community. Jim Moloshok, for many years a top television marketing executive at Warner Bros., correctly asserts that the closest thing to community for traditional TV is the laugh track—the recorded laughter meant to make viewers feel like they're laughing with the rest of the equally isolated members of the audience. Television programmers simulate community. Television is a genus of dynamic manufactured communications media, and species of television include broadcast, cable, and satellite.

In industries where media is not the core product (as it is for television, film, and music companies, for example), linear media have been relegated mostly to a marketing, advertising, or publicity role, or to specialized training and marketing functions, such as the "industrial video" or "corporate training." Mostly, "nonmedia" industries employ the manufactured static communications medium of print, but more and more they are using dynamic media like videotape and DVD. But the same limiting constraints apply: centralized media departments or outside production houses are enlisted to create "stories" consigned to tape or CD/DVD and distributed to staff members, customers, or business partners. Again by design, viewers cannot customize the programming in any way, and community is consigned to discussions, say, when a video is watched (passively) en masse.

In all cases for linear media, there are no elements of community, commerce, or code, since by definition linear media are incapable of accommodating those programming elements.

Interactive Media

These are the primary characteristics of interactive media:

- They are nonlinear—that is, participants can choose their
  path through the media or can access any part of the media

programming randomly. By this definition, board and card games classify as interactive media, albeit analog interactive media. Among those media classified as interactive media are: phonograph (vinyl LPs), pay-per-view, CD-ROM, DVD-ROM, console games, and arcade games. The advent of digital technology gave rise to three additional characteristics:

- They are bidirectional—users can impart an action or send data, and receive an action or response in return.

- Programmers employ both content and code—this enables participants to change the programming itself (like games) or the flow of programming (like pay-per-view or channel surfing).

- Like linear media or analog interactive media, the programming possesses limited or negligible ability to connect one participant to another—a requirement for creating community.

The compact disc (CD) is typical of interactive media. Whereas an audio-cassette tape require a listener to move through a predetermined order of programming (even fast forwarding) as programmed by the record company, thus making it a linear medium, a CD provides for instantaneous random access of tracks in the order the listener desires. Many CD players allow the listener to preprogram the order of tracks on a single disc or across multiple discs. Each disc contains content (audio) and code that enables the disc to play in the CD player device.

Today, virtually all CD or DVD games for the PC and various game consoles are interactive media. "Halo" is one of the top selling video games of all time. Available for the Xbox, Mac, and PC platforms, the series is designed to blend a franchise science-fiction back-story with an evolved first-person experience rooted in the legacy of classic action-shooter games such as "Quake" or "Doom." The game is a combination of content (animated renderings of a lead character—Master Chief—heroically exploring beautifully constructed landscapes, fantastic vehicles, and clever mechanisms) and code (instructions to the computer or game console given by the player that drives what happens on the screen). A successful experience includes conquering various challenges that enable players to proceed further into the game environment, further along in the story and, if they're skilled enough, eventually finish the game adventure. But it is similar to a TV show in that players have the experience alone or with a very few people immediately around them; it doesn't provide a truly communal event (unless in a "massively multiplayer" mode, which moves the experience into a networked medium). Some game-based interactive programming strives to simulate community dynamics. Lorne Lanning's "Oddworld" series is designed to encourage the player to enlist characters within the game for help in negotiating difficult passages. The "Oddworld" series is quite effective at engendering a feeling of community—though it is community with computer-generated avatars.

Interactive media programmers can also incorporate bidirectionality to employ commerce elements into their programming. For example, pay-per-view allows the consumer to pay for programming as they please, without having to go out-of-medium, such as to use a telephone to make a credit card purchase. The purchase of programming is simply charged to the cable bill. It is now common to find CD-ROM and DVD programmers who create titles that connect to the internet—so-called CD-ROM/DVD-web hybrids. Users can communicate with a server that unlocks hidden content on a disc—for free or for a fee—or enables them to download new game levels. These hybrid titles don't classify as "in-media" commerce—that is, the medium might be DVD, but the programmer had to use a separate medium, the Internet, to enable a supplemental transaction—but are an important first step since the programmers have brought commerce elements into the creative process.

Overall, digital interactive media have been widely hailed as the ultimate end point in media's evolution, but it turns out to be only the chrysalis between the caterpillar and the butterfly of linear media and networked media, respectively.

Networked Media

More than 90 percent of human DNA is the same as that of a mouse. If you've kept up to date on what's going on in genetic engineering, it's not outrageous to assume we may one day have the technology to apply gene therapy to a mouse and slowly morph it into an entirely different animal, or even into a human. It gives new meaning to the old phrase, "are you a man or a mouse?"

Now, what if you could do the same to all families of media—change their DNA so that they evolve into a new form of media? That's exactly what's happening. All electronic media are on an irrevocable evolution-ary march towards two confluent end points—becoming both digital and networked.

The ramifications of digital networked media are vast and go far beyond just the emergences of the new devices we're now using to experience text, audio and video, or the uniquely influential emergence of the internet. Even so, a medium does not have to be digital to be networked. For many years, the telephone industry was not digital, but instead evolved using the arcane analog technologies rooted in the manipulation of time-varying electromagnetic signals. The same is true of the telegraph or ham radio, and even, as j2 Global CEO Scott Jarus cited, nonelectronic analog technologies like "... the smoke signals or drumbeats of primitive indigenous peoples."

Networked media allow all endpoints on a network to be producer, distributor, vendor, marketer, or consumer, and connect to all other end-points in an exchange or conversation. Networked media can mimic linear media or interactive media, whereas the latter two cannot reciprocate; digital networked media provide a native environment for the four C's of code, content, community, and commerce to flourish equally. The first two, code and content, underscore the convergence in the use of the term programming—content programming and software programming. Con-tent programming, or community or commerce programming, cannot exist in networked media without some component of software. Any networked media device, from computer to mobile phone to set-top box, requires some element of software code to manipulate content, com-munity, and commerce functions. All four must be treated with equal consideration in this context.

The ancestry of networked media includes the telegraph and the tele-phone, and the future of networked media is not limited to the internet. Networked media is the fusion of the $500 billion-a-year telecom-munications industry, the $220 billion-a-year media industry (motion pictures, video, magazines, books, games, and music), and the $188 billion-a-year advertising industry that fuels $3 trillion-plus in annual retail sales in the U.S. market alone (in itself an inevitable participant in the growth of networked media). It doesn't end there. Fold in virtually all other industries profoundly affected by telecommunication, tradi-tional media, and retail—like education, health care, manufacturing, travel and leisure, transportation, and many, many others—and then give the general population a framework through which they can effect combinations. That is, network them in ways that close the feedback loop, aggregate their desires, virtually assemble, or take on new roles they couldn't easily take on pre-network.

The general population, of course, has always been the backbone of commerce, politics, society; we were simply missing the "connectivity"— the nervous system, if you will—that allows each part of this extended body to speak to the other. Networked media are capable of moving critical information from one part of the economic corpus to the other, while simultaneously flattening the topology of media. Of course, the parallel to a biological nervous system isn't perfect. In networked media, there is no central organizing structure like the brain that ultimately ties a biological nervous system together—there's no centralized programming and no distribution structures of linear and interactive media. It's more accurate to compare the structure to a distributed brain—a colony—where each little brain has the choice to work independently or in unison with other colony members.

Stan Davis and Christopher Meyer, authors of the book *Blur,* note that the economy is experiencing "a meltdown of traditional boundaries" where "neat value chains become messy economic webs." While they are absolutely correct that the boundaries are blurring, the "mess" they allude to is superficial. We're simply dealing with new and different organizing principles. An ant colony may look messy, but in reality it possesses sophisticated social order. This networked media community dynamic is very close to that what we see in physical, "real life" communities. Any limitations faced by members of a networked community have to do with the physical devices they use to connect to the network, not time or distance, as would be the case in a physical community. Today, a connection to a network via a full-blown computer is capable of richer media interaction than that enabled by a cell phone or PDA (true today, but changing rapidly). As devices become more sophisticated—everything from television sets to PDAs to car radios and, eventually, even what we've traditionally known as paper are all destined to be digital—all media will become networked media. All digital devices will be connected to some degree, and all media will embody the ability for the consumer to connect with the creators, distributors, marketers, and other consumers of programming—and to assume those same roles themselves.

Networked media will permeate all industries and all aspects of the economy, becoming a superset that will virtually subsume linear and interactive media. In this respect, it will act as a kind of global economic gene therapy—a change agent that relentlessly transforms the basic DNA of commerce, communications, information, and entertainment. This will profoundly affect social and individual human behavior. We understand pretty well the human conduct surrounding linear media, interactive media, and even rudimentary networked media (like the telephone) after decades and sometimes centuries of experience; but we're entering an age where networked media will become the rule instead of the exception. It will become clearer year to year that networked media adheres to a different set of rules, rules that are still just beginning to emerge.

CHAPTER 5

Networked Media

All men are caught in an inescapable network of mutuality.
—MARTIN LUTHER KING, JR.

Before a recent trip to Montreal, where I'd never been, I did some research. I used two sources: friends who had traveled there before and the internet. My online research centered on looking for a place to stay: somewhere nice, but not a large local hotel or hotel chain. I went to Google and searched "bed and breakfast in old town Montreal." The results were predictably well targeted. The third highlighted listing seemed particularly apropos, based on the short description, so I clicked on it. The detail page provided on that site—bbcanada.com, a compendium of bed-and-breakfast offerings across Canada—further fueled my interest. After searching around for a few more choices, I settled on a small B&B in Old Town Montreal called La maison du Patriote, and booked it.

In terms of location, the lodgings turned out to be right-on—smack dab in the middle of Old Town—and the price was right: about US$60. The owners, a young couple with a baby on the way, had established the B&B only a few months earlier. It was in an historic building—by definition, "old"—and they were clearly working to turn it into something really special. I was charmed by the ardent generosity and hospitality of my hosts—for my tastes, a hallmark of a good B&B. I asked how they started their business, how it was doing, and how they were marketing. For someone like me, steeped in internet technology and lore, the answer shouldn't have surprised me, but it did.

Originally, La maison du Patriote generated its business from three sources, in order of effectiveness: word of mouth, overflow from nearby hotels (another form of word of mouth) and walk-ins. The couple had no ad budget to speak of. While they were included in various freebie listing services, they were still just one of hundreds of other B&Bs. Before founding the B&B, the primary business of the wife in the couple was graphic and web design. She was pretty web savvy and knew the internet could be employed to market their new business. They could only afford one method of advertising, and they chose Google.

On many Google search results, you'll find a group of highlighted results listed on the right side of the results page. Individuals and enterprises pay for those; they actually "bid" on key words and phrases, agreeing to a maximum per-click payment (usually tens of cents) and subjecting themselves to the market forces arising from others bidding on similar key words and phrases. The bidding process determines what position an ad occupies in the paid search results. The proprietors of La maison du Patriote chose key phrases like the ones I typed, "bed and breakfast" and "old town Montréal," and bid enough for those key phrases to rank in the top three search results consistently over their first three months of participation in the ad program. But they only had to pay for each person who clicked through to their web page—again, that would normally be tens of cents per click, but it could go higher (up to their maximum bid) based on market dynamics.

By tapping into Google's massive search audience, La maison du Patriote was able to employ a supercharged word of mouth (or word of mouse) in a highly efficient manner. They created their own web page "brochure" using off-the-shelf hardware and software that already existed on their computer; included testimonies of reviewers and past lodgers; employed a highly trafficked internet search engine that afforded them reach to the entire networked planet; and engaged in a free-market dynamic that determined the amount they had to pay for each click from Google to their web page. The result was, by the owners' own admission, startlingly effective. During the first three months of their Google "campaign," their ad in Google's paid search results was viewed nearly 163,500 times (each view called an "impression"). But the little B&B didn't even have to pay for those. They only paid an average of $0.46 for each of those 1,710 times Google users clicked on their ad and came to their website. Those 1,710 "qualified leads" resulted in more than 60 percent of the B&B's business during the Google campaign. To that point in time, they had generated more than $13,000 of business directly attributable to $800 they spent on the Google campaign. That is, for every dollar they spent with Google, they generated $16.25 in business.

The word of mouse into which the owners of La maison du Patriote tapped is a powerful dynamic of networked media—without being wholly conscious of it, they employed networked media to program a marketing and advertising campaign that leveraged dynamics native to the family of media, and they did it without spending a lot of money. On a larger scale, Google and other sites like Yahoo! and MSN have found a way to monetize a service for which people are willing to pay, and it is demonstrably effective. But this dynamic is only one of many enabled by the power of networks; all are indicative of an inevitable future, and businesses (and the rest of us) would be well served to identify, learn from, and employ them. The age of networks has arrived, and it is enabling media—and us—to do things never possible before.

The Nature of Networks

In the 1960s, American psychologist Stanley Milgram tried to form a picture of the network of interpersonal connections that link people into a community. He sent letters to a random selection of people living in Nebraska and Kansas and asked each of them to forward the letter to a stockbroker friend of his in Boston whose address Milgram purposefully withheld. To forward the letter, he asked that each of them send the letter to someone they knew directly who might be more socially proximate to his stockbroker friend. Most of the letters eventually made it, and many in startlingly few hops—more often than not, six or less. The work became famous and inspired the phrase "six degrees of separation."

Advocates for the fishing industry in South Africa long argued that culling the seals off their coast would increase the number of hake, a popular commercial fish. Seals eat hake, of course, so linear logic would seem to support the theory that killing seals will result in more hake. Fortunately for the seals, it's not that simple; it turns out that the food chains we learned about in school are not chains at all. They're networks—webs—and intricately woven ones at that. Ecologist Peter Yodzis of the University of Guelph in Canada estimates that a change in the number of seals would influence the hake population by acting through intermediate species in hundreds of millions of interconnected pathways of cause and effect. "In nature, each species exists within a complex web of interactions with other species, yet almost all ecological research, both empirical and theoretical, focuses on one or two species as the object of study," explained Yodzis. He has spent half a life's work investigating "multispecies interactions"—interactions within community food webs containing at least twenty species. Using experimentation and sophisticated mathematical models, Yodzis and others doing similar work have virtually eradicated the notion of food chains, and given credence to the notion that all species are related to or dependent on each other to one degree or another within a diverse bionetwork.

This is the point in this book where reductive categorization would fail us in further pursuit of understanding networked media. "[All] networks share deep structural properties with the food webs of any ecosystem and with the network of business links underlying any nation's economic activity," wrote Mark Buchanan in *Nexus: Small Worlds and the Groundbreaking Science of Networks*. "Incredibly, all these networks possess precisely the same organization as the network of connected neurons in the human brain and the network of interacting molecules that underlies the living cell."

The study of networks is exploding these days. Some of the hottest research in economics, sociology, biology, genetics, and (obviously) telecommunications is rooted in the concept of looking at the world as a network of interconnected parts; this is the study of complexity theory—any collection of interacting parts, from atoms to bacteria or traders on a stock market floor. "Some of the deepest truths of our world may turn out to be truths about organization," wrote Buchanan, not absolute knowledge of the nature of constituent parts. Albert-László Barabási, in his book *Linked,* pointed out that we've spent "...trillions of research dollars to disassemble nature over the last century, [and] we are just acknowledging that we have no clue how to continue—except to take it apart further." Most people's first reaction to this new knowledge might be exasperation—how in the world can anyone, or anything, at once keep track of the millions of possible interconnections and relationships in the billions of systems and organisms that comprise the universe as we know it? But books like Barabási's and Buchanan's show how for the first time in history, the "math" to back up holistic views of the universe is arriving.

Complexity theory holds that matter, or more complex organisms composed of matter, tends to intermingle—whether this means galaxies colliding, a jungle rapidly overgrowing man-made structures, herd or flocking behavior among animals, or the circumventions of humans defying ineffectual governmental models of regulation in order to pursue some popular activity (think prohibition or the illicit drug business). All are examples of network dynamics. To the extent that the intrinsic nature of the universe tends toward networks, media technology is no different than the rest of the universe. Media technology is on an evolutionary march toward being networked because systems want to be networked. As we move from linear to interactive to networked media, the nature of that which moves through a medium—the programming—changes.

It should be no surprise that networking increases the complexity of any system. In fact, it could be argued that networked media programming is logarithmically different from linear programming. That is, networked media is probably as different from television as radio was from, say, cuneiform—the earliest form of writing. In short, networked media, while eminently understandable, is more complex because it has more elemental dimensions and constituents with which to program.

The Pillars of Programming

The term "programming," remember, evolved separately in the fields of media and computer science. For the former, it connotes the stuff that flows through mass media like television or print. For the latter, it refers to software created to allow computer-enabled devices to perform a function. Programming for networked media includes both, and can be represented by the four C's of content, community, commerce, and code. These are the pillars on which all programming efforts for networked media should be based. The better we understand them, the more effective we will be in creating compelling, effective, and profitable programming. (The way I'm treating the four C's here does not entail "technical" definitions, but rather derives from a programmatic viewpoint.) That is, how do we use programming to entertain—to divert, engage, compel, or amuse humans? The C's reflect the "how to" in engaging people to buy, watch, or do what we'd like them to do, employing media in the service of precipitating specifically desired action, response, or behavior.

When it comes to programming for networked media, community, commerce, and code are of equal (if not greater than) importance to content. For example, a chat room, as a mechanism, exhibits a community dynamic, but the text that shows up on chat boards is content—it just happens to be content created by the people chatting. Buying a subscription to the *Wall Street Journal* is commerce dynamic, but the text and graphics a subscriber gets are content. A multiplayer game has content comprising sophisticated graphics, text, and audio, and might enable community by allowing people to play the game simultaneously across vast distances, but it is useless without the code used by each respective player's computer to render the experience. With some notable exceptions, much internet programming created to date is poor. In too many cases, the four C's are thrust together clumsily, making it difficult and unpalatable for people to use and enjoy. One of those C's—code—is consistently underestimated by traditional media programmers.

In February 2003, some of the biggest video game publishers announced major delays in several of their much-anticipated titles, sinking the stocks of some and emphasizing the increasing technical demands on game developers. Electronic Arts, or EA, the world's biggest video-game software company, announced it would delay "Medal of Honor: Pacific Assault." The main problem seemed to be that the development team was slowed by a growing technological complexity that only added to the inherent unpredictability of software development. Industry insiders speculated to *Wired* that the game was pushed back because the console version of the game, released in fall 2003, took a critical drubbing, and that Activision's "Call of Duty," released that November, had set the new standard for World War II combat games—one that EA felt it had to surpass. Pushing back the release date of a major entertainment franchise is nothing new. Films and television shows get that treatment frequently. However, in the case of "Medal of Honor," it wasn't story or acting performances that had to be retooled; it was the very software code that enables the fidelity and complexity of the entire experience that had to be upgraded. Modern games are fundamentally reliant on software code; it is as important as content, perhaps more important, and both are key elements of this kind of programming.

In networked media, there is no separation between the four elements, unless by design or omission. The four C's are equal partners in a new kind of dance. But in the past, "content" has been synonymous with "media" or "programming." Community, commerce, and code were never consciously considered elements of media programming. Television and radio over the years aggregated some of the largest audiences in history, but both were missing the ability to accommodate community, commerce, and code elements. There was never any means of providing an "in-media" mechanism for them to connect with each other, interact (save for the remote control), or transact. Furthermore, producers of radio and television programming had to know little about the technological infrastructure necessary to deliver the experiences they authored. Writers need know nothing of printing presses; radio talk show hosts can know little about how their voices get across the country, or how radios reconstitute their signature utterances for the listeners. For better or for worse, these are not luxuries shared by those who would harness the dynamics of networked media at this stage of its evolution.

Radio, TV, and Commerce Interruptus

For radio, content means one thing and one thing only: audio. Radio provides no mechanism for allowing listeners to connect with each other in-medium. To engage a consumer in community activities, a programmer must go out of medium, either by getting listeners to use the phone or to physically go somewhere to connect with other people. Radio call-in shows create the illusion of community, but only a handful of audience members, out of the millions of listeners, can participate. Commerce in radio is similar. Consumers cannot transact through the radio itself. They must physically pick up the phone or travel to a commercial outlet referred to in an advertisement—a significant barrier to transaction. Code is simply nonexistent. As yet, radio programmers are unable to build anything into the broadcast signal to execute some function in the home, car, or wherever the receiving device sits.

Pillars of Programming	Radio	Television	Networked Media
Content	Audio	Audio Video	Audio, Video, Text, Graphics, Animation, 3-D, etc.
Community	Nothing "In-Programming" Requires out-of-medium action	Nothing "In-Programming" Requires out-of-medium action	Email, Chat, Instant Message, Blogs, SMS, multi-player games, etc.
Commerce	Nothing "In-Programming" Requires out-of-medium action	Nothing "In-Programming" Requires out-of-medium action	Hard & Soft Goods, Pay-Per (View, Play, etc.), Subscription, Microtransactions, etc.
Code	Nothing "In-Programming"	Nothing "In-Programming"	HTML, XML, VML, Java, C++, Perl, ASP, JSP, etc.

Figure 5.1. Palette of Programming: A Comparison of Radio, Television, and Networked Media

Television has twice as many content elements as radio (adding video to audio), but, interestingly, the complexity and cost of producing that content is many times greater than in radio programming. Visit a television studio or a movie set, and then visit a radio studio. The difference in the amount of equipment and personnel is striking: perhaps five or ten times more complex, not two times. As with radio there are few, if any, in-medium community, commerce, and code elements. HSN and QVC have a community element that is typically one-on-one and relies on the out-of-medium mechanism of the telephone. Game shows like *Who Wants to Be a Millionaire* or *Jeopardy* have a limited community element and now routinely go out-of-medium (into the web, wireless, or DVD) to capture other naturally occurring audience behavior. Like the home shopping channels, telethons successfully conduct live transactions over the phone, but the hurdles for viewers are not insignificant, and programmers rely on a blanketing, real-time approach that requires them to hope people are available to tune in at a specific time.

Ironically, the foundation of the American television and radio industries *is* commerce—thus the "commercial." Every advertiser on the planet is looking to sell something, and most of them use television and radio to support that effort. Yet, television and radio suffer from the inability to "complete the act"—to allow a person to *transact*. Both media, and other traditional media, have evolved with a fundamental flaw: they suffer from *commerce interruptus,* the inability to close a transaction within the medium itself. This puts them somewhat at risk as media evolve.

For starters, the television commercial is under assault. First came the remote control, which allowed viewers to zip away from television advertising without having to leave their chairs. Then came the VCR, which enabled viewers to record their favorite shows and watch them at their leisure, allowing them to fast-forward through the commercial breaks. Now, digital video recorders (DVR) and personal video recorder (PVR) services such as TiVo have given viewers even more power to bypass commercial messages. A PVR is a set-top box that enables viewers to record television shows on a hard disk for concurrent or later playback. Advertisers see PVRs as a threat and the television networks have been uncomfortable with this technology—though most have invested in it. This new technology will give everyone the capacity to delete commercial messages from daily programming. An entire industry will need to find new methods for generating revenue.

Television first began to cure this affliction—its dependence on the commercial—with the advent of cable, pay-per-view, and satellite. By 2003, roughly 86 percent of US households received some form of these paid services, up from 79 percent in 1998. By 2004, cable and satellite subscriptions accounted for more than two-thirds of the estimated $59 billion in total television-related revenue. Before cable, 100 percent of television revenue came from advertising; today, advertising provides only 30 percent of that revenue.

The trend in television is clearly headed towards an environment where viewers foot a bigger and bigger piece of the tab. A large portion of a U.S. subscriber's monthly cable bill (the U.S. average for basic cable is now more than $38 per month) goes to paying not just for delivery, but for content. For example, according to Kagan Research, in 2004 average cable subscribers paid $1.50 per month to ESPN whether they watch it or not. ESPN generates 70 percent of its revenue from subscriber fees, even though most subscribers aren't aware they're actually paying a subscription. These subscriber fees account for between 27 percent (MTV) and 100 percent (Disney Channel) of each cable network's revenues.

The commerce at work in the cable and satellite industry is akin to a wholesaler-retailer relationship. The television network is the wholesaler and the cable or satellite company is the retailer, and both take a piece of the pie. The creators of such programming aren't actually employing commerce dynamics within the programming. With pay-per-view, on the other hand, programmers understand that the only way their programming will succeed is if they can create a direct connection with an audience, each member of which must make the effort to transact in order to view the programming. The percentage of television's overall revenues that comes from pay-per-view is small but growing, and it clearly falls into the definition of commerce developed herein. Before much longer, pay-per-view television (and other on-demand offerings) will simply become part of the larger scheme of networked media.

Programming for Networked Media

Unlike radio and TV, most networked media typically have many different classes of content elements, which might include text, static and 3-D graphics, animation, dynamic database-driven information, and game elements. On top of that, networked media have a dozen or more intrinsic community, commerce, and code elements that can be considered when developing programming. Taken together, these different tools make for an incredibly rich and complex palette for the creative programmer looking to capture and nurture a particular behavior. Truly viable networked media are defined by the fact that they find ways to deploy all of the four C's to one degree or another and integrate them into a relatively unified media experience. To this point, hard examples of fully mature networked media outlets are hard to find, but they are evolving at such a rapid pace that it's as though they're taking shape before our eyes.

Thousands of examples may be found all over the internet of relatively ineffective or superficial applications of networked media programming. For example, Passitalong.com did a brilliant job of building a community-content site that at one time vaulted it into the Jupiter MediaMetrix Top 50. Unfortunately, the site built no commerce elements into the mix other than advertising. Result? It's dead. Amihot.com started out similarly, but that site's still alive because its owners found a way to add commerce elements to its programming that tapped into the explosive growth of online dating. Individuals post images and data about themselves, or sometimes unwitting friends, and then subject them to "rating" by other internet users. Amihot.com left its core programming—the ability for users to post pictures of themselves or acquaintances for rating—as a free service to capture audience, but laced in a premium subscription service that allows members to send private mail to users, read their bios, view private photos, and post up to ten photos. Pictures of paid subscribers also show up on the home page, and their profiles always show up in the top of any searches by other users. They can customize their level of exposure. People seek out paid users because they know they can contact them. Amihot.com also employs auctions that enable users to "buy" the homepage. A minimum bid of $2.50 puts users in the running to win the prime position for their photo, with market dynamics the ultimate arbiter of who wins the placement. This site figured out the networked media commerce dynamic and, so far, is surviving. Individuals and institutions alike must realize that—unless they're doing so for personal, altruistic, or nonprofit reasons—creating programming for networked media that doesn't incorporate community and commerce elements is tantamount to economic suicide. Only a few can hope for success by following the traditional media models of radio, television, and film. Advertising alone simply cannot support the diverse sea of programming that is networked media. The history of the cable industry, again, is instructive here—even the most successful channels generate less than 50 percent of their revenue from advertising. But even disregarding commercial necessity, programming that lacks all of the four C's will almost always fall short when it comes to fully satisfying audience members.

As treated earlier, networked media possess many mechanisms that allow humans to connect to each other—email, instant messaging, text messaging, message boards, fan pages, multiplayer games, chat are available to connect humans with other community members. In the commerce space, hard goods, soft goods, subscriptions, pay-per-play, pay-per-view, pay-per-download, and (more and more) microtransactions are all being exchanged. Networked media programmers would be wise to use all of these elements. In fact, there are only three reasons why a programmer should omit any of the four C's:

- *Creative* There is some creative statement to be made via the inclusion or omission of programming elements.

- *Technological* The technology may not be sophisticated or mature enough to allow people to engage, interact, or transact with the programming easily, as envisioned by the programmer

- *Economic* Some programming elements may simply be too expensive to justify their use and still recoup the cost of building the programming.

It's not easy to create programming that deploys all of the four C's in effective ways that, ideally, are intuitive and transparent. The better the programming does this, the easier it will be for users to enjoy, and thus the easier it will be for the programmer to monetize the programming. In this context, going out-of-medium is not in and of itself bad. Game companies that distribute their games on DVD and then provide upgrades, updates, and supplemental content via the internet are an example of this cross-media programming, as are television shows that use phone, web, and wireless for voting *(American Idol),* supplemental programming (the *Who Wants to be a Millionaire* phone-a-friend lifeline), or commerce (any home shopping show). It can sometimes be very effective and for now at least it reflects a pragmatism necessary in the contemporary business and technology climate. There are still some things that cannot be done with quality, reliability, and economy in networked media.

The core power of networked media lays in the element of community—the ability to attract other members of the network to a specific topological level of connected commonality where they act in a way that is monetizable. Television has been very good at attracting folks to unconnected commonality. *The Apprentice* routinely attracts 20 million simultaneous viewers, yet they are unable to speak to each other. (except for very small numbers via telephone, which is not a part of the linear television medium). The telephone is a networked medium separate, though employable, by television programmers. The producers of *American Idol* have used this out-of-medium process to attract huge numbers of voters. Tens of millions of votes are logged via mobile phones and landlines each season of the show. Television has also been very good at monetizing that unconnected commonality through a contrivance of the "commercial" and, more recently, subscription cable and pay television. But once you allow audience members to interact with each other, the dynamics become vastly more powerful and complex.

If a programmer in any medium believes it's necessary to go out-of-medium to build a multifaceted and complete media experience, by design the task then becomes to orchestrate that experience—to program symphonically across the multiple media. However, most traditional companies, and most programming formats, aren't organized properly to create this kind of programming. Consider how major music companies are trying to ram their increasingly outmoded economic model down the throat of internet users. In the face of users displaying obvious and rampant natural behavior, they should be doing everything in their power to harness that behavior, not ban it.

Whether within networked media, or across multiple complementary media, the great challenge for creators/programmers is to reconsider their efforts and try to figure out how to base them on a new foundation supported by the four-C pillars.

Networked media marks a profound change in the relationship between creator and consumer. As McLuhan emphasized, the specific form of any widely adopted medium evolves human cognition; networked

media is evolving human cognition in directions unfamiliar to programmers and producers of media product that have come before. In
addition to the multiplicity of programming elements, and the increased
complexity in the creative process they beget, our perceptions of how
networked media effectively "rewires" our brains and behavior, in
McLuhan terms, must be addressed. Like the hunter learning to stalk a
new kind of prey, the manner in which we treat the audiences that are
the targets of a programmer's efforts, how we engage, divert, or compel
some desired behavior, passive or active—that is, entertain them—must
change as well.

CHAPTER 6

All Business is Show Business

ENTERTAINMENT, n. Any kind of amusement whose inroads stop short of death by injection.

—AMBROSE BIERCE, THE DEVIL'S DICTIONARY

Eyeballs: every business wants them. Those "businesses" ultimately want the wallets and bank accounts behind those eyeballs—or ears, or taste buds, or noses—but they need the eyeballs before they get to the lucrative attachments. Whether literally, or as a euphemism for engaging the awareness of a potential customer, capturing the attention of any human sense is essential to imparting a message, attracting an audience, or compelling some collective (often commercial) behavior—getting humans to transact in some way.

It is inarguable that media are inextricable from all human-to-human interaction. It would follow that my assertion that "all companies are media companies" is also irrefutable, as any organism composed of human beings looking to compel other human beings to adopt some desirable behavior is, by definition, human-to-human interaction. So, as a commercial enterprise looking to engage eyeballs and then compel the brains behind those valuable orbs to absorb a message or to take some kind of action, what dynamic or technique do you employ? How do you get them past the first page of a brochure? How do you construct a television commercial to maximize the probability a viewer will run out and buy the featured product or service? How do you get scores of executives afflicted with attention-deficit disorder to read more than the first paragraph of your proposal? How do you get someone to come to your website and stay? Or play a game from beginning to end? Simple. It's called entertainment.

As with the term "media," we could profit from refining our understanding of the term "entertainment." Is a television commercial "entertainment"? Some. Is a really good teacher "entertaining?" Too few.

Are you "entertaining" at your dinner party on Friday nights? Only after a few highballs. Do we "entertain" the opinions of others? Not often enough.

We often use the term "entertainment" to refer specifically to mass media such as television, film, and radio—mainly because these are entertainment forms that can and have been commercialized and monetized on a large scale. This use of "entertainment" is limiting because the act of entertaining is important to all aspects of commercial and social interactions, not just the traditional entertainment business commonly associated with media companies. Simply put: entertainment can be anything that engages, compels, amuses, pleases, or diverts. A shopping spree or an afternoon picnic can be entertaining. Playing a game of hoops or a challenge match with your weekly tennis foursome is entertainment. Some social historians believe that many people participated in the crusades as much to escape the boredom of medieval village life—in other words, for the entertainment value—as out of religious fervor. Whatever the experience, message, or action to which one wishes others to ascribe, if it can be represented as entertaining, the chances are much better others will participate. "Entertainment programming" refers to any experience or information presented in a way that engages, diverts, or compels the recipient of the information, or participant in the experience, to some end.

So, from the standpoint of a creator/communicator, whether the creation is a film or a technical manual, every bit of message is entertainment, however utilitarian its purpose. Anyone who has ever flown Southwest Airlines knows it has forever changed the boringly repetitive airline safety briefings required by the Federal Aviation Administration. They allow their flight attendants to improvise their safety briefings, often encompassing a few jokes and plays on words while still imparting the important information required by regulations. They've turned something tedious and functional into entertainment. A sales presentation should be entertaining as well as informative. Television news programmers discovered long ago that they could boost ratings by mimicking the network's entertainment division and infusing news stories with a sense of drama, rhythm, and (sadly) marketing hype.

Bran Ferren is the Oscar-nominated former president of creative technologies for Walt Disney Imagineering. One would not expect someone with Ferren's background to be hired as a consultant by the U.S. Navy, but in fact he was brought in to explore cross-pollinating the art of war with the art of the entertainment business. He explained the incongruity this way: "I have never known a great teacher, a great political leader, or a great military leader who also wasn't a great storyteller. Education is a storytelling problem. Leadership is a storytelling problem." Franklin Roosevelt's fireside radio chats during the Great Depression had the aim of influencing and galvanizing public opinion, but they were also superb performances—which had a lot to do with their being so memorable. Later, the popularity of television changed the very nature of the presidency, requiring our leaders to become more telegenic and "entertaining."

A strong leader is intrinsically a good entertainer, but the ability to engage, divert, or compel isn't restricted to the mode of storytelling. It's true that individuals imparting information to one or more people are generally doing it in storytelling fashion. In fact, entertainment as a whole is often mistakenly equated with a storyteller entertaining a passive audience. But entertainment is multifaceted, and it's certainly not always one-way or linear—that is, not always in a storytelling form. A military leader managing a wargame simulation where thousands of soldiers and officers are "living" a game is not engaged in storytelling. Citizens attending a town hall meeting, where the attendees are allowed to interrupt, ask questions, and change the "flow" of their leaders' stories are not participating in storytelling. A group of friends drinking wine and playing a spirited game of "Cranium" are certainly not passively being told a story, either. So if these folks aren't engaged in storytelling, what are they doing?

There's No Such Thing as Interactive Storytelling

"Interactive storytelling" is just the type of oxymoron against which legendary comedian George Carlin is famous for railing (others include "jumbo shrimp" and "military intelligence"). Storytelling is just that—storytelling. Storytelling is one-directional—from storyteller to audience—linear, and fixed. Interactivity is bidirectional—actions proceed from programming (or programmer) to participant(s) and, in turn, from participant(s) back to programming, which is altered by the participant's response. This composite term has an inherent incongruence that has misled many. If it's true that "interactive storytelling" is a fantasy, then is storytelling the only form of entertainment? Certainly not. Consider an increasingly popular pastime—the computer game. It is most certainly entertainment; but is it storytelling? Not to the player, no. What about playing chess? It is not storytelling, nor is it interactive storytelling. Playing in a pickup basketball game is also entertainment, to most of us who play, but it's no more storytelling than a game of cards. It is intuitive and reasonable to assume there are other forms of entertainment that differ from storytelling. But what are they?

Entertainment suffers from an ailment that afflicts media in general—a lack of taxonomy to differentiate its various forms. Fortunately, there are far fewer forms of entertainment than there are of media. In fact, there are three: storytelling, storyforming, and storydwelling. While entertainment in any of these forms can be staged across the spectrum of all media, this discussion of entertainment is limited to the context of the three families of media—linear, interactive, and networked. Just as networked media is a superset of interactive media, which is itself a superset of linear media, so do storytelling, storyforming, and storydwelling build upon each other, with storydwelling subsuming the former two in its ability to mimic them both.

Storytelling

Storytelling has been around as long as mankind, going back at least as far as when humans scratched drawings on cave walls and adventurers regaled small groups with oral recitations of myth and fact. It is typified by a one-directional flow of programming centrally conceived by one (a storyteller) or more persons. Examples of storytelling should be intuitive to us all. They include everything from the books of the Bible and Homer's *Odyssey* to *The Da Vinci Code,* films from *The Great Train Robbery* to *Finding Nemo,* television shows like *Friends, The Apprentice,* and *CSI,* and countless other poems, plays, films, books, radios, television series, and radio shows. Works of music—from symphonies to single songs—are also forms of storytelling, as is dance. Even paintings and sculpture, forms of art that date back to mankind's earliest days, are considered effective modes through which to "tell a story." From an audience's point of view, a storytelling experience is passive and one-directional—auteur to audience—and desirably so.

Storyforming

In storyforming experiences, which have been around as long as story-telling, the audience can change the flow of programming, or the actual programming itself. Historically, storyforming has taken the form of games—checkers, chess, or board games—that is, anything that allows one to affect the outcome of the event. But with advances in technology, like the television and its now inseparable consort—the remote control, storyforming now also includes behavior like channel surfing. Channel surfing may not comprise a three-act story structure, or adhere to the stages of Joseph Campbell's mythic-hero's journey, but channel surfers are shaping their own story and experience nonetheless.

Storyforming has been exalted over the last twenty years or so through digital technologies developed primarily through the video, PC, and console game industries. More than 20 million copies of the popular series of computer games, "The Sims," had been sold through the end of 2003. While numbers of units sold indicate a very broad appeal game, one of the demographic groups the series is most popular with is preteen and teenage girls. Little wonder. The Sims games allow players to build and define characters, neighborhoods, and relationships and set parameters through which a social simulation takes place. Simulated characters interact, get married, get jobs, have children, and get divorced—all subject to the godlike power of the human players, manipulating the simulation through the choices they make. Players are storyforming in a way that combines the Barbie, Colorforms, and pretend-tea-party activities so popular with past generations of girls, and supercharge it with the graphics and networking technologies so popular with the present generation of girls.

Many electronic games are not even pure storyforming experiences. While many well-crafted games give the impression of infinite ways to play them—to form the story as a player chooses—storytelling is still their main component. In popular video games like "Halo," "Half-Life," "Splinter Cell," or dozens of so-called "platformers" like "Ratchet &

Clank," "Crash Bandicoot" or "Jak & Daxter," the player is said to be "on rails." That is, there is an overarching structure to the game—a storytelling engine—that result in a finite (and very small) number, of possible outcomes. Most often there is only one. Within this encompassing storytelling structure, there is a storyforming experience—an infinite variety of choice-compositions along the way. It's a bit like riding on a train: there are essentially infinite ways to ride inside—where you sit, for how long, who you talk to, what you eat—but ultimately the train and all its passengers will end up in the same place.

Collectively, billions of dollars have been spent to enable storyforming (especially in the form of games) to become a more articulate and compelling experience, and collectively account for the fastest growing segment of the worldwide entertainment industry. Furthermore, while traditional pastimes like board games and card games will remain storyforming activities ad infinitum, technology is enabling many digital-based storyforming experiences to graduate into the ultimate of entertainment experiences: storydwelling.

	Telling	Forming	Dwelling
Programmer's Role	Auteur/Presenter	Story Engine Builder/Manager	World Builder/Manager
Audience Role	Passive Observer	Puppeteer	Participant
Audience Psychology	Empathetic	Influential	Experiential
Audience Sensorial Experience	Passive	Interactive	Immersive

Figure 6.1. Audience Attributes for Different Types of Entertainment

Storydwelling

Storydwelling includes and subsumes both storytelling and storyforming. While storyforming allows one to control or direct programming, or the flow of programming, the individual still stands outside the experience, looking in, like a puppeteer managing his charges. Storydwelling, on the other hand, involves immersion into actual participation in the evolution of a story, or a deep psychological association with characters or avatars within the "story."

Simply living one's life can be looked at as a physically immersive storydwelling experience. In the context of a shorter time frame, playing sports classifies as the quintessential storydwelling experience—a sporting event has a beginning, middle, and end, and the players are fully immersed participants directly affecting the outcome. Similarly, gambling is storydwelling. Cards, chess, checkers, and the board game "Monopoly" are storyforming, but "Dungeons & Dragons" is storydwelling. Why? Except for pathological situations, players do not psychologically identify themselves with a jack of diamonds, a chess rook, or a black checker; the creation of a "Dungeons & Dragons" character, however, is an intensely personal process—the avatar is in some way a little piece of the creator, the player, the participant. Stage actors are storydwelling during a performance. Even though the script has been written, the sets have been built, and they've run through the production dozens of times, they are still dwelling within a story, participating in the performance's unfolding. Rehearsing for a keynote speech or role-play practice for a presidential debate are storydwelling activities. Live war games, reality television game shows (for the contestants only), or a children's game of "Cowboys and Indians" all classify as storydwelling experiences. Storydwelling entails immersive experiences requiring the physical or psychological presence of participants, whether representing themselves or playing roles. If it doesn't require either sensorial immersion, or a specific manifestation/projection of the participants' psyches, the experience remains in the realm of storyforming.

As we continue to develop technologies for fooling the senses, the virtual and the actual intermingle in storydwelling more and more. It's no longer just physical participation that serves as the primary distinction between the storyforming and storydwelling. To the uninitiated observer, the physical action necessary to play "Pac-Man" on a Game Boy is virtually indistinguishable from playing "Halo" on an Xbox console or "EverQuest" on a PC. They're all just games, right? Not right. It's the experience inside the head of the participant that distinguishes between storyforming and storydwelling experiences.

To qualify as storydwelling, the "audience" must contribute as participant; their level of psychological engrossment must be fully experiential; and they must undergo either full or partial sensory immersion.

Remember, storydwelling is a superset of telling and forming. That is, in a storydwelling experience one can generally choose to be a full participant and actually be a character within the story (storydwelling mode); one can directly affect the evolution of the story—through coaching, kibitzing, or puppeteering—without actual participation (storyforming mode); or we passively watch the storydwelling experience unfold (storytelling mode). In this way, storydwelling is an analog for our real lives: in a sense, we are literally dwelling within a live story (we might even call that "storyliving"). For example, playing "Pac-Man" or "Donkey Kong "or "Super Mario Brothers"—all classic video games—clearly entails manipulating an iconic character: the little man, the big monkey, or the mustachioed brothers. Whereas in, say, playing ice hockey, it is the actual player winning or losing, not a separate entity controlled by the player. It's a fine line, but a clear one. Let's take a contemporary example: Sony's massively multiplayer game "EverQuest." By 2003, hundreds of thousands of people were paying Sony $10 per month to participate in the popular role-playing action game. Subscribers create a character or characters (often several) called avatars to represent them in the game's virtual world—a highly graphic and animated realm inside the computer. It's role-playing on steroids. Now, most of the well-adjusted, sane players know it is not them in the virtual world, but they have specifically crafted the avatars to represent them. Sometimes participants even create and train an avatar, then sell it in the marketplace—often on eBay. However, the avatar is still meant to represent the player—whether the creator or second-hand buyer—when meandering the virtual landscape.

This is the first way modern role-playing storydwelling games have separated themselves from storyforming games: there is a one-to-one relationship between the in-game avatars created by role-playing gamers and the gamers themselves. In a piece entitled "Confessions of an Ultima Addict," online gamer Tabitha King wrote about her experience with the massively multiplayer game "Ultima:"

> My game starts when the sun goes down and the lights go off. Darkness sets the stage for my alter ego. The surroundings could be described as a mystical medieval setting, with various towns and villages, day and night, plants, wildlife and characters all programmed to give you a sense of realism. Even though I'm a woman, I can log onto my account to create

a maximum of five different characters, male or female, with any length or color of hair (which you can change later, if you can find a shop that sells dye) and, of course, your skill.

Skills are the key to your character's success, so choosing wisely is a matter of life and death. The concentrated effort in building the skill you choose is the best part of the game. Alchemist, blacksmith, healer, magery, tailor, scriber, and many more, including begging and stealing. Carpenters build furniture, tailors make clothes, blacksmiths make armor and weapons, and healers can cure you from snakebites, illnesses, and even death. Pick one, and then develop those skills to become a master at your craft.

If you believe this is a simple and quick effort—it's not. The only way to build your skill is to use it, continuously, and that can take months.... Neglect your skills and your skill level and attributes will suffer, leaving you as a vulnerable victim and a miserable existence.

During play, if someone distracts you (in the real world) and you step away, leaving your character vulnerable, a vicious monster may come by and kill you. Leaving your dead body to the looters and wildlife.

Notice King's narrative voice blurs the identification of characters in "Ultima" with the players who create and deploy them—"Leaving your dead body to the looters and wildlife." That blur indicates how "Ultima" and "EverQuest" tend towards storydwelling entertainment, away from storyforming. Even so, computer role-playing games in general still border on the storyforming. King still refers to her "alter ego" as a "character" she controls; of courses she knows it's not her in the virtual world, but an avatar fully under her control. Regardless, her passion for this kind of immersive experience is evident.

The psychological aspect of storydwelling should not be underemphasized. As stated earlier, any entertainment experience—telling, forming, or dwelling—can be staged via any medium. The skill of the telling/forming/dwelling creator and the susceptibility/willingness of the audience determine how deeply an audience "buys in." Regardless of where the entertainment experience is rooted—film, book, television, sporting event, electronic game—there is a psychological trigger that graduates a person from one to another. To a rabid fan of soap operas or other television programs—storytelling experiences—audience empathy can become so deep that some fans become convinced the scenarios and characters presented on-screen are real. Believe it or not, some people think Ross and Rachel of *Friends* are real people living real lives. For the average chess player, the game is a storyforming experience. However, intense players or masters can create powerful psychological associations with their pieces—their queen, for example—the loss of which can result in profound visceral reactions. The average card player is typically storyforming, casually disassociated from the actual cards and the experience; but anyone who has watched the world poker championships knows those players are living that experience. Every card dealt, drawn or flipped can be life-changing. Similarly, average players of storyforming electronic games like "Halo," "Half-Life," or "Medal of Honor" know they are not characters in the game; but having played these (and many other) games from beginning to end, I can assure you there are times in any well-crafted storyforming experience of similar ilk that one easily loses themselves in the experience, becoming completely immersed, losing the real world, and dwelling within the game. While the feeling is fleeting, it is legitimate. When the association with a playing piece, card or character is intense enough, a telling or forming experience can cross into the realm of dwelling—a psychological threshold is crossed, making the telling or forming experience "real" to those experiencing it.

For most of us, there still exists a technological gap between "actual" storydwelling experiences and emergent digital ("virtual") storyforming experiences. In live sports, if you get hit, you get hurt. When you throw a ball, it moves according to the laws of physics and can be caught by another physical human. From that physical immersion follows psychological immersion. For synthetic storydwelling experiences, though, physical immersion—that is, the immersion of our senses—lags far behind psychological immersion. Physical immersion is limited by technology. We have flat, window-like screens and abstract apparatus like a game pad or mouse to control "action," giving us only partial sensory immersion. There have been many means developed to improve such "immersion" for all kinds of communications experiences—teleconferencing, 3-D projection and glasses, large-format projection like IMAX, ride films at theme parks. But as good as many of us are at psychologically submitting to a synthetic experience—television, movie, book, radio—none approach full sensorial immersion into an authentic synthesized storydwelling experience. The best we have today can be found in the business of simulation.

Simulation is, by definition, storydwelling. The simulation industry attempts to fool the human senses with state-of-the-art technologies, most of which (thus far) have been developed for training purposes. They've done a good job. According to engineers at CAE, the largest builder of commercial airline simulators in the world, in order to qualify to fly a new type of aircraft today, already certified commercial pilots can take all of their training on the new type of aircraft in a simulator and then step directly into the cockpit of the real thing—loaded with passengers—without ever having actually flown the new aircraft. These superreal simulators can cost tens of millions of dollars each, but they represent the highest level of realism technology has yet been able to achieve, designed specifically to fool all but the sense of taste. Industries that utilize any form of vehicle are adopting simulation technology to provide a realistic but ultimately safe environment to run trainees through thousands of scenarios—scenarios that are essentially stories.

Several of the world's militaries have spent billions on the creation of sophisticated simulation centers. The Combined Arms Tactical Trainer (CATT) facility in Warminster, England is one of the most sophisticated. Dozens of ground vehicle simulators—blank metal shells containing realistic copies of the interior workings of tanks, armored vehicles, and personnel carriers—are networked together in a vast warehouse space. This austere real environment hides a robust virtual one: the CATT facility can drop the virtual position of the simulators into a synthetic universe such that all the sensory input reaching the trainee makes them feel like they are traveling and fighting through one of three high-fidelity representations—one of southwest England, one of a region of northern Europe, and one of an unspecified desert terrain. Whole companies of armored cavalry can train for hours at a time, fully immersed in completely virtual world. When I met with him, CATT commander Lieutenant Colonel Anthony De Ritter told me, "This is no game. This is serious kit... and may be the difference between life and death for these lads." Technology continues to enable the evolution of these kinds of immersive experiences. There are many "EverQuest"-like alternative universes that defy the essential definitions of storytelling or storyforming and demand to be classified separately—as storydwelling.

Today, the use of networked media is trending toward the storydwelling mode. Projecting oneself into a virtual world of stores, travel agents, communal centers, news desks, editorial opinions, and game boards is by definition a storydwelling experience. The world of networked media is a virtual abstraction of a variety of real world constructs mixed with constructs that simply could not exist in the real world (like a massively multiplayer game world). For programmers, it may be most appropriate to treat networked media as if users' psychological avatars (or variants of them) are negotiating a virtual universe. Analogies of networked media (like the internet) that liken these types of media to physical spaces are insufficient. The evolution of technology is helping programmers in their efforts to create programming that is participatory, psychologically experiential, and sensorially immersive. Technology is already continuing its inexorable march toward virtualizing the actual, notably through telecommunications technologies like mobile wireless, and actualizing the virtual, through the further development and distribution of simulation technologies.

Using entertainment for any purpose—commercial, political, personal, military—requires an understanding of how to program in its various forms. Storytelling programming is pretty well understood; even story-forming programming has come quite a long way—recall that the electronic game industry is currently the fastest growing segment of the entertainment marketplace. But there still exists a dearth of understanding of how to create articulate synthetic storydwelling programming. Much of this is due to current limitations of technology, but not entirely so. Contemporary storydwelling experiences created on purpose within existing contemporary media are still rare.

Orchestrating those various forms of entertainment—within one medium or across multiple media—is a key to employing entertainment more effectively and more profitably.

The Spectrum of Experience and the Octaves of Entertainment

Media pundits have produced much discussion about the so-called "lean forward" and "lean back" experiences. The lean-forward type are more interactive experiences that require frequent interfacing by the participant; lean-back types are usually more conducive to the participant remaining passive and unresponsive. The distinction is too superficial. We've all seen audiences at sporting events—from the fan point of view, normally classified as a storytelling type of experience—who were anything but lean-back passive and noninteractive. American football has even adopted the term "the twelfth man" to describe the effect a passionate crowd of fans can have on the outcome of a game. Lean-forward experiences are characterized as more "immersive" than lean-back experiences, "immersive" implying a certain level of engrossment, direct interaction, or suspended disbelief. But it is easier to immerse a viewer in a well-made film (lean-back) than a mediocre electronic game (lean-forward). Immersivity is a measure of the success of a piece of programming, not a type of programming in and of itself. Storytelling, storyforming, and storydwelling experiences can (and should) always be as immersive as possible.

It may be more instructive to refer to entertainment experiences as "ten foot" or "two foot" experiences. When offered any form of entertainment at two feet removed and at ten feet removed, people will respond in different ways. Some are comfortable answering email at ten-feet through their internet-enabled television, others are not. Some enjoy watching a movie on their laptop or desktop PC, others do not. Most everyone likes playing the same game on a console (connected to television) as they do on a PC.

This suggests that the boundaries between these classifications of entertainment aren't perfectly delineated. In fact, the three families of entertainment form a continuum with an uninterrupted scale from passive to active, just as in real life. Programming can be created that lies anywhere on the passive-active spectrum—or an experience may move along the spectrum over time. Imagine watching a sporting event on television (passive, linear storytelling), then moving to the console player or PC after the event to play a game based on the sport (interactive, storyforming), and then moving online into a fantasy league with chat rooms, trading opportunities, and other community activities (active, networked, storydwelling). Think of this breadth in the range of experiences as like the scale of a three-octave musical instrument. For practical purposes, the infinite shades of real experience can be binned into discrete experiences, much like the keys of a piano correspond to discrete set of notes. As author Doug Floyd has said, "You don't get harmony when everyone sings the same note." A composer doesn't use all the notes on the scale when writing a musical piece, and even if he or she did they wouldn't use them all at the same time. Entertainment programmers should heed the metaphor. Effective programming for networked media may, in fact, be more like building a musical instrument and giving users basic instruction on how to use it. Everyone will use it differently. Moreover, while a single person can play a single note at any given time—notes being analogous to some activity along the spectrum from creation to consumption—many people playing together can create infinitely diverse harmonies.

Some level of literacy is necessary on the part of both creators and consumers to explore the broader possibilities of networked media, in particular to learn the implications of how multiple contributors/players/users create unique experiences in which all of them participate to one degree or another, and which all of them experience in ways that are partly shared and partly unique to each individual. Humans utilizing networked media become different kinds of creatures than the purveyors of product and programming have encountered before. In fact, those who were relegated to consumer are no longer restricted to that role (nor satisfied with it). Combine networked media with humankind and you get a web of multifaceted humans with attributes unknown to their prenetworked brethren. You get a unique type of human. You get humanodes.

CHAPTER 7

The Humanode

Everything that is really great and inspiring is created by the individual who can labor in freedom.

—ALBERT EINSTEIN

History has shown that whenever there are new discoveries or inventions, certain terms are reinvented in light of those discoveries. The term "channel" had very different meanings before radio and television, mostly referring to bodies of water. "Broadcast" was originally an agricultural term referring to the spreading of seeds, yet it suited its new application so well that the new definition has almost completely replaced the original meaning of the word for modern generations. As discussed in earlier chapters, the evolution of networked media requires just such a reevaluation of traditional vocabulary associated with media and entertainment. But certain aspects of the changes networked media portends require entirely new terms to describe them.

Remember, we're talking about a future world where every digital device will be linked to every other digital device. Regardless of the apparatus—cell phone, PDA, computer, or even your TV, car stereo, or refrigerator—people will be able to interact, in real time or asynchronously, as smart nodes on a network full of other such nodes. Each of these nodes can just as easily be an individual as a major corporation. The exchanges among the nodes can be personal, social, commercial, or political in nature, and together they will create a new kind of linked society. Linear mass media tend to isolate people into experiences that are shared, but disconnected; networked media connects (or reconnects) people, groups of people, enterprises, governments, and all manner of institutions (or humans working on behalf of institutions) in virtual and digital analogs of meeting places, forums, and marketplaces.

Networked media has the potential to be orders of magnitudes more powerful than face-to-face interaction between physical humans. Spheres of influence or interest can be widened without boundary as physical barriers drop, enabling new dimensions of human interaction that conceivably have the power to change the very nature of humans themselves. This kind of networked human might be different enough from our ancestors to warrant a special taxonomical classification; if you accept an assertion that McLuhan also once claimed, technological advancement directly affects not only human cognition, but also associated biological and sociological evolution.

An Unconscious Collective

How do we classify human beings—you, me, our friends, family—within the framework of evolution and the diversity of life forms? Hominid is a term that applies to any bipedal primate mammal that belongs to the biological taxonomy family *Hominidae,* which includes our species, Homo sapiens. The family has also included Neanderthals, or *Homo sapiens neanderthalensis* and other forerunners of today's humans, such as *Australopithecus, Homo erectus,* and *Homo habilis.* Today's human beings are the only surviving hominids, and as far as conventional science is concerned, we represent the current state of human evolution. However, a strong case can be made that we have experienced, and continue to experience, an evolution that differentiates us from our *Homo sapiens* brethren of even a few centuries ago.

Father Pierre Teilhard de Chardin (1881–1955) was a French Roman Catholic priest, geologist, paleontologist, philosopher, and theologian. Teilhard was noted for his interpretations of humanity, technology, and the universe, and he insisted that his views were compatible with his devotion to God. One of his more compelling arguments claimed that with the emergence of humanity, evolutionary development entered a new phase.

Teilhard observed that all elemental material—rocks, earth, water, air—comprised the basic stratum on and in which all life grows. He called it the lithosphere. He went on to claim that the lithosphere provided the necessary elements that enabled the emergence and sustenance of the layer of living things covering the earth, and he is, in fact, the first one to use the term biosphere to describe it. Finally, as technology advanced, he observed that the earth was being laced with faster and faster modes of transportation—from roads, shipping lanes, air routes, and all the vehicles we build to traverse them, carrying goods and information and more and more articulate forms of communication media—telegraph, telephone, radio, television, and so on. He believed that this wiring of the planet was linking humans in a way they'd never been linked before, and that these interconnections were creating a sort of hive dynamic, a mind layer surrounding the earth that manifests a collective consciousness. He called it the noosphere, "noo" from *nous,* the Greek word for "mind." This mind layer, or collective consciousness, generates increasingly complex social arrangements that in turn will give rise to a higher consciousness. One interpretation of Teilhard's theory is that with the emergence of consciousness, evolution was taken off of autopilot and put into the hands of mankind and, according to Teilhard, guided by the control tower of God. Whether God plays into the equation or not, Teilhard didn't believe the next step in evolution would be characterized so much by another incarnation of Homo sapiens, but by what he called a collective "sphere of reflection, of conscious invention, of conscious souls."

Teilhard's own life spanned the emergence of the telegraph, telephone, radio, and television, so his assertions were based on relatively modern observations. His theory still has merit. Before and since he wrote and worked, science has given credence to parts of his theory, with dozens of examples of interlinking plant and animal life dependencies substantially supporting his concept of a biosphere. Since his death, we've witnessed the accelerated wiring of the planet with terrestrial telephones, satellites, mobile phones, internet, fax, overnight shipping, and dozens of other mechanisms that have sped up the man-made worldwide nervous system.

While there is still little or no conventional scientific evidence of a noospheric collective consciousness, most of us would probably agree that information is communicated very quickly to vast portions of the planet, making large portions of the world population "conscious" of certain knowledge. Most would also agree that a significant portion of the human race acts and lives differently today than they did 100 years ago in terms of how improved transportation and communication have shrunken the world to an astounding degree and profoundly changed the pace of life. But is that reason enough to assert that a tick has passed on the evolutionary clock for the human race? It's difficult to justify on a biological and morphological basis. We still look the same as our circa

1900 ancestors. But if the criteria for classification were different—say, behavioral instead of morphological—we might more easily make a case for mankind having evolved beyond *Homo sapiens*.

In a 1997 article on artificial intelligence, software developer Denis Susac claimed that in the future, *Machina sapiens*, part man, part machine, would best describe the nineteenth- and twentieth-century man. Using a negative argument, perhaps one can justify Susac's classification. That is, there are some modern humans who would simply die without the aid of machines and modern conveniences. They would not know how to keep themselves warm, where to find food or water, or how to protect themselves from the elements. But are these people a different species from those who could survive under more primitive circumstances?

Perhaps both Teilhard's and Susac's assertions are more palatable as predictions. Perhaps it is reasonable to foretell physiological changes that will follow technological ones. Susac may very well have predicted a future where technology is so wired into our lives that it actually invades our physiology, turning some of us into cyborg-like hybrids of biology and machinery. But these ideas are subsumed by the scope of Teilhard's assertions. Humans have transcended their incarnation as *Australopithecus, Homo habilis, Homo erectus,* and now *Homo sapiens*. While each of those stages in human evolution is marked by morphological changes in the body, each is also marked by stark changes in social behavior. By that measure, I believe we are indeed evolving into a different species. As a group we are becoming *Homo telanimus,* "a living or conscious web of man." As individuals, we are humanodes, a single node within that web.

I'm Only Humanode

The term "node" is commonly used to describe endpoints on a network. In fact, the common technological definition is as follows: In a network, a node is a connection point, either a redistribution point or an endpoint for data transmissions. In general a node has programmed or engineered capability to create, recognize, process or forward transmissions to other nodes.

By now, the concept of the network and the node is pretty common to many of us. We have a social network of nodes we call friends. We have a business network of nodes we call contacts. Television networks are made up of nodes called local stations. So the term "node" is an accurate description of a generic network, but what term is an accurate description of a node in networked media? Each networked media node is essentially an individual human, and the node is powered by a human regardless of the device through which they are connected. Thus, a humanode represents an individual endpoint, or node, in networked media.

Anyone who wishes to harness networked media, commercially or noncommercially, must come to grips with this concept. Each humanode possesses the individuality, freedom of choice, and social dynamics that the word "human" implies—but supercharged with the potential to connect to every other humanode on the network, unlimited by physical distance. This enables them to take on roles that belie their traditional classification as mere consumers of products, programming, or services. In fact, classifying them according to that traditional role is a serious mistake.

Through networked media, humanodes have the choice to consume media in a traditionally passive fashion, or become wholly involved in the process of creativity or commerce. The term may seem somewhat dehumanizing at first—a faceless node on a global network. To the contrary—used properly, networked media is tantalizingly empowering. Humanodes can insist on their individuality and express themselves freely, as many have already done by proudly displaying their distinctiveness on their personal web pages, or by ranking books, evaluating sellers from whom they made a purchase on one of zillions of commerce sites, or posting to the countless weblogs, commonly referred to as "blogs", throughout networked media. Humanodes can *choose* when and where they want to be lumped in with a larger group. Spheres of interest will thus be multiplied, magnified, and enlarged, as will spheres of influence. Individuals are rapidly becoming part of a collective group of linked humanodes all contributing opinions, exchanging information and/or talent, and generally fueling the networked ecology.

These humanodes are the neurons and nerve endings of the networked economy. Today we are at a point where this conscious web is learning to know itself, its power, and responsibility. Information will continue to move more and more freely through the collective, but until a sort of global ego develops and asserts itself, that consciousness will remain without a collective conscience, and thus be scattered, unfocused, and child-like, its intrinsic power largely dormant. While most in the modern world are conscious of the myriad problems affecting our world, they collectively lack the will to do anything about it. Just as importantly, most lack the knowledge that there is now a mechanism that gives them the ability to do something about it, should they have the will. Like a child, *Homo telanimus* is unconsciously growing, learning, adapting; generations born and raised networked will have the best chance of transcending technology, and naturally rejecting or transforming the imperatives of autocratic traditional institutions like government and big business.

The Telacorpus

It's important to make a distinction between the "network of man"—*Homo telanimus* or noosphere—and the superstructure through which we are connected to each other. Just as the human body serves as the vessel or infrastructure through which our consciousness is expressed, there is an analogous infrastructure of technology that enables our collective connectedness.

While Teilhard, I believe, correctly identified the constructs of the lithosphere and the biosphere, he did not predict the technologies that have arisen in the last fifty years. This technology and the networking it enables have created a sort of cybernetic layer that lies on top of the lithosphere and the biosphere—fiber, copper cables, harnessed wireless spectrum, and the countless specialized computing devices that deploy them. It forms the corpus of *Homo telanimus*: the body of networked man. It is a layer as physically real as the lithosphere and biosphere, yet man-made. All those wired pathways on the surface of the earth, the subterranean and submarine cables and fiber, the invisibly airborne wireless transmissions and constantly pulsing constellations of satellites orbiting the planet, all make up the body of *Homo telanimus*: the telacorpus.

The literal Latin translation of telacorpus is "body (corpus) of the web (tela)." The telacorpus serves as the body for the collective mind (Teilhard's noosphere) of millions of humanodes. In the parlance of Teilhard, it would be the telasphere. The telacorpus isn't organic like the biosphere, nor is it the ephemeral noosphere. This is the vehicle through which networked media flows and within which native networked media dynamics occur. It is a distributed prosthesis for the biosphere—an inorganic construct that, as it turns out, mimics biological behavior.

Consider virulence, for instance. The word "viral" has become commonplace in discussions about networked media like the internet. It refers to the quickness with which a message—an email, for example—can duplicate and spread around the world. It's also used in reference to small bits of computer code written by mischievous or malevolent programmers to disrupt the normal function of individual computers or whole computer networks. Certainly a virus can be bad, but the characteristic to which Steve Jurvetson and Tim Draper first referred when they claimed that Hotmail and ICQ had spread through "viral marketing" was the ability of the virus to multiply and spread. They could have dubbed the dynamic "rabittish," or "kudzal," after the kudzu vine famous for its ability to spread at incredible speeds and envelop all in its path. But they didn't. The term they chose probably resonated so strongly because most folks have experienced first-hand the kind of freakish speed of infection to which they are subject anytime flu season rolls around. It's not so much that networked media like the internet are "viral" in and of themselves; it's that networked media behaves somewhat biologically.

The fact is, a computer or network virus, or virulent behavior of organisms of any kind, cannot flourish without a host—a body. In the case of networked media, this is the telacorpus. A computer virus doesn't infect each of us as humanodes; it affects the devices we employ to connect to and through the telacorpus. Excepting our emotional reaction to the ease with which our computers succumb to invading code, a computer virus doesn't attack our bodies directly (yet). The bits of malicious programming attack the prostheses we use to become part of the body of networked media, a body created with a relatively weak immune system. The disparate engineers, scientists, and businessmen who all helped create networked media couldn't anticipate what tasks the ad hoc telacorpus would be asked to perform.

"Attacks" on the telacorpus come in many forms. Spam emails and computer viruses—whether intended as a nuisance or to generate a network-threatening plague—are analogous to the bacteria and viruses that are constantly laying siege to biological organisms. Human immune systems are perennially battling would-be bio-enemies, but there are some organisms that give us particular trouble. For those, mankind's microbiologists and medical researchers have created chemical aids—anti-viruses and antibiotics—designed to help us stave off infection by these microorganisms. Those head-on approaches often work, but only for a while. According to *Wired,* in the America of 2003 there were more than 1,000 antibacterial hand soaps, detergents, lotions, bandages, and toothpastes, whereas in the early 1990s there were only a few dozen such products. Now everything from socks to chopsticks—and most liquid hand soaps—contain antibacterial agents. The backlash to these blitzkrieg techniques are a microcosm of what we see in fighting wars based on ideology—attempts to eradicate offenders simply breed stronger, more virulent strains. *The New England Journal of Medicine* says our attempts at germ-free living may result in kids who develop lifelong asthma and allergies. Superstrong staph bacteria are already resisting our potent last-resort prescription antibiotic, vancomycin. Seventy percent of bacteria now resist at least one of the common drugs used to treat infections, and about 30 percent of the bugs causing sexually transmitted diseases resist penicillin, tetracycline, or both.

For frustrated network engineers, website managers, or individual computer users—humanodes whose roles include acting as agents for the telacorpus's immune system, staving off infection—the first reaction to spam and e-viruses is an "antihackterial" direct frontal assault on the transgressors: prosecution of those humanodes who originate these offending bits of programming. It's the equivalent of trying to eradicate bacteria with antibiotics. It simply makes those organisms that survive the direct frontal assault stronger and smarter; in the case of the telacorpus, as in biological bodies, the intrinsic weaknesses are perpetuated. Hackers and spammers are performing a much-needed service. In fact, they spawn whole new industries in virus protection, antispamming and security software. There will always be small numbers of humanodes perpetrating mischief. We should let the problem solve itself—if there is an offensive behavior occurring within networked media, you can bet there will be an individual or company running full-speed to capitalize on the software antidote and create solutions that make the immune system of the telacorpus stronger. Just as infant children need to be exposed to bacteria and virus, and sometimes actually get sick, in order to strengthen their immune systems, the dynamics of the telacorpus are robust enough such that it can be relied upon to develop its own immune system. If we've learned anything from microbiology in the last few decades, it's that aggressive, head-on fights have unwanted ramifications. Blast bacteria with antibiotics and they fight back even harder. Try and wipe out a virus with chemicals or radiation, and the few that survive (and it only takes a few) become stronger or adapt into entirely new, more deadly, strains.

Would-be network immunologists should be taking a page from microbiology researchers, who are now advocating a kinder approach to the bacterial war. Instead of trying to kill the offending microorganisms, they are employing techniques perfected by Mother Nature to prevent those microorganisms from getting a foothold—don't kill them, just discourage them. Simple examples of these kinds of biomechanisms are plentiful. Mother's milk works its protective magic on newborns by infusing them with complex sugars that prevent bacteria from binding to cells. Cranberry juice, well known as a folk remedy for urinary tract infections, has been proven to have an anti-adhesive effect on the bacteria typically found in such infections. Network and software engineers should look to the latest in research on biological organisms to inform their efforts to maintain a healthy telacorpus. Even so, the telacorpus is overdue for a major evolutionary upgrade. If it doesn't get it, it might very well succumb to the effects of attack and misuse. Fortunately, that upgrade seems to be forthcoming.

An estimated $3.9 trillion in business transactions took place over the internet in 2003. The medium's reach is increasingly global—an incredible 24 percent of Brazilians, 30 percent of Chinese, and 72 percent of Americans went online at least once a month during that same year. Still, despite its indisputable effect on the planet and its inhabitants, to bring the internet up to modern day standards, observed Wade Roush in *Wired,* would be like taking a "1973 Buick [and refitting it] with air bags and emissions controls." Its decades-old infrastructure was originally designed and built out for noncommercial research and educational applications. Granting that the internet's originators deserve their monikers of "genius" and "visionary," they (like the progenitors of harnessed electricity) couldn't possibly predict the revolution their invention sparked. On top of their invention are countless sprouting applications: the World Wide Web (itself host to a thousandfold applications), streaming media, e-commerce, file sharing, telephony, and video conferencing, among others.

One grassroots group of nearly one hundred computer scientists, backed by heavyweight industrial sponsors like Intel, Hewlett Packard, and Google, aim to give the internet more than just a facelift. Dubbed PlanetLab, their effort is based on an idea that's been around for sometime: "the network is the computer," a catchphrase popularized (and quite probably trademarked) by Sun Microsystems. The main idea is to move data and computation off the desktop and fragment and distribute them throughout the collective network, but a network smart enough to protect, distribute, and parse that data and computation in a way that is anonymous while still maintaining the intention of the individual humanodes. It would be as if you were able to take a math problem occupying your brain, or a large chunk of your childhood memories, and break them down into individually unrecognizable fragments in order to distribute them throughout the brains of thousands or millions of your fellow humans, who might be better suited to handle that math problem, or who might have more unused memory capacity. Ideally, this would leave individuals with more processing power to devote to whatever were their greater priorities. An appealing thought. PlanetLab accomplishes this by first supplementing, then ultimately replacing, the relatively "dumb" computers called routers that traffic data around the internet with "smart nodes"—more sophisticated computers capable of employing their own processing power and disk space to take on small pieces of much more complex tasks distributed throughout the network. "If the internet is a global, electronic nervous system, then PlanetLab promises to give it brains," wrote Roush—a significant upgrade to the telacorpus, and only one of a long series of upgrades to come in future years.

Within the telacorpus, adapted corporate organisms and individual humanodes can thrive in powerful ways. One of those involves the capacity to engender virulence at will. Another entails collections of nodes that work together for a specific purpose, in the way a human organ is a collection of specialized cells working to a single purpose within the human body. Within networked media, these are called organodes, or supernodes.

Supernodes and Flash Mobs

Institutions, or the humans representing them, are always the first to be networked. Telegraphs, phones, faxes, mobile phones, local area networks, and wide area networks were first adopted by institutions because when brand new, such technologies are typically only affordable for enterprises that either can bury the cost in the overhead of their core business, or that gain a crucial competitive advantage by using the technology.

The internet belies those cost-curve dynamics. While it was incubated by government and educational institutions, it was adopted by and proliferated among individuals. Its intrinsic nature as a decentralized network of networks demanded this. Now, anyone in urban, suburban, and even some rural worlds who wants to be networked can be networked, to one degree or another. The command-and-control nature of previous networked technology—like telephone networks—was missing from the internet, despite the continued best efforts of various institutions that feel threatened by it and wish to umbrella it under a hegemony of institutional supervision. It's unclear whether they will win their fight to make the internet and related networked media more "supervisory." Personally, I hope they don't.

Colonizing animals like ants or termites have autocratic control structures centered on a queen, whose death will throw a colony into turmoil and effectively dissolve it. While the disarray is substantially less, similar disorder occurs in human society when strong leaders take leave of this world or centralized command structures break down. By design, this doesn't happen in networked media. The telacorpus doesn't blip when a single humanode of any stature dies or leaves the network. In that way, networked media is more like coral than an autocratic colony.

Small, sedentary marine animals, most corals form colonies by budding, a form of asexual reproduction in which an outgrowth develops on a parent organism that detaches to produce a new individual. The individual animal, or polyp, then secretes a cup-shaped skeleton around itself. In coral colonies, the skeleton of each polyp attaches to the skeletons of its neighbors. As the colony grows, more polyps are produced and build their skeletons on top of the older polyps' skeletons, and the lower, older levels of the colony eventually die.

Networked media are like a coral reef in that it there is no center or core. If one cell dies, it doesn't affect the whole. Individual humanodes within the telacorpus act of their own volition, or at least they believe they do. The collective of humanodes forms the "reef" of the telacorpus, but unlike natural corals, each humanode can connect to any other. Sometimes, voluntarily or involuntarily, humanodes group together to create super-centers or supernodes. This strange dynamic leads me to assert that it's useful to consider all humanodes as being at their own "center" of the telacorpus. Unlike coral, humanodes have volition—a will. Humanodes can choose to aggregate in subreefs or to square off against other individual humanodes in the collective for communication, play, or debate. They can choose to log-off the colony and separate themselves from the telacorpus completely, whether for a time or forever. The lack of a definitive single center underscores the need for programmers to treat networked media as having many centers. Every endpoint to networked media is a center since every humanode is enabled similarly in the activities they can undertake as desired by an effective programmer.

Radio and television have aggregated the largest audiences in history, yet lack the capacity to connect audience members. The telephone connects people over large distances, yet cannot offer a way for millions of people to share the same phone call, or share programming as rich and articulate as television (yet). Networked media combines the best of these other media. Moreover, while networked media allows an individual humanode to be heard by many other humanodes, collections of humanodes can wield considerable power if harnessed to a common goal. Networked media helps like-minded humanodes to connect, aggregate and motivate around common causes or themes. These connections result in the creation of two kinds of connected superorganisms, or supernodes—autocratic and communal—which in certain respects are simply new ways to look at some very traditional entities.

An autocratic supernode is a formally structured organization in which the individual humanodes within the organization derive more benefit from the supernode than they do acting as individuals. Those benefits may take the form of a steady and secure paycheck, health insurance, or the social comfort of the community of fellow workers they see every day. This kind of supernode is hierarchical and has a leadership that is autocratic in the pursuit of the supernode's mission. Microsoft is an autocratic supernode—tens of thousands of connected humanodes who serve the same corporate purpose. It's not even that the leadership of the company is micromanaging the actions of individuals, but rather the culture of the Microsoft collective that ultimately guides the majority of humanodes under its aegis. Microsoft is not alone, of course—all kinds of organizations hold such sway over their constituent members. Often

times, individuals will actually take action on behalf of the greater organization in direct contradiction to the action they'd take were they acting
as an individual. Meter maids might feel sorry for hapless motorists, but
they'll still give the tickets. Judges may empathize with defendants, but
they'll still serve the letter of the law. Autocratic supernodes motivate
individual humanodes to believe that what's good for the supernode is
ultimately good for them. The wired constituencies of any organization
of size—whether commercial enterprise, religious community, government, or other—will generally employ networked media and technology
for the greater benefit of the larger organism, which ultimately benefits
each individual humanode within the supernode in some way that serves
to subjugate individual will or value system.

Willing or unwilling agenting of supernodes doesn't stop with those
humanodes on the payroll, either. Operating systems, personalization,
browser start pages, or custom-consumption technologies like personal
video recorders (such as Replay and TiVo) all subtly pull in untethered
humanodes to do the bidding of a supernode. Everyone who owns a
Windows operating system essentially works for the Microsoft supernode;
traders on eBay are, by definition, cells in their supernode; those who
swear by their TiVo are willing members of their supernode; and weekend
warriors sporting the Nike logo on the basketball court, golf course, or
softball field are effectively doing the work of the brand-holder.

However, individual humanodes possess the potential for individual
creation and innovation. Properly nurtured, that kind of energy can
be harnessed by a communal supernode. In contrast to an autocratic
supernode, a communal supernode is an informally structured organization of humanodes, often with no formal hierarchical structure or leadership. A communal supernode can, however, be a formidable organism
when harnessed, with the capacity to build great value. Newsgroups
and home page communities are examples of communal supernodes,
and collective buying or demand aggregation is another. Demand aggregation combines orders from multiple humanode buyers into powerful high-volume transactions, providing the means to increase buyers'
purchasing power. Humanodes come together in different combinations
on different occasions for a specific products or purposes—all those
buyers looking for blue Corvettes, say, or all those travelers looking for
a flight to Miami from Los Angeles, or all those voters looking to vote
for a particular candidate.

The primary difference between autocratic and communal supernodes is based on time and need. Autocratic supernodes are generally "always on." Communal supernodes are generally "on demand." As long as there is general ignorance regarding how networked media work, autocratic supernodes will benefit at the expense of individual humanodes and communal supernodes, since autocratic supernodes have humanodes working around the clock to further their agendas. This has a twofold significance. First, most autocratic supernodes themselves are ignorant of the true nature and power of networked media, but are figuring it out more quickly than the average humanode. Second, there will eventually be a conscientious awakening of individual humanodes and communal supernodes to the intent of autocratic supernodes, ultimately lessening the egregious behaviors of the latter. Institutional intelligence senses and reacts to the threat of new technologies, and they will do anything they can to mold them to their advantage. The more controls and tracking that autocratic supernodes are able to build into networked media for the "protection" of individuals, the sooner we'll all see the other side of that protection coin—control, allowing autocratic supernodes greater ability to monitor, to manipulate, and to perpetuate whatever methodologies, technologies, or policies benefit them. Look at the ever-more-prevalent realities of the workplace: today, data entry operators in many major companies are watched every moment they're on the job. Software monitors their every keystroke and phone call, collecting information on words per minute of typing, average call lengths, and anything else that can be tracked through their networked tools of work (which today, of course, is just about anything that uses electricity).

Individual humanodes are accustomed to feelings of futility when it comes to effecting any real change outside their normal spheres of influence—if they perceive they have any influence at all. They are afflicted with countless personal worries about things like paying bills, taking care of children, chemicals in their water, and other sundry concerns in their daily lives. Professional media programmers have learned well how to fuel individuals' fears and desires; institutions, in general, have become expert at manipulating perception to their advantage. For example, consider a major company threatened with a strike by its workforce. While negotiating, they hire a firm that sends in whole families of industrial spies to infiltrate the local workforce—not to try to talk people out of striking, but only to fuel doubts and fears already held by average

workers' worried about their families' well being. They were successful. The strike never happened, and the union was forced to settle. In the
"war of electrical formats" during the turn of the twentieth century—the
battle between AC and DC—General Electric and Westinghouse Corporation both hired "stock manipulators," a legitimate profession at the
time, to effect changes in each other's public share prices. To this day,
this kind of manipulation on behalf of superorganisms continues—spin
doctors manipulate public opinion, lobbyists influence the votes of
Congress, and advertisers use almost any means possible to capture the
attention of potential customers. Networked media will only make it
easier to practice influence peddling, much of which is perpetrated by
supernodes. These ideas may seem anti-institutional. They are not. They
are anti-propaganda. Institutions of any kind, being always-on, tend to
perpetuate whatever agendas they favor and use propaganda techniques
to further those agendas, and they're generally better at it than individuals. Some of those agendas are altruistic; most are self-serving.

Fortunately, technology always beats technology. That is, the basic
nature of networked media makes it difficult to control outright. Even
if a majority of humanodes don't have the time in their daily lives to
vet or challenge the messages of always-on autocratic supernodes,
watch dogs will always exist to challenge overweening institutions (the
Electronic Frontier Foundation is one of these watchdogs that is using networked media to its advantage). And the democratic nature of
networked media empowers the voice of the motivated individual—for
better or for worse. We've already witnessed several cases of stock manipulation where a single short-selling trader posted an anonymous
"tip" on an internet message board that spread through the internet
like the smell of predators through a herd. Stocks often plunge on that
kind of disinformation, making a tidy profit for the single perpetrator.
Just as networked media gives new power to institutions in furthering
their aims, networked media vastly amplifies the voice of the individual,
no matter who they are and what they espouse—from stock tips, to
virulent hate messages, to medical advice, to conspiracy theories, to
legitimate knowledge or groundbreaking ideas. Whether from individual
humanode or institutional supernodes, authenticity of information will
become incredibly important as networked media continues to evolve,
and initially, people will turn to traditional authorities as sources for
that kind of credibility.

Networked media, at least, endows individuals with the ability to exercise a collective will that was hitherto unavailable to them. Some recent examples from the American scene: Howard Dean predicated his presidential campaign on the ability to assemble "flash mobs" on short notice to generate contributions and popular support. He quickly came out of relative obscurity to become, briefly, the front-runner for the Democratic nomination, forever cementing networked media as a critical campaign tool for politicians. Roy Disney, after resigning from the board of the company that shares his name in a dispute with other directors allied with CEO and Chairman Michael Eisner, took his battle to the web. He established SaveDisney.com to seek support from Disney shareholders and fans of the Disney brand. By early 2004, shareholder discontent had led Eisner to give up his role as Disney chairman. Networked media has become the mechanism to enable on-demand masses of individuals to rally around a cause, create economic leverage and economies of scale, and assert a shared opinion—in ways far faster and more efficient than ever before.

Even the idea of government through elected representation will change as it becomes easier for individuals—as individuals or communal supernodes—to express their opinions issue-by-issue. In November 2003, *Time* showcased MoveOn.org as a group of progressive-minded internet entrepreneurs who are enabling just that. On its website, MoveOn asserts, "Our international network of more than 2,000,000 online activists is one of the most effective and responsive outlets for democratic participation available today." In early 2004, MoveOn had all of seven staff members, and that staff serves only to focus its fluxing constituency on a topic du jour. One day, MoveOn's email armada pushed a petition against the FCC's relaxing rules on media ownership; the next, a fund drive that brought in $1 million in 48 hours to support the Texas state senators who had left the state to stop a G.O.P. redistricting plan. There are no membership dues, and gratification is as instant as a mouse click. "MoveOn is easily the largest political-action committee in the country," said Professor Michael Cornfield of George Washington University. At the end of 2003, MoveOn mounted an ambitious $10 million drive to fund anti-Bush campaign commercials to air in U.S. states expected to play a key role in the 2004 presidential election. Billionaires George Soros and Peter Lewis offered to give $1 for every $2 given by MoveOn members, up to a cap of $5 million. Pop star Moby and a group of his celebrity friends (like Jack Black and Janeane Garofalo) judged the best commercial made by members, which MoveOn aired around the State of the Union. MoveOn founders Wes Boyd and Joan Blades are visited by a steady stream of consultants and candidates coming to pay homage. Those who seek endorsement are in for a disappointment. "I don't spend any time figuring out who the right candidate is," said Boyd. "All I want to do is evangelize populism, so [politicians] go away thinking, 'Whoa—there's someone other than wealthy donors I have to impress?'"

Even with the early successes of MoveOn and other such groups in bottling collectives of humanodes on demand, autocratic supernodes still have the most to benefit from networked media, at least initially. In the face of a growing array of choices, most people will seek out the messages that make them feel most secure. In the case of "news and information," the masses have historically relied on mass media—print, radio, and television—for the "truth." Those autocratic supernodes that espouse journalistic objectivity at least have some checks and balances in place. Many news editors require their journalists to produce two or three independent sources before they'll approve a piece. But institutional integrity is a fuzzy thing. Even if they are accountable to self-policing ethical practices (legitimate news organizations) or regulatory bodies (the FCC, FDA, or other purported watchdog agencies), autocratic supernodes are mostly driven by their bottom line—profit, in the case of commercial institutions, or the dissemination of a subjective message, as in the case of religious groups or nonprofit organizations. Whether veracious or not, networked media gives new power to the armies of humanodes working in the service of these groups.

A Manifold Awakening

This will continue until a critical mass of humanodes awaken to the manifold ways networked media are empowering them. Eventually, collective consciousness within networked media will evolve to the point that it surpasses collective ignorance—a collective conscience, if you will. Humanodes and communal supernodes will gain more influence relative to the autocratic supernodes. "Trusted sources" will become less

about reliance on autocratic supernodes, and more about a web of connections to humanodes of like mind or purpose. It has already begun
with nascent forms of networked media.

In 1989, when the Loma Prieta earthquake hit the San Francisco Bay
area, I was very alarmed—all of my relatives lived there. Based on the
information I received from mass media like television, it looked like
a localized Armageddon had befallen my hometown. Of course, I was
unable to query the television reporter interactively to find out more
specifics of the event. So I used the networked medium of the telephone
to contact friends and family there. All were OK and all gave me more
specific information—chiefly, that while the entire area had been rocked,
only a few specific locations had suffered severe damage. The fact I was
networked to them via phone made it possible for me to pierce the veil
of mass media supernodes and not have to accept prepackaged reports
whose mission was to entertain me—that is, hold my attention for as
long as possible—as much as it was to inform me. It's not that news
organizations were reporting falsities; it was that they were selecting a
sampling of what to show us based on what was most sensational, not
a comprehensive picture of the state of the San Francisco Bay Area. My
broad sampling of trusted humanode sources gave a better picture of
"reality" than that which news organizations would, or *could* show.

While I knew each of the people I called when investigating the Loma
Prieta earthquake, the anonymity of networked media has the potential
to engender as much misinformation as authentic information (think of
that unscrupulous short-selling stock trader). Until dynamics emerge that
provide intrinsic authenticity, many humanodes will continue to rely on
autocratic supernodes for important information. Thousands of shopping
and auction sites on the web have feedback loops allowing receivers of
service, product, or information to "rate" their veracity or quality. This
feedback loop is essential, and unique to, networked media.

"The media" as we collectively consider it today is a collective
of autocratic supernodes. There is no substantial feedback loop for
humanodes to debate or vet information or programming. The editorial
pages of newspapers and phone calls to the local television affiliate pale
in comparison to the feedback power of networked media properly programmed. The traditional use of commercial media (or manipulation of it
by advertisers, governments, and institutions) is predicated on the intent
to engage, compel, or divert attention—to entertain—and more often

than not, to capitalize on our attention in some way. That's not to say that communal supernodes don't have a cutting edge. Networked media are agnostic in that any group—from neo-Nazis, pedophiles, conspiracy theorists, and terrorists, to the more innocuous alien abductionists—can "virtually assemble" and disseminate powerful and compelling messages ranging from hate and xenophobia to love and humanitarianism. But the desire to spread these messages is not a characteristic of networked media, but rather a characteristic of humanity, which will be perpetuated in any new milieu. This is not a reason to change the open and frictionless nature of networked media.

With freedom comes responsibility. With power comes responsibility. These are common refrains, but should not lead us to conclusions that result in autocratic and paternalistic control structures over networked media. That "responsibility" should appropriately be left in the hands of the humanodes. While the dynamics of networked media will not cure humanity's ills and foibles, it will provide a better, more profound way to interact with our fellow humans. Joe Trippi, the former manager of the Dean presidential campaign (which was noted for having such unprecedented success and influence online), told *Wired* about an epiphany he had regarding networked media: "You will absolutely suffocate anything that you're trying to do on the internet by trying to command and control it." Yet traditional autocratic supernodes are still having trouble adapting to the emerging networked media landscape. They are institutionally mired in philosophies born of linear media and the centralized infrastructures created for the linear distribution of physical goods. From the music industry's overblown battle against piracy, to government's paternalistic attempts to control the internet to "protect" citizens from terrorism or pornography, to the failures of internet businesses that based their strategies on enterprise models derived from the industrial revolution, all are missing one of the most basic, most profound, and most powerful effects of networked media: how it changes the relationship between the programmer and the humanode.

CHAPTER 8

The Value Net

In the midst of one of the largest media company mergers in history—that between AOL and Time Warner—Richard Bressler, one of the handful of executives presiding over that ill-fated corporate marriage, made a statement as to what he claimed was the linchpin to their future success: that the new company would be based on a "relentless focus on the consumer." While this statement no doubt echoed AOL Time Warner's (now, once again and appropriately named Time Warner) internal corporate mantra, the terminology underscores an ignorance at the top of the most powerful media companies. This doesn't bode well for innovation; nor does it demonstrate a clear understanding of the media milieu.

The makers of products or programming refer to human beings as consumers because, consciously or not, that is how they view them—as capable only of consumption. That's not much more credit than one would give a domesticated farm animal. According to this view, consumers can be temperamental, moody, and unpredictable, but if they're good consumers, they swallow what they are given and do what they are told, so that they can flourish only enough so that they can go on consuming more product or programming. Harshly put, this herd mentality is the true key to the worldview of most major consumer-oriented enterprises. In an increasingly connected world, seeing humans this way is not only perilous but also erroneous. The goal of business should no longer be to simply encourage people to consume, but to enlist them as producers, distributors, marketers, and vendors—roles that, with few exceptions, traditionally have been restricted to companies' owned value chain.

The Value Chain

Whatever the elemental functions into which one chooses to break down the value chain, humanodes employing networked media can assume any of those roles. For the purpose of this discussion, consider the value chain as possessing five constituent steps: production, distribution, marketing, vending (or retailing), and (with every intention) consumption.

- *Production* is the creation and manufacturing of products or programming. In the case of media, this applies to both media programming and the form it takes for consumption. One might produce a film in a native form of celluloid, and distribute it as such, but it can be reconstituted for television, cable, or home video distribution as well. Production, therefore, refers to product or programming as essence and form—for instance, a film's essence is a two-hour story told through audio and video; but its form may be celluloid, VHS tape, DVD, a television signal delivered via broadcast, or a video stream delivered over the internet.

- *Distribution* is the process of gaining proximity to a consumer. Note that distribution does not describe the actual process of a consumer consuming, or even acquiring, the product. In the feature film business, distribution means getting a film onto 3,000 screens. While the film may be showing in those venues, there is no guarantee anyone will actually come to the theaters to see it. In television, distribution is getting your show on a network like NBC, CBS, or any of a plethora of broadcast and cable channels. Anyone with a television can tune in to NBC with little effort, should they choose to do so. In retail, distribution is getting a product into physical locations close to the consumer and acquiring the kind of shelf space that enables customers to easily find the product. A familiar mantra in business is to "control distribution." In linear media—film, radio, television, publishing—a typical producer of products is beholden to the distributor, who takes a nice chunk out of the revenue stream. Hollywood is famous for this via the legerdemain of "net profits." Every once in a while, though, a producer possesses something everyone wants (e.g., George Lucas and his Star Wars franchise), whence the power shifts to the producer. The point is that both the enterprise and the individual naturally seek the weak points in the value chain and try to control them.

- *Marketing* is the process of telling the potential customer what the products or programming are, and how, where and when they can be consumed. (This refers to transaction marketing, specific efforts to get a human to take specific action, not brand marketing, which relates more to the creation of awareness or buzz around a specific product or piece of programming.)

- *Vending* is the exchange of value (usually money) in return for product or programming. Retail stores, movie theaters, restaurants, Coke machines, and Amazon.com are all vending venues.

- *Consumption* is the act of <verbing> product or programming—buy it, watch it, eat it, play it—<pick-your-verb> it.

In linear and interactive media, the value chain is typically linear, and companies vertically integrate their operations around production-distribution-marketing, and sometimes vending (retail) whenever possible or viable. How do companies "listen in" on the consumer? How do they get feedback so they know if their products or programming are working or not?

There is a term in electrical engineering, the "feedback loop," which refers to a circuit that has built-in self-sensing. The human sensory and nervous systems are an example of a biological feedback loop. Our nerve endings tell the brain when the environment is too hot or too cold. Our nose alerts us to smoke before a fire might come close enough to cause harm to the body. In linear media, the same feedback loop principle is true. How can you push the programming to consumers without measuring what they think of it? How will advertisers know the best way to place billions of advertising dollars?

The problem in linear media is that the feedback loops from consumer to producer-distributor-marketer are often unreliable or sub-optimal. That is, mostly they rely on flimsy filaments of information that make their way back from consumers—and invariably a tiny sampling of those consumers. Television programmers rely on arguably flawed measurement techniques like the Nielsen ratings, which measure the viewing habits of some 6,000 homes and extrapolate them to represent the preferences of more than 100,000,000 homes (that's approximately one family in 17,000 determining what programming does and does not succeed in television). Billions of dollars in advertising are wagered according to the Nielsen ratings, and nobody wants to rock that boat—until a demonstrably better (and easily adoptable) boat comes along, of course.

For feature films, the feedback loop is often a test screening of a few hundred people prescreening a film; that single audience, ostensibly selected to represent the demographic cross-section the filmmakers wish to reach, exerts profound influence over the fate of a film. "For one of our films, after our initial test screenings we were able to re-shoot and re-edit certain scenes to which the test-screening audience didn't initially respond well, which ultimately increased our test scores by 20 to 25 percent in subsequent test screenings," says Oliver Eberle, producer of films like *Universal Soldier* and *Stargate.* Test screenings are the most important feedback loop for filmmakers and studios, but by no means are they bulletproof. Many films test well and go bust at the box office; conversely, some test badly and become breakout hits. Again, here is feedback loop dynamic where a few hundred people influence what millions may or may not see. The other feedback loop used by movie studios is the exit poll. Employed after a film's release, pollsters capture the off-the-cuff comments of perhaps a few hundred or few thousand people leaving theaters after the film. The data is used to determine the ongoing evolution of a film's distribution and marketing strategy. By that time, though, hundreds or even thousands of prints of the film have been made. At that point filmmakers can't change the programming, only the way it is marketed.

In general, market research involves sampling—the selection of small, statistically representative groups of people to represent the tastes and tendencies of large groups of people. Even with the best intentions, this process is inherently flawed. Even if the sampling techniques used are mathematically sound, once transferred to real-world application, they are prey to numerous imperfections. Werner Heisenberg, upon whose work much of quantum physics was built, once said, "An event comes into existence only when we observe it." Said another way, measuring or observing an event changes the event.

Take the focus group, a popular form of market research where perhaps a few dozen people are selected to sit in a conference room answering questions and reacting to product or programming presentations. Many elements involved in the process of performing a focus group can easily skew a genuine response, including the questions asked, how they're asked, the attitude of the focus group leader, the group dynamics, the setting in which the focus group occurs, the mood or state of mind of any or all of the participants at the time the focus group takes place—just to name a few. I've personally seen a focus group leader—a professional at eliciting responses from strangers—expertly guide focus group attendees in desirable directions. I've seen focus group attendees be generally upbeat about a product until one person in the group with a strong opinion and reasonable communication skills turns almost the entire group around. But while there are plenty of market researchers who would like to—and do—manipulate market data to the advantage of their product or programming, I believe most would prefer to have accurate information. That is, I suspect that if marketers could find better, less intrusive, more accurate metrics and methodologies for gauging public attitudes, they would embrace them. Fortunately, networked media are providing just that.

Be-Bits: Weaving the Value Net

In a world of networked media, the value chain dynamic is very different. We are better served by thinking of the value chain as more of a value net—a nonlinear collection of humanodes, who can do more than just consume. These humanodes can take on multiple states.

In computer lingo, multistate dynamics can be described in binary language with dual-state bits. Each bit has an "on-state" and an "off-state." Humanodes can take on many combinations of the five "pure" states—producer, distributor, marketer, vendor, consumer. They can act as both consumer and marketer simultaneously, depending on how the networked media programming is constructed. For example, sellers on the eBay site have their producer bit turned on (posting an auction and creating/uploading the relevant data/images), their distributor bit turned on (responsibility for shipping the item when auction ends), their marketer bit on (using the eBay format and listing engine to make the item appetizing), their vendor bit on (engaging in an actual commercial transaction), and their consumer bit on (paying eBay directly for the privilege of using their commerce engine). Whereas Kazaa users have only their producer bit on (ripping and uploading files), and sometimes their marketing bit (compelling file annotations), distribution bit (offering the best songs and broadest bandwidth), and consumer bit (downloading songs themselves). Networked media programmers should be trying to create programming that activates these five behavioral bits, or be-bits, in combinations that sustain their programming and evoke the desired humanode behavior. They should be asking themselves, how can my programming turn on or off each of those states in my audience members?

Herding the Humanodes

Most media programmers are not doing a particularly good job of motivating consumers—as anyone who has done a random click-through of television channels, or surfed the web, can attest. The perennially effective ways to encourage others to spend money are to appeal to the head, the heart, and (politely speaking) the groin. (The fourth way is through the stomach, also a powerful motivator but not one that has much relevance to networked media at the moment.)

The appeal to the head is based on logic and reason—the belief that one will get things faster, cheaper, or more efficiently if one does the programmer's bidding. In networked media, a "head appeal" may include new kinds of services or features not available in other media, such as data research or real-time stock quotes.

The "groin appeal" is based on sex, pure and simple. Sex-oriented programming contributed greatly to the success of both the cable television and home video markets, and is doing so again in the internet networked media. Of course, sex-oriented programming need not be pornographic, per se.

"Heart appeal" employs elements like passion, suspension of disbelief, pity, empathy, altruism, and fanaticism. Entertainment is uniquely suited to tapping into "heart" since the programming relies on the ability to draw in audiences emotionally and move them to cry, to laugh, to be afraid—to emote. Advertising campaigns aimed at getting customers to "consume" often focus on the consumer's emotional side. Some examples exist of networked media programming that have touched the heart. Such disparate entities as eBay, chat rooms, Epinions, the marketing efforts behind *The Blair Witch Project*—all have shown how the emotions of consumers can be harnessed in the world of networked media. In fact, eBay is to the internet—to networked media in general— what *Your Show of Shows* was to television: the first hit entertainment programming as measured by the two most important criteria: audience, and monetization of the audience.

When considering the difference between the head and the heart, consider this observation: the dynamic that drove people to see *The Passion of the Christ* multiple times (heart) is very different from the dynamic that drives businesspeople to subscribe to the *Wall Street Journal* online (head).

Knowing how to motivate the humanodes is intrinsic to efforts to program for networked media, since "programming" is moot unless there are humanodes for which to program. How do we turn those be-bits on and off, to take on roles valuable to a programmer that has them part with value—their time or efforts—that may or may not include money? How do you get humanodes to act as producer, distributor, marketer, vendor, or consumer on your behalf? Here are the eight motivational dynamics—the "motive-eight," if you will—that are the most powerful programming attributes for encouraging humanodes to do what you want them to do.

Utility

Utilitarian motivators make it possible to do the things humanodes need for everyday life and business in ways that are simpler, faster, and better. Enabling one to buy and sell stocks via sites like eTrade is of obvious utility to people who play the stock market. Amazon.com makes it more convenient to buy a book or any number of items now on their massive web store. Ticketmaster.com makes it easier to buy a ticket to a live event, providing seating charts, directions to venues, and other bundled services all from the comfort of home. Text messages on mobile phones are a hugely efficient way of sending short, simple messages to friends or colleagues.

Compensation

Find ways to compensate people to do what you want them to do, and you'll have hordes of folks lined up at your door. For instance, airline mileage reward programs that provide value, if not outright cash, fall into this category, as does any system that provides a usable value in return for an action taken on behalf of the giver-of-value. When I was doing some research for this book, I stumbled across a Salon.com article that came up in a Google search. Not being a subscriber, I could only read a short excerpt from the article. If I wanted to read the whole article, I was encouraged to spend $36.50 for a year subscription. ("Ten cents a day," teased the offer.) I would have been happy to spend the ten cents for the day or even $0.70 for the week, but I wasn't prepared to spend $36.50. However, Salon gave me another clever option. If I watched a full ad presentation from one of its sponsors, I would be allowed a one-day pass. I watched the ad, and then read the article. They compensated me with the value of a one-day pass to their site for an action they wanted me to take. It was a bonus that the ad actually appealed to me—a SaveOurEnvironment.org request for me to sign a petition to preserve the Clean Water Act—and so I received additional value beyond the one-day pass I initially needed. It was coincidence, perhaps, that Salon's advertiser further appealed to my intrinsic value system (see "superego" below) in getting me to sign the petition showcased in the advertisement.

Ego

The ego dynamic is based on an appeal to self-interest: recognition, self-aggrandizement, fame, power, control, and sometimes even simple self-expression. Hecklers.com is a humor site that capitalizes on the contributions of visitors, particularly in their hilarious, topical, David Letterman–style top-ten lists ("Ten Least Popular Items for Sale on eBay"). In exchange for providing ideas for the list (Number One last time I looked: "Napster stock"), contributors receive recognition by having their email addresses posted along with their contributions. Amihot.com is another example—people post their picture, or that of a friend/enemy, and other folks vote on how "hot" that person is, or bid in an auction to get their image on the front page.

To some extent, weblogs also fall into this category. While not always rooted in ego, self-expression can provide a boost to it nonetheless, especially when blog sites frequently build in editorial engines that bring various blogs to the forefront; it is certainly ego-gratifying for your blog to be on the front page of a well-trafficked site.

Superego

The superego dynamic relates to people's value systems. If, say, animal preservation is important to a particular individual, there's not much effort required to enlist that person in an animal preservation effort. The Amnesty International website mobilizes thousands of people in calls for support of political prisoners around the world. The thousands of Howard Dean supporters who enthusiastically blogged him to political prominence in 2003 were also expressing their superego. Networked media, properly employed, provides a peerless mechanism for superego-driven behavior to emerge.

I'd also include "passion" in this category: that is, the kind of passion that's rooted in selflessness and creation—a channeling-like dynamic that removes the expressers' actions from reward schemes and self-aggrandizement. This is one of the most difficult shades of motivation to assume in humanodes, as it naturally entails suspicion of the programmer, and the encroachment of other human emotions that might devolve the idealistic "passion" into "ego," "compensation," or "fear." Nonetheless, it remains a viable mode. Members of People for the Ethical Treatment of Animals are likely to be passionately selfless about helping animals, and their intrinsic value system tells them hurting animals is wrong. True art lovers may be highly motivated by their passion to do something on behalf of a networked media programmer working with that subject, without any basis in value system, social mores, or political bent.

Communal

The desire to belong to a group is a powerful motivator for many individuals, particularly the young. Human beings naturally differentiate themselves by association (or disassociation) with other human beings. Success in employing networked media will often be related to the ability to create virtual spaces where humanodes can associate "at will," using programming that employs only code and community, leaving the content creation to those humanodes using the virtual space. These are communal engines—like chat rooms, instant messaging, weblogs, or persistent worlds—where humanodes choose topics and purposes around which to commune, effectively creating their own zones within the virtual space (whether public or private), with the mechanism abstracted from the subject matter of the communal exchange. Other times, a communal viewpoint or purpose can be established that appeals to a certain set of humanodes. These are communal engines created by the networked media programmer with a very specific purpose in mind. Online dating sites are a good example, where the communal motivation is quite specific.

Social networking sites like Friendster.com, LinkedIn.com, and Tickle.com trace their popularity directly to this motivator. These are sites where one can actually manifest a map of human connections—friends, business colleagues, and, by association, all the connections through them that may be one to several degrees of separation away from one's direct contacts. Often, the point of using a social networking site is to potentially harness those connections to some end—employment, business development, sales, romance—which incorporates other motivators.

Addiction

Tapping into people's addictive, habitual behaviors can be extraordinarily powerful. The approach is simple and time honored: give people something for free first, and then, once they're hooked, they'll come back and pay for more. Gambling sites are proficient at this, as are sports fantasy leagues and dating sites. Pornography websites are particularly adept at using this strategy. Even lowly email has an addictive nature to it. Anyone who has dealt with a friend or colleague who cannot stay offline for any significant period of time has witnessed the effect.

Diversion

Diversion is addiction's tamer sibling. Anything that helps consumers divert their mind from the vicissitudes of everyday life can be a powerful motivator. Entertainment is virtually synonymous with diversion. Television, radio, and film are of course famously diverting, but games are an ever-rising power in this regard, as are web-based activities like eBay, day trading, and random web surfing.

Fear

The catch-all for the opposite of pleasure. Fear is a hugely powerful motivator: fear of reprisal, fear of losing something valuable (like human rights), fear of destitution, and any of a hundred phobias rampant amongst modern humans. All motivate behavior in different ways.

In 1999, hacker David Smith unleashed the Melissa virus onto the net. Before it was stopped, some estimated the bug did more than $80 million in damage. As quoted by the Associated Press, "When I posted the virus, I expected that any financial injury would be minor and incidental," Smith told the judge while pleading guilty. "In fact, I included features [in the virus program] designed to prevent substantial damage." Imagine his horror as he faced federal judge Joseph Greenaway, who could have sentenced him to as many as ten years in prison. But Smith had acquired an ace. Within weeks of his arrest, the FBI had "convinced" Smith to help root out other computer hackers—using a fake identity with which he communicated with and tracked down hackers from all over the world. "Smith provided timely, substantial assistance to the United States in the investigation and prosecution of others," wrote New Jersey's U.S. Attorney, Christopher J. Christie, to Greenaway during Smith's hearing. The letter also confirmed that Smith gave the FBI the name, home address, email accounts, and other internet-related data for Jan DeWit, the author of the so-called Anna Kournikova virus in the Netherlands, which the FBI passed to Netherlands authorities who arrested DeWit. Christie's letter ultimately resulted in the reduction of Smith's sentence to a mere twenty months.

Regardless of the moral question as to whether hacking is right or wrong—or the equally moralistic question as to whether Smith was heroic in helping find others like himself whom the FBI considered dangerous, or a traitor to his creed—the FBI effectively used the powerful motivator of fear (of a decade in prison) to persuade David Smith to do their bidding, taking actions he would likely never normally do—turn evidence on fellow hackers.

There are, of course, more subtle forms of fear employed naturally and regularly. Dating sites naturally incorporate fears of loneliness, undesirability, or ultimately dying alone. To some extent, all community elements of the networked media incorporate this intrinsic fear. Diet sites incorporate a fear of obesity, job sites a fear of unemployment and destitution, and so on. Fear and pleasure are two of the most powerful motivators of humanodes, and the former is ubiquitous.

The Networked Marketing Model

These eight motivators are universally applicable, but they may be particularly powerful in the relatively frictionless realm of networked media's value nets. Rudimentary value nets have been created before in the form of networked marketing schemes made famous by companies like Avon, Mary Kay Cosmetics, and Herbalife—enterprises within traditional industries that employ individuals as agents to distribute, market, and vend for them. In fact, they call it networked marketing, and have for some time. Agents for these networked marketing companies are motivated by compensation (money), ego (internal competitions between agents), superego (self-employed, they work at their own pace), and communal (they often focus on their own circle of acquaintances, or on extending and maintaining their community of clients).

Avon is a 117-year-old enterprise that made its mark selling cosmetics door-to-door to American women. In addition to going door-to-door, Avon's independent contractors, the proverbial "Avon ladies," have sold their wares at their homes or in their workplaces—to the tune of $6.23 billion in 2002. According to an Associated Press profile by Anne D'Innocenzio, Avon is enrolling a new generation of Avon ladies, re-creating direct-selling for the sixteen-to-twenty-four age group and reinventing its marketing model. "You would have never thought of the Avon lady as cool. But for the teen community, the sense of gals marketing to other gals—this whole tribal marketing—is very timely at the moment," said Wendy Lieberman, president of WSL Strategic Retail, a consulting firm. Younger Avon reps are now selling via community settings matching the lifestyle of young women—slumber parties, sororities, campus events. Now, and then, Avon has motivated its reps to distribute, market, and vend its product through compensation (money), ego (awards for top saleswomen), superego (self-employment), and community (leveraging saleswomen's existing networks of friends and acquaintances, and offering them tools to expand and maintain their client lists). Similarly, Avon has motivated customers to buy its product through utility (easy access), compensation (giving them a good deal), and ego (ensuring the Avon brand represents quality). Even these successful applications of networking are constrained by "real world" limitations and outmoded philosophies regarding how to engage in commerce.

Networked media is, not surprisingly, intrinsically well suited to tap into the power of networked marketing. As networked media proliferates, distribution becomes more of a commodity. That is, the proximity from product or programming is the same for every humanode—one web address away. Marketing is just as important in networked media, but the dynamics of networked media provide whole new ways to market that are (at first) counterintuitive to broadcast-oriented marketers.

In networked media, value chains give way to value nets where, by definition, all networked media programming can and should enroll humanodes in multiple be-bit modes—the programming should capture and nurture humanodes to do the bidding of the programmer, including marketing. Value net feedback loops, through which information and activity flow back and forth from programmer to humanode and back again, should not be built solely for the act of humanode consumption, but for production, distribution, marketing, and vending as well; it should be laced into programming, regardless of the humanode motive that programming activates or ensnares. Using the powerful humanode motivators without ensuring that such feedback loops are in place wastes both time and money. Even then, as we've discovered, the humanode cannot be controlled in a traditional sense, only motivated. Using the be-bit programming techniques and the basic eight motivators can help harness and monetize naturally occurring humanode behavior within networked media.

But these guidelines are best employed with a healthy love of chaos.

CHAPTER 9

Traders in Our Midst

We have a unique partner—millions of people.
—MEG WHITMAN, CEO, EBAY

I watched the television concert/documentary *Paul McCartney in Red Square* a while back, which dealt in part with the powerful effect McCartney and his erstwhile band mates, The Beatles, had on the Soviet Union when they emerged on the international music scene circa 1964.

Before the mid-Sixties "the Russian people, and the Russian youth in particular, felt quite enthusiastic about what was going on in their country," said Artemy Troitsky, sociologist and author of *Back in the USSR: The True Story of Rock in Russia,* but then a number of events conspired to help the dissident movement there make great strides. The youth of the USSR no longer wanted the same thing as their government and were not as likely to buy into the less and less credible Soviet propaganda. "We all had to decide whether to stay loyal or look elsewhere," added Troitsky. They didn't have to look far. Something was fueling dissension among the young people, and it was the same thing fueling youth rebellion across the civilized planet at the time—rock and roll, and specifically Beatlemania. "They were affecting the superstructure of the society and it literally brought about the collapse of the communist-style economy and the entire system," said Timothy Ryback, director of the Salzburg Seminar and author of *Rock Around the Bloc.* "In a sense, Paul McCartney and the Beatles acted out exactly what Lenin feared would happen—a scenario ultimately played out seventy years after he predicted it. So, in the end, Lenin was right."

Lenin was right? About one thing, most definitely. "Marxism and Leninism, the very foundation for the Soviet system, preaches that the economic structure—the very basis for [in this case, Soviet] society—affects what [Lenin] called the 'superstructure'—that is, *everything*: religion, music, commerce, the way people think," explained Ryback. "[Communist doctrine] alluded to something called the dialectical relationship, which [asserts that] the way people think affect the way the economy functions; and the way the economy functions affects the way people think. Therefore, [in Communism] you needed censorship to control the system." The government of the Soviet Union controlled the media and heavily influenced not only what people saw, heard, and bought, but *how* they bought and consumed it. "The Beatles started a whole, huge movement in the Soviet Union, a movement that didn't involve thousands or even hundreds of thousands. It involved *millions* of young people, who became, as Communist publicists have said, *inner immigrants*—they still lived in the Soviet Union with their bodies, but mentally and spiritually, they were somewhere else," summarized Ryback.

The Beatles were just one of many termites undermining the foundation of Soviet life, helping along the eventual implosion. But what most struck me about the story of the Beatles' impact on the Soviet Union were the striking parallels to the internet revolution of the latter half of the 1990s.

Capitalism, in general, tends towards monopolies or oligarchies. Once these achieve power and influence, they use it to do whatever they can to protect and perpetuate that power. They design rules and regulations to enforce their will, and they lobby to etch those rules into laws, effectively conscripting the government to enforce their dominance. Typically, they try to defeat any less-agreeable government regulation to maintain their power. Monopolies and oligarchies, and the institutionalism they champion, are not unlike communist regimes in that they use their power to either co-opt, control, or crush the emergence of anything that threatens their dominance. But users of networked media—humanodes—have already moved on. Regardless of how tightly institutions hold onto legacy models of production, distribution, and marketing, humanodes have become inner immigrants—they're already thinking and behaving in a way that will ultimately take years for institutions—autocratic supernodes—to catch up.

One of the most recent and best publicized examples of this has been the music industry's battle against file sharing. Regardless of whether the law supports the music companies' argument with file sharing, their consumers have already emigrated away from the commercial model that the music industry holds on to so tightly.

Launched in mid-1999, Napster's ingenious software introduced the public to the previously unimagined abilities of peer-to-peer network computing. For those of you (somehow) unfamiliar with its story, Napster was the most famous of a family of file-sharing software products that found their way onto the networked media scene in the late 1990s. This ilk of software provides a mechanism for individual humanodes to assemble a collection of all kinds of digital files on their own computer and make them available to any other internet-connected humanode with the same software. While any kind of file can be shared, digital music fast became the favorite. The relatively small file size of a song (compared to, say, a feature film), the broad popularity of music, and the simple search and retrieval functionality provided by Napster enabled this particular new behavior to spread at lightning pace. According to *Fortune,* at its peak in March 2001, Napster was enabling its users to copy some 165 million music files per day—the majority of which were copyrighted works.

In late 1999, not long after Napster hit the scene, the Recording Industry Association of America (RIAA) sued Napster for copyright infringement, even though it was not technically Napster that was infringing. Suing a software manufacturer for the way its buyers use the software is analogous to suing Microsoft for someone using its word-processing software to plagiarize a book, or suing a gun manufacturer for the sins of a murderer who used the weapon in a crime. The product, in this case a software program, is just a tool. Even so, the RIAA persisted. Ironically, the suits served as free marketing for Napster, augmenting the already swift adoption of the software. By early 2000, over 15 million people had downloaded the file-swapping client.

The RIAA looked at the emergent file-swapping behavior as wholesale piracy. Humanodes looked at it as manna from heaven—something they took to naturally. A few enlightened music industry pundits looked at it as a new consumer behavior to be studied, harnessed, and (inevitably) exploited. Bertelsmann, the multinational media company with interests in broadcasting, publishing, and music, and almost $20 billion in annual revenue, had just such a vision. In *Fortune,* R. Bruce Rich, chief Bertelsmann litigator in New York, explained that "Bertelsmann had a vision that has come to be true: that peer-to-peer file sharing is a phenomenon that was here to stay. The best thing that could happen was to find an approach to licensing that would, over time, get royalty money flowing from Napster to the record labels." More accurately, this vision was that of their chief executive at the time, Thomas Middlehoff, who made his career in 1995 by convincing the Bertelsmann board to invest $50 million in the still-nascent AOL, a gamble that would eventually pay off to the tune of $7 billion. Bertelsmann believed Napster would do for file sharing what AOL did to promote internet use.

For many years, one of the gems in Bertelsmann's corporate crown had been BMG (Bertelsmann Music Group), a division that, in 2003, was the leading distributor of singles in the United States, and had either a first or second market share position for local repertoire in ten countries around the world. Its subsidiary, BMG Music Publishing, was the world's third largest music publisher. Clearly, Bertelsmann was "one of the boys" in the music business. Yet its leaders saw the potential in the firestorm of natural humanode behavior unleashed by Napster, not to mention amazing brand recognition Napster had gained in less than a year, and made it their business to try to make the service compliant with the prickly and often fluid rules of intellectual-property licensing.

On Halloween 2000, Bertelsmann kicked off a strategic partnership with Napster, providing it with the first of a series of loans that would eventually total $90 million, convertible to stock. The loans were intended to convert the free Napster service into a compliant music distribution/ sharing business. Numerous documents were circulated to support the stated claim that, to Bertelsmann, legitimizing Napster was top priority. Phrases like "Support the move of Napster to legal environment"; "Loan is intended to turn Napster legal"; and "Legalize file-sharing model for business use" peppered the documents that papered the agreements.

Even though Bertelsmann's intentions were clearly commercial in nature, competing media companies that owned music labels launched an assault that could not be confused as anything but a bid to kill Bertelsmann dead. Bertelsmann was made a co-plaintiff in the $17 billion lawsuit brought against Napster by the RIAA—even after Napster shut down its service in July 2001 after deciding it could not find a way to comply with an onerous court order precipitated by the actions of those same competing music labels. Any assertion that Bertelsmann was somehow motivated by some illicit purpose in partnering with Napster is ridiculous. "The purpose and intent of exploring with Napster what became a series of loan transactions was to prompt Napster to move to a fully licensed pay service," explained Rich.

Here was a situation where a magical transformation took place among the customers of music companies—they were displaying a posi-tively rabid behavior with regard to their product—and music companies for the most part were trying to kill it dead, instead of yoke it and mone-tize it. The fact that humanodes weren't paying for the opportunity to exercise this file-swapping behavior was not reflective of their appetite for doing so. In fact, several studies over the years have shown that the majority of file swappers would indeed pay for the right to do so.

Now, the merit of the RIAA's argument is obvious; a pandemic of free music simply isn't an option. But neither is shutting down file swapping. If the music companies behind the RIAA suit had saved the money they invested in legal battles and spent it instead on technological development to solve the genetic programming defect in Napster's original model and those of other file-swapping services—Napster software was missing the "commerce" gene—and on the marketing efforts necessary to mold this chaotically popular humanode behavior into a commercially acceptable service, the file-sharing war would have been over without a shot fired.

Institutional hegemony goes only so far in affecting individual thought. Just as the Soviet youth took to the Beatles (and rock music in general) like ducks to water, circumventing their government's power-ful and oppressive doctrine, contemporary youth around the world have adopted the internet as their own and embraced new behavior like file swapping with little regard for the desires of the institutional powers, and their sometimes antiquated modes of commerce, that rule the day. Trying to crush this behavior is folly.

However, much as the greed of financial markets arrested the devel-opment and understanding of the internet and networked media, Napster retarded the evolution of file swapping and peer-to-peer technology by being irresponsible and innocently ignorant in its approach. Much of the controversy generated by Napster and other the file-sharing services could have been avoided if the makers of the software had observed all of the pillars of programming. Napster and others incorporated the content, community, and code genes admirably, but took a laissez-faire approach to commerce and a self-righteous position against the prevailing music hegemony, thus failing to monetize the behavior it was responsible for humanodes adopting so rapidly.

Yet hindsight is 20/20, and it is Pollyannaish to assume that every one of the file-swapping software programmers omitted that commerce gene through ignorance or accident. Some were deliberate in their efforts. There are folks who feel "information should be free." While I take great issue with the "intellectual-property police" approach of many institutions with large IP holdings, I do not feel information should be free. I don't even think those free-information advocates really believe it should be free. I think we all simply want information to be binned and priced fairly, given actual production and distribution economics, and subject to true free-market dynamics.

Vin Crosbie, one of my favorite contrarians and a well-informed authority on free-to-fee dynamics in networked media, reminded me that Stewart Brand, in his 1987 book *The Media Lab: Inventing the Future at MIT*, wrote about an economic trend Brand had noticed years earlier in his roles as editor and publisher of *The Whole Earth Catalog,* organizer of the first Hacker's Conference, and founder of the pioneering Whole Earth 'Lectronic Link (WELL) electronic community. Brand wrote: "Information wants to be free because it has become so cheap to distribute, copy, and recombine—too cheap to meter. It wants to be expensive because it can be immeasurably valuable to the recipient. That tension will not go away. It leads to endless wrenching debate about price, copyright, 'intellectual property,' the moral rightness of casual distribution, because each round of new (technological) devices makes the tension worse, not better."

The truth is there is a value for *everything.* In actual free markets, all product and programming will find its pricing level, which can change from minute to minute, hour to hour, day to day. But there's a problem. Textbook theories about free markets are phantasmal. In practice, it's not just about supply and demand; what govern markets are limitations in technology, actual costs of distribution, and the pricing idiosyncrasies of different industries. Why is a music CD $14.95? Why couldn't we (until iTunes) buy the one song we liked instead of all ten on the CD? Why is a DVD movie $19.95? For that matter, why are all DVD movies pretty much the same price? I'd pay twice as much for a *Spider-Man* or *Lord of the Rings* DVD than I would for a much lower-budget movie. Why does an industry research report cost $1,995? Why do I have to buy the whole report if I only want to refer to one paragraph? The answers to those questions pre-Internet were based on economic models born from the production and distribution of hard goods. As Brand astutely observed, technology shepherds intellectual property in more egalitarian directions—as the costs of production and distribution go down, there is downward pressure on pricing. But of course profit-focused enterprises will resist this downward pressure if they can, often by manipulating the metering systems they put in place to monetize their product.

In the age of networked media, there is less and less justification for using the costs of duplication and distribution to keep the price of information artificially high, or to keep traditional product-bundling structures intact. Digital information is essentially free to duplicate, manipulate, or reconstitute, and microtransaction technology is removing the low-end barriers to pricing that were often subject to the (also artificial) minimums imposed by credit card clearing systems. Then again, it's hard to agree with arguments like these when considering a $100 million-plus movie. We wouldn't have *Lord of the Rings* if media programming were free or significantly cheaper than the box office or DVD prices we're paying now. Certain forms of information or entertainment require gating into business models that support the expense of creation.

For all goods and services, but particularly digital programming products, networked media *does* provide lower duplication and distribution costs, and they potentially lower marketing costs, and technology and techniques do exist to take us into the microtransaction realm (which iTunes and others are already employing). Of course, even if Napster and others had built a reasonable commercial model into their original software product, major music companies would have found it in some way insufficient, because they didn't own/control it. Like most technological advancements that occur outside the control of major corporations, they would likely have tried to crush it anyway. This is exactly the kind of corporate behavior that fuels the ire of hackers—just because it *was* one way, doesn't mean it *has* to be that way. However, it's juvenile for file-swapping hackers to fan the already raging flames burning the major music companies—the RIAA can barely keep its website alive under the constant attack of hacker-sympathizers. These actions don't help the situation. File swapping has already demonstrated a cheaper and more effective way to market and distribute music. By simply applying their cleverness in a more informed manner, file-swapping software programmers could have spliced commerce into their already brilliant code, and there would have been no claims of "wholesale piracy," no $17 billion lawsuits. The focus would have been on refining file-swapping programming—content, community, commerce, and code—to satisfy both avid humanodes and the controllers of the intellectual property being shared. Even so, the music companies would still have to accept the realization that networked media models for commerce are different than their traditional models, which they appear grudgingly to be doing.

Further confusing the issue, the marketing departments of music companies are engaged in what many could construe as subversive behavior. Charged with the simple tactical responsibility to ensure that their artists receive the quickest and widest exposure possible, low- and mid-level marketing staffs have no choice but to use the internet—and file-swapping services—to aid their efforts. More and more it's where the music customer base is making its music-consumption choices.

Several upstart labels, like Magnatune, Loca Records, and Opsound, are wholly embracing file sharing, making it a core part of their business strategy. Berkeley-based Magnatune calls its approach "open music," a blend of shareware, open source, and grass-roots activism. The idea is to let users try music before they buy, and when they do buy, to give half the revenues of every sale to the artist. Every track in Magnatune's fifty-artist catalog is available for streaming and downloading. Humanodes can download, swap, and remix songs as much as they like for noncommercial use. But if they want to make money from their use of the song, they must pay. Licensing works on a sliding scale—using a song by soprano Beth Quest for a wedding video costs $5; using the same song for the opening credits of a $5 million feature film with worldwide distribution costs $2,600. Again, half of the proceeds go to the artists, who maintain control of their library, both unheard-of practices in the vaunted halls of the major music industry.

Each of these companies—and let us not forget the artists—wants to make money. They are simply moving forward in ways that mesh more naturally with emerging humanode behavior in the world of networked media. Will their models evolve? Yes—just as the models of the bigger media conglomerates will have to evolve, too. It's likely one of the industry behemoths will eventually acquire the most successful of the upstart networked labels, using its (by then) proven-out model to effect an internal change. It's simply a matter of time, as is most change. But the change is inevitable. Large companies will still have the leverage or money necessary to buy loads of media time to promote their artists in brute displays of commercial might, but those prohibitively expensive marketing modes will become less important (and less desirable) as networked media spreads, as natural word-of-mouse techniques become better understood, and as the humanode marketplace demonstrates how it wants to purchase music.

So why has the RIAA taken a litigious, witch-hunt approach to the problem? Lots of reasons, but most of them boil down to issues of institutional fear and control. They're coming around to networked media slowly, but unless specifically designed to adapt, institutions resist change, especially change that threatens a business model that has afforded relatively stable livelihoods for thousands of employees. This is not a new dynamic, nor one that should be unfamiliar to any living, breathing human being dwelling in the twenty-first century. Institutions fear innovation that comes from outside of their control structure, much as average individual humans fear change that is not of their choosing. Contemporary institutions are built for control, not change or adaptability. They prize control as their best means for amortizing capital costs and creating economies of scale. But this dynamic is less and less applicable as more companies and more consumers embrace contemporary models of commerce, technology, research and development, distribution, and marketing—as more and more consumers become humanodes.

The music labels don't own radio stations, but radio is (or was) the most important showcase for new music: the level of radio exposure often makes or breaks an artist. Motion picture companies don't own theater chains in the U.S. anymore, yet they are reliant on them to expose their products to moviegoers. Distributors of any kind of product don't want someone standing between them and their consumers if they can help it. They don't want new MTVs to crop up—intermediaries to their consumer marketing efforts that become more powerful than the product-sellers themselves. The distribution, marketing, and vending methodologies on which companies grew up are simply inappropriate for the networked media environment. They don't match the messiness of natural humanode behavior.

A Messy Business

In Greek mythology, chaos was the vacant, unfathomable space from which Gaia (the earth) sprang and became the mother of all things. From chaos, then, grew order. Networked media are fairly chaotic themselves.

In comparison, a beehive looks sedate and an ant colony looks like an orderly military parade. If we could actually visualize it, we'd see millions of humanodes connecting and disconnecting, billions of bits fluxing through copper and fiber, and the entire telacorpus pulsing with an arrhythmic virtual life force powered by an actual life force—us. This kind of chaos makes us nervous. We're simply not capable of comprehending supercomplex systems in a deterministic and linear fashion.

Most technology inventions are wittingly or unwittingly designed to order chaos—to linearize it—since we abhor disorder in our world and try to minimize it. In practice, our inventions don't truly order the chaos, but simply harness it—sometimes, if we are lucky, for purposes that can be commercialized. When our inventions fail, it is often because we tried too hard to impose order and control—a point the creators of programming for networked media should bear in mind.

The human approach to understanding the world, and thus the way we organize it and our societies, is linear, compartmentalized, and rooted in reductionism. Logic is linear and partitioned. Its employment via analysis provides us with linear equations, processes, functions, algebra, and most of our sciences, all molded into simple, understandable contexts for the human mind to ingest and process. Time itself is the ultimate linear device we've imposed on ourselves. Some emerging sciences—parallel processing, fractals, fuzzy logic, swarm computing, and distributed systems—promise to break us free of linear mindsets in our approach to mathematical analysis, but logic remains the root of our fundamental approach to computing—a procedural, step-by-step process from which we've only just begun to evolve. All these simplifications were for our benefit, giving us sanctuary from the fear that there may not be any real order to the universe, and giving us a mechanism to harness nonlinear dynamics.

But our universe is not linear. It is messy and chaotic. Yet the world works, and evolves, despite and perhaps because of its chaotic nature. Despite our love of order, on some level we've always appreciated the chaos around us. Consider fire, the rapid chemical reaction of combustible substances to generate flame. Fire can be destructively wild and unpredictable. Yet, when harnessed, it can keep an abode warm during the cold winter nights, light our way through darkness, or drive an internal combustion engine. Struggling to force-fit linear systems to the nonlinear world around them, scientists of the nineteenth century became burdened with the task of creating a new science and mathematics to measure, or attempt at least to understand, the chaotic complexities of actual life. Thus, chaos theory was born.

Manus Donahue's succinct essay on chaos theory describes it as "the qualitative study of irregular, unpredictable, aperiodic behavior in nonlinear dynamical systems." Simply put, a dynamical system refers to time-varying behavior of an actual system. A dynamical system can be as simple as a ticking clock or as complex our planet's weather system. Aperiodic behavior is simply a behavior or dynamic that never exactly repeats itself. As it turns out, there is no such thing as a truly periodic behavior, since every repetitive dynamic, no matter how precise it seems, never exactly repeats itself.

All processes feature some level of chaos. Even a ticking clock may appear to be periodic, but any small disturbance in what appears to be an identical, repetitive dynamic (each tick of a clock's second hand) will continue to manifest its effects. This is familiar to most of us who've seen our watches lose or gain time. Another result of microscopic aperiodicity might result in a bald spot on your car tire. For all you know, it looks like the wheel spins the same way with every revolution, but small disturbances in its rotation caused by misalignment, road conditions, and a dozen other variables ultimately cause the tire to wear more quickly in one area. The study of chaos theory helps us understand the processes occurring behind the economy, history, weather, and even the human brain. As humans are inclined to do, once we understand something, we try to harness it and then, inevitably, commercialize it. Humankind has always attempted to harness the chaos around us, so we can do things better, faster, and cheaper.

Media are no different. All media technologies attempt to capture and organize ideas, concepts, and experiences and store them for later consumption. This applies to everything from the Dewey decimal system of library organization to electronic television programming guides, from Homer's *Odyssey* to a primetime television program. This mindset often emerges in the programming itself. The homogenized world of 1950s television attempted to portray very structured systems and boundaries where we could easily recognize linear elements of the world. But we've always known that father doesn't always know best, and an FBI agent usually takes longer than an hour to catch a bad guy. Networked media defy linearization. We are better served embracing the macrochaotic behavior of the telacorpus instead of trying to control individual humanodes. The purpose of the networked enterprise is to engender a desired humanode behavior, or "capture" a target humanode behavior when it occurs independently, and then apply dynamics that provide a higher probability of reoccurrence, or generate different but equally desirable behavior. Put another way, it's to acquire and retain an ever-shifting, empowered sea of humanodes, and ultimately harness and monetize their behavior.

Enginets

The pre-Industrial Revolution use of the word "engine" was related to "ingenuity"—a sense of skill, a clever device, an invention, or an innate ability. Philosophers and poets used it metaphorically. Sir Walter Raleigh alluded to "terrible engines of death" when describing the emerging weapons of mass destruction of his time.

Whether literal or metaphorical, an engine describes the process of yoking something—most often something fuzzy, messy, unpredictable, or chaotic—into the predictable service of another thing. An internal combustion engine harnesses little chaotic explosions through a complex bit of controllable machinery built most commonly to turn automobile wheels. The sail rig on a sailboat is an engine designed to convert the wind into locomotion. Any computing device is an engine. Even Charles Babbage, one of the fathers of computer science, saw fit to call his rudimentary (circa 1844) mechanical stored-program computer an "analytical engine." The term has survived many steps in the evolution of computer science. Today the term "engine" is used to describe specific software—database engines, search engines, game engines, auction engines. While there is no moving machinery per se, the meaning is the same: building a device—in this case, a virtual device composed of software instructions—to organize information, process data, or harness user behavior.

Networked media are well suited to programming efforts that incorporate the concept of an engine, but a specific approach to the engineering of those engines must be considered. In this context, the sail rig is a good metaphor for the kinds of programming we should be designing. A sail system itself is a somewhat inexact—and arguably *nonlinear*—system of canvas, ropes, masts, and pulleys designed to harness the nonlinear, chaotic energy of wind. In a gasoline engine, as long as there is gas in the tank, spark in the battery, and a source of air, the engine will work pretty much the same under any circumstances. Conversely, sailors rely on their own skill to adjust a sail rig in real time to optimize whatever energy they can milk from relatively unpredictable wind conditions at any given moment.

In networked media, the most successful programmers have consciously, unconsciously, or accidentally, employed network engines—*enginets*—or an "enginetworking" approach. These have been like sail rigs designed to harness humanode behavior. But these enginets are also capable of fueling themselves. A well-programmed enginet will allow for resonant behavior to occur. Put another way, and in keeping with the metaphor, enginets can help the "wind" of humanodes resonate to higher levels of energy and usage. It would be equivalent to a sail rig capable of making more wind by itself.

Elance built an enginet that connects people seeking a specific expertise with a vast and geographically distributed pool of freelancers—programmers, artists, and others. Most dating sites exponentially benefit as the numbers of humanodes using them increases—a bigger dating pool implies better chances for success in romance (though anyone who has used an online dating site will tell you that quantity doesn't necessarily lead to quality). LinkedIn and Friendster created powerful social-networking enginets that allow humanodes to connect for all sorts of reasons, completely abstracted from the managers of the enginets—that is, Friendster has no idea why people on its site might connect, what they write in their profile, or what they do after they "network." Companies like eBay, Yahoo!, and Google have made optimal use of their enginet programming by tracking and scrutinizing how networked behavior is shifting. The volume of search on Google or Yahoo! often heralds a number-one box-office opening weekend for a movie—an attractively tangible benefit of measuring where the wind is blowing.

In networked media, think of the molecules that make up "the wind" as the humanodes. The sail system to harness their behavior can come in a limitless number of forms. Three of the contemporary forms of enginet deserving further discussion, and that are relatively easily employed, are (1) the exchange; (2) peer-to-peer; and (3) free-range agents.

The Exchange

Most of us have been to county fairs or giant swap meets where hundreds, perhaps thousands, of people paid the organizer for the right to sell anything from antiques to tools to baseball cards, and thousands more people paid to get in to shop, haggle and buy. Today, we get that same sense of excitement and awe by logging onto eBay.com. Whenever the words "internet" and "profits" are used in the same sentence, eBay garners attention.

In 1995, eBay founder Pierre Omidyar developed a website for his girlfriend. She collected Pez dispensers, and Omidyar's software enabled her to buy and sell Pez dispensers with fellow collectors online. Others found the site and started selling things other than Pez dispensers. Six months after putting up the site, Omidyar realized he'd accidentally started a company. He quit his day job to focus on the business full time. In June 1997, Omidyar received $3 million in venture capital from Benchmark Capital. Silicon Valley legend has it the money remains untouched in the bank—one of the benefits of having operating profits to draw from in order to manage growth. From day one, eBay made money. According to *Business Week*, in 2003 alone, eBay was host to at least 30 million people buying and selling more than $20 billion in merchandise; it remains the number-one e-commerce site in the world.

Of course, eBay doesn't produce or distribute any of the items sold on its site; humanodes do this for them. The company provides the context for this experience, an enginet with a monetizing stopcock to siphon off profit. It's the networked media equivalent of a marketplace—an exchange, with a networked infrastructure where anything can be bought and sold; where prices are set dynamically based on supply and demand; and where the enabler of the exchange—eBay—makes money off of every transaction. Many of those dealers who, in another era, would have traveled the country like gypsies, setting up tables at conventions and fairs to sell their collectibles and wares for a day or two, are now able to sit in the comfort of their own homes and reach not just a few hundred people, but millions all over the world.

Whether by accident or by design, eBay created the near-perfect paradigm of an exchange-enginet for a networked media environment. It has all the elements of a well-programmed networked media experience. The company admirably employs all four C's:

- *Content* The text of product descriptions, comments, and trader reviews, graphics, photos, et cetera.
- *Community* Mechanisms to connect buyers and sellers.
- *Commerce* In-programming monetary transaction capability.
- *Code* The software "engine" that pulls it all together in a humanode-friendly experience.

eBay also capitalizes on all five humanode be-bits:

- *Producer* eBay provides the tools for humanodes to write descriptions and scan images. The humanode actually creates the product listing.
- *Distributor* eBay's servers allow any humanode in the world to "distribute" their auctioned item to every other eBay user worldwide. Once sales are complete, humanodes actually distribute the physical products themselves.
- *Marketer* eBay has built in several marketing functions. One is the feedback mechanism. Buyers and sellers can rate each other; the collective rating becomes a powerful message, for good or bad, to other eBay users. Also, eBay's search and directory system becomes the voice for sellers trying to connect to buyers, and vice versa.
- *Vendor* eBay users are their own shopkeepers.
- *Consumer* Any humanode can bid and buy from eBay.

Furthermore, eBay touches just about every one of the eight humanode motivators:

- *Diversion* Often people bid for the item on eBay because they enjoy the experience far more than "just shopping." It's entertainment, whether or not they get a better price for the object of their desire.
- *Compensation* Humanodes sell products for cash. For some, eBay is their sole source of income.
- *Ego* Humanodes using eBay are self-empowered, and sometimes eBay actually provides their means of self-employment.

- *Superego* eBay appeals to the free-market mentality of many humanodes—a specific value system.

- *Utility* eBay provides a fast, easy, broad-reach way to engage in commerce.

- *Community* eBay is extremely efficient at connecting buyers and sellers, and grouping sellers and buyers of like mind.

- *Addiction* Talk to any avid eBay user for more on this one.

- *Fear* To one degree or another, any auction participant fears losing.

Again, a key factor in the success of eBay is that it didn't try to predict what humanodes would do; it only built a mechanism—an enginet—that enabled them to do it in a way that made eBay money. Edward Ciliberti, a successful antique dealer based in Monterey, California, at first thought that selling on eBay would be "difficult." This perception is one of the primary barriers for increasing exchange on networked media, which are still unfamiliar to many people: how hard is it to do business with them? Ciliberti later discovered that "eBay made it so simple and effortless to sell what I have and this is the key to my success." The value proposition for online sellers is in enabling humanodes to transact with others in the easiest, most cost-effective manner possible.

There are, of course, numerous other examples of exchange enginets, and many have less to do with direct commercial product transactions. The year 2004 saw social networking sites come into vogue. While specific features vary from site to site, companies like LinkedIn, Friendster, Tickle, and others basically do the same thing: create a mechanism for humanodes to connect with other humanodes for social or commercial exchanges of their own design and taste. Friendster founder Jonathan Abrams, in his keynote speech to the 2004 SXSW Interactive Conference, described it thusly: "At this conference, we're wearing name tags with our real names. That's the kind of experience I wanted to create with Friendster. The beta for Friendster went up in March 2003. It's grown pretty fast. We never did any marketing. We still don't have a PR firm. I just put this thing up. And my friends invited their friends, who invited their friends." At this writing, the company claims 7 million users and growing. He states no marketing, but his enginet was built—Friendster's *programming* was built—with intrinsic marketing: word of mouse.

Social networking enginets are not online communities where people veil their identities; it's where they flaunt them, as well as their connections to other humanodes. I'll let the reader decide how well these social networking companies have implemented the Four C's, how well they've activated the humanode be-bits and what kinds of motivators they've employed; but I will also point out that none of these enginets has reported, as yet, making money.

Most exchange enginets—auction sites, dating sites, social-networking sites—have made a deliberate effort to allow site transactions to be as unmediated as is practical. This hands-off approach has enabled humanodes to come together in unpredictable but often fruitful ways. Social-networking enginets and dating enginets are predicated on transaction anonymity. It's unlikely they would have any chance of success if they demanded editorial control over the information exchanged between their humanodes, unless, of course, that editorial control was a feature of the site—a theme, perhaps. Even JDate, a dating site for Jewish people, has numerous non-Jewish members, none of whom are dissuaded from joining. Pressures have grown for eBay, in particular, to take greater responsibility for what is sold on its site—the 2001 controversy over the sale of Nazi memorabilia being a case in point. I certainly abhor Nazism, or fascism of any kind, but I am an ardent supporter of freedom of speech and the right of like-minded humanodes to assemble, physically or virtually. Commerce is a simple extension of those rights. Not only is it a burden on its business to try to edit an exchange, it's not particularly feasible. As David Bunnell put it in his book, *The eBay Phenomenon,* "it's hard to see how anything less than a small army of employee-sleuths could effectively monitor the site's millions of auction listings," and guarantees or warranties on items sold would both be costly and would suck company personnel into endless disputes.

Besides, different people will define appropriateness differently. While eBay does its best to monitor its site for egregious behavior, and technologies to aid and automate those efforts continue to improve, I personally think eBay is better off staying out of the editing business. But that's a purist approach to networked media that doesn't take into account the political pressure contemporary public companies must endure. Unless specific products or programming are banned or regulated specifically in the statutes of our state or federal government, networked exchanges should be allowed to perform freely.

Peer-to-Peer

The drug trade in the United States can accurately be described as illicit networked marketing.

While it is difficult to assign completely accurate numbers to a business so shrouded in secrecy, the Associated Press reported that in 1998 the United Nations estimated the worldwide drug trafficking trade as a $400 billion-per-year industry, equaling 8 percent of the world's trade. This is greater than the exports of the automobile industry worldwide, and it rivals annual "legal" drug sales for the global pharmaceutical industry. The same 1998 estimate found that marijuana was the fourth most lucrative crop in the United States, after corn, soybeans, and hay, and the biggest grossing crop in several states. The U.S. spends more than $5 billion every year in the "war on drugs," but to no avail. The illicit drug industry is bigger today than ever and shows no signs of abatement. Efforts to end, or even diminish, the drug trade don't seem to work; and history has witnessed this kind of behavior before.

The prohibitionists of the early twentieth century were adamant about stopping the use of alcohol. But even after alcohol was banned by a constitutional amendment passed in the 1920s, America's thirst for alcohol was so great that illegal liquor sales swiftly became one of the country's largest businesses. The changing political climate, and the admission that prohibition simply wasn't working, eventually saw prohibition repealed in the 1930s, and the government switched to regulating liquor instead. The U.S. and state governments installed an infrastructure that oversaw the distribution, consumption, and taxation of alcohol, and set legal drinking ages. Does that mean there still isn't abuse of alcohol? Do some minors still drink? Do some people still drink and drive? Absolutely. But with regulation in place, those have become more the exception than the rule. Modern-day prohibition focuses on drugs like marijuana, cocaine, and other mind-altering substances. Why do people continue to flout the government's mandate? The answers have to do with the illicit drug business's deployment of several of the basic eight motivators: drug dealers receive monetary *compensation*; a percentage of users develop either psychological or physical *addiction*; many of those not addicted enjoy drug use as a form of *diversion*.

Prohibition never works in human societies. Not for long, anyway. According to PriceWaterhouseCoopers *(Global Entertainment and Media*

Outlook: 2002–2007), the *projected* 2007 global markets for theatrical box office revenue ($22 billion), consumer book publishing ($52 billion), broadcast and cable advertising ($137.5 billion) and electronic games ($40 billion), a *combined total* of approximately $250 billion, falls well short of the size of the worldwide illicit drug trade *today*. It is ironic that the illicit drug trade's more legitimate entertainment industry cousins rely on mass-media marketing and advertising—significant portions of their costs—and the only consumer marketing available to the illicit drug industry is word of mouth. Comparatively, drug dealers spend zilch on marketing. Clearly, "traditional" forms of marketing are not necessary for success in business if the product or programming itself is attractive enough.

Any institution fighting to eradicate an undesirable human behavior (to it) is better off installing a visible regulatory infrastructure that monitors and manages the environment, and that possesses informational and financial feedback loops that can be used to evolve that infrastructure in desired directions. Keep your customers close, and your pirates closer. The latter can end up being the most valuable of humanodes.

The plethora of technologies that enable us to "file swap"—epitomized in online song trading—across the internet are even more effective than the networked marketing schemes that evolved organically in the business of illicit drugs. It's a digital bazaar—a great example of the increasingly popular peer-to-peer environments—and employed correctly, it can be a powerful enginet to drive preferred behavior and, if desired, resultant commerce.

After Nullsoft completed the first version of its software Gnutella (a competitor to Napster that appeared shortly after and was freely available on the internet), employees briefly posted the program's code on the internet. However, AOL, Nullsoft's parent company, quickly yanked the data off the servers. Too late. A few humanodes flipped on their distributor be-bit and the code began to spread like a virus. Within hours, it was on computers around the world. Meanwhile, other humanodes flipped on their producer be-bits to continue tweaking the Gnutella software outside of AOL's control. Before long dozens of websites provided access to different versions of the Gnutella software and updates about the latest developments. There were parallel dynamics going on here. First, the software itself didn't require traditional production, distribution, and marketing techniques to proliferate. There quickly emerged a distributed group of coders who took responsibility for evolving the software, and the internet provided a relatively frictionless method for networked marketing to take root. For example, Napster gained 7 million users in fewer than six months after its initial release. That's some powerful word of mouse. Second, the programming—files of all kinds, including music—moving through the peer-to-peer lattice didn't require traditional distribution and marketing techniques. Users of Napster and Gnutella were acting as much as producers (ripping songs), distributors (posting them on their peer client as available for download) and marketers (intrinsic search capability built into the software client) as they were consumers!

Both Bill Gates of Microsoft and Andrew Grove of Intel have publicly stated that they believe peer-to-peer (often called "P2P") networks will continue to be very important in the networked media environment. I believe they are more correct than probably they suspect. But what is peer-to-peer? Why does it work so well? And why would it behoove institutions to adopt the P2P model (in a form that adheres to the pillars of programming, of course)?

Concentrate a 10,000-pound load on one square foot of floor on the top story of a building, and that load will be in the basement before you know it, after leaving a nice one-square-foot hole through each of the floors in between. In traditional client-server computing environments, the individual humanode's computer software—called a client, like a browser or email application—must query and connect to master computers in order to move information. When you open your browser and type in yahoo.com, your browser (client) shouts out to the network until a Yahoo!-owned or -controlled computer (server) answers. The server then negotiates an upload or download of programming depending on the original query. The widely publicized outages at eBay a couple years back were a result of the load-scalability problems that can result from this kind of client-server architecture. Even with *hundreds* of servers and as much bandwidth as they could pipe in, they still failed under the weight of millions of passionate, regular eBay users. It's the same thing that would happen if millions of people all over the country tried to see a movie that was available in one theater in one neighborhood in one city. Even if we could imagine a theater big enough to hold everyone, the airports, bus stations, train stations, and highways would choke with incoming theatergoers. Now, if you take that same 10,000-pound load and spread it over a thousand square feet, you'll support it with no problem. Distributed computing technologies like P2P spread the load across the network and are intrinsically capable of better network management if coded properly.

Bottlenecks in the internet are creating a great need for distributed computing technology to help spread the load away from giant, centralized server farms. This architecture of computing is called distributed client-server, a classic example of which is the SETI@home project. SETI@home conscripts the unused disk space and idle computing power of volunteers' personal PCs across the world to help the California-based SETI (Search for Extra-Terrestrial Intelligence) Institute create the equivalent of a distributed supercomputer, which is then employed in SETI's quest to investigate extraterrestrial life. It manages distributed clients in a holistic, centrally coordinated fashion.

True P2P is a little different: clients are linked to other clients and are theoretically capable of bypassing the centralized servers that might seek to manage what the clients do. The result is a sort of "client-client" architecture that enables clients to act like little servers themselves. Foregoing any discussion of copyright infringement issues for the moment, users of ideal P2P technology are seamlessly connected to each other, and they have the ability to share media of any kind with anyone else on the planet. P2P is a point-to-point synchronized connection between individuals, anonymous or familiar. Meanwhile, as distributed computing proliferates, PC power is also increasing, while simultaneously becoming less expensive. Add to that the demonstrated humanode demand for P2P systems made popular by the likes of Napster, Gnutella, Morpheus, and Kazaa, and a crucial confluence of elements is in place to ensure the continued emergence of distributed systems, if the pillars of programming are observed.

There are actually two forms of P2P. The first is *chaperoned peer-to-peer* (CP2P), where centralized servers monitor peer-to-peer activities and provide services like indexing, activity tracking, authentication, and authorization. CP2P is a bit like ants going about their daily business doing their individual ant-to-ant thing, but still turning to the queen when permission-required functions are attempted. Even when permission isn't required, though, the central authority tracks the P2P activity. Kazaa, Napster and pretty much any other file-swapping service fall into this category. So do telephones and fax machines that have been employing this kind of system for years. One of the reasons Napster and other CP2P sites could be targeted for lawsuits was because of something called "vicarious copyright infringement": because CP2P sites have central directories and can track what people do, they are thought (by plaintiff lawyers) to be complicit in any act of copyright infringement that may or may not happen within their enginet.

There are two main ways CP2P can be used. *Messy* mode describes classic P2P, where individual humanodes initiate their own actions and use of P2P network resources. Messy mode is many-to-many. *Managed* (or *permissioned*) mode requires the peer essentially to ask permission to do what it plans, or desires, to do; if programmed properly, this allows for managing and measuring any commerce transactions. Permission needn't necessarily be explicit: it may take the form of a simple agent that alerts a central server of the intention of the peer, which in turn approves or disapproves the action subject to the peer's status within the system (e.g., if the peer's subscription tier doesn't allow it access to a particular piece of programming) or status of the programming (e.g. it's illegal or of sub-par quality). The "permissioning" can be built into the code of the peer software.

For distributed peer-to-peer (or DP2P), the Gnutella protocol is a good example. As originally conceived and developed by Justin Frankel and Tom Pepper at Nullsoft in March 2000, Gnutella is not a company, a particular application, or a website. Rather, it is a name for an open-source, peer-to-peer networking protocol unique to the Gnutella standard. Many companies are still building services and software based on the Gnutella open standard, including Morpheus, Bearshare, Gnotella, and Limewire. DP2P clients are truly independent, and network-wide services are done in a more organic, distributed fashion. There is no one controlling authority and it is difficult, if not impossible, for a (messy or managed) centralized application to run without the express buy-in of the individual clients, or the humanodes controlling those clients. A small piece of software resides on every peer computer, each of which functions as both client and server, thus the derivation of the term "servent" (SERVer+cliENT) used within the Gnutella community for a node on the network. Each servent, also spelled "servant," allocates a customizable set of resources usable by the peer client—CPU power, disc space, memory, et cetera. The collectives of peer clients are designed to manage themselves without human intervention. The strength and weakness of these DP2P enginets are the same. The decentralization of the information being shared across the network arguably absolves makers of this kind of enginets from "vicarious copyright infringement"; but distributed peer-to-peer often suffers from drops in quality of service. Since there is no central directory server—no single authoritative source index—many argue that DP2P searches don't find all that's on the network, because the search algorithms quit after a few, pre-defined hops to topologically proximate servents. It's also more difficult to create a feature-rich software client environment and consistency of features across servent nodes, since by nature the software development is hands-off and open-source.

The emergence of P2P systems is inevitable, and both software developers and purveyors of product, or programming with intellectual property ramifications, should embrace them, not eradicate them. P2P systems are enginets perfectly suited to the cost-effective distribution, marketing, and consumption of digital works through networked media, which can be designed to profit purveyors of programming from the chaos P2P enginets engender. For now, let it suffice to say that P2P is one of a few powerful new technologies taking root in networked media; it is not going away, and programmers need to understand its dynamics, embrace them, and use their sweat, brains, and attorneys to find ways to cultivate this humanode behavior, which is naturally arising within the telacorpus and which is being embraced by the humanodes that populate it. P2P is a natural enginet for chaotic behavior waiting to be harnessed and commercialized.

Free-Range Agents

The telacorpus—the body of networked media—is an entity capable of supporting pseudobiological dynamics. Take that paradigm one step further and imagine a future where the telacorpus plays host to "virtual life forms," some smarter, some dumber. At the most basic level of networked media infrastructure—physical layers of routers and transceivers—packets of instructions are racing across the networks trying to find their homes or destinations, or fulfill some purpose. Computer viruses are the telacorporeal equivalent of biological viruses or bacteria. That is, the "eDNA" of a computer virus is made up of instinct more than intelligence. Their

genetic makeup limits them to simple, parasitic consumption and duplication activities; some computer viruses are cleverly created to go so
far as to act like a biological retrovirus, capable of simple mutation that
circumvents eradication efforts.

Intelligent agent technologies promised (but as yet have not succeeded) to simplify our lives by learning from us humanode "masters."
These agents are meant to act as virtual valets to perform mundane tasks
like researching subjects in which the master is interested, staying alert
for shopping bargains, and serving as proxies for eBay bidding wars for
that particular item you've just got to have. But most agent technology
is based on procedural software, code programs that must be written by
a humanode. The agent has to be reprogrammed by someone whenever
a new assignment is desired.

Fortunately, human reprogramming of agents may soon be a thing
of the past. Coming on fast are the free-range agents (sometimes called
"mobile agents or "virtual life forms"), which are among the newest developments in artificial intelligence. One of the defining characteristics
of free-range agents is mobility. They move freely across the network,
using whatever computing resources they can find to perpetuate their
existence and becoming quiescent only when none are available. Free-
range agents are also autonomous; they are imbued with the type of
genetics that allows them to grow and evolve, subject to their initial
gene-configuration and the environmental conditions of the network.
Finally, free-range agents are emergent: coherent patterns are formed
by interactions between two or more agents, and collectively they form
a virtual consciousness. As I see it, there are three potential classes of
free-range agents.

Changeling or *proxy* agents are autonomous free-range agents in-
fused with basic human cognitive characteristics that are designed to
act as virtual replacement selves, growing and carrying out our wishes
based on the genetics with which we imbue them. Creating a changeling agent involves anthropomorphizing a free-range agent to create
an individual's proxy to roam freely through the telacorpus. People
may have a relationship with changelings for years, both teaching and
learning from them.

Itinerant agents are autonomous mobile agents built on basic business principles that roam the network at the behest of enterprises that
create and control them for commercial purposes. They are essentially

a proxy agent designed specifically for commercial enterprises, their genetics limited in scope to require them to perform the boring functions of a business. Generally, they are hobbled so that they can't grow beyond their original genetic programming. This may include a limited lifespan—like a free-range itinerant agent genetically coded to "negotiate" a deal with a brief time limit. When the deadline passes, the agent self-deletes.

Chimera agents are intelligent life-forms that couldn't possibly exist in the real world. They are primarily created for entertainment or diversionary purposes, and can "live" in virtual environments created within networked media (like massively-multiplayer game platforms). They are fanciful. They live only in the telacorpus, or a virtual world that exists virtually within the telacorpus.

Free-range agents can be as diverse as our ability to imagine them. None require a permanent singular computer host. If a humanode creates one of these agents and shuts off the computer on which it was created, the agent will move to another system before the first is shut down. The free-range agent persists not because electricity is powering the computer, but because the entire telacorpus provides a sea in which these agents can swim, unabated by the actions of a single humanode or a single device.

Ostensibly, we'll be able to maintain our tether on these agents. For example, I may have a free-range itinerant travel agent that I imbue with initial genetic conditions that limit its lifetime to the duration of my business trip. From my work or home computer, I set it in motion and shut off the computer. The migrant is already wandering through the network, using available resources (most likely from a peer-to-peer platform) to "survive" and carrying out its task of monitoring my trip. When I arrive at my destination, I log on to any computer or mobile phone and "whistle" for the agent to come. The agent accesses whatever local memory and processor resources it needs to tell me there's been a change in my itinerary due to weather. I modify my trip parameters and send the migrant on its way again.

Inevitably, these free-range agents will be evolving from the inside out. Just as we have ways of "virtualizing" ourselves into networked media via digital prosthetics like computers, mobile phones, and game machines, mobile agents may find ways to manifest themselves into the actual. This process may start with simple "permissioned" control of our devices—send an email, make a phone call or stock the refrigerator—allowing the agent to express whatever we've employed it to do for us. It's even conceivable that a traffic free-range agent created to monitor road conditions might reprogram my futuristic car's navigation computer to modify its route without my having to inquire into traffic conditions or make the route adjustments myself.

As with most technologies, I'm sure such agents will be used for bad and for good—but what is certain is that they will emerge, and soon. If we focus now on discussing and developing the systems, laws, and technologies in which they can thrive, we have a better opportunity to assure that the majority of agent usage will be legitimate and sanctioned.

Sumner Redstone, the chairman of media behemoth Viacom, has said that the best way to deliver shareholder value is to foster an atmosphere in which "the unpredictable, surprising, and essential elements of creativity can take root and flourish." It's likely he was referring to the people whom he employs, or talent with whom his company has relationships, but his sentiment can be extended to his customer constituency, who are avidly partaking of networked media. I'd say it a little differently—let chaos thrive, but charge at the door and for the drinks.

Chaos naturally occurs within networked media. The lightning is there (highly motivated humanodes), as are the bottles: enginets, exchanges, peer-to-peer networks, free-range architectures, and more will emerge. The trick is to discover means by which we can monetize them for commercial value—the key being to employ the commerce gene when developing networked media programming.

The chaotic systems discussed above can all be harnessed, though not linearized, and they promise to usher in yet another stage of networked media evolution; but all roads lead back to the humanode—the most important variable in the networking equation today. How might we unleash and harness, in the near term, the power of humanodes? With all this innovation, unpredictable consequences can arise. What consequences and possibilities arise in cutting loose thousands or even millions of humanodes furnished with the abilities to produce, distribute, market, vend and consume? We have seen a glimpse in the emergence of a buccaneer mentality with regard to trade in copyrighted intellectual property, and especially music; but as we've discussed, the approach was flawed and ignored prescient application of native networked media programming techniques. There is a better way.

Trading Posts

According to estimates from Jupiter Research, spending on download-able online music in the U.S. totaled less than $1 billion in 2003; that number that will rise to $3.3 billion, or about 26 percent of all U.S. music spending, by 2008. Companies like Apple, with its iTunes service, are leading that charge.

On the whole, the contemporary incarnation of Apple seems to "get" networked media. Under Steven Jobs's aegis, it has a legacy of champi-oning the needs and desires of the user and has led by example in design of both product and programming over the years. They have more often than not given us what we want. In the case of iTunes, they have prag-matically walked the line between what is native to networked media, and what is acceptable to mostly risk-averse, institutionally minded music companies. What Apple has created is simply an online music store—digital, yes, but a command-and-control center for download-able music. That in itself gives music companies comfort. Let's not kid ourselves, though. Apple has not cured the piracy issue. There already exists software to bridge the security systems built into the iTunes client software, allowing users to illegitimately share files bought legitimately on the iTunes service. But Apple is on the right track: by designing an easy-to-use digital music player—iPod—and an intuitive, humanode-oriented music download website—iTunes—they have had a bigger effect on piracy than any antipiracy technology or legislation could. Most folks couldn't be bothered with the less well-engineered and amateur-ishly programmed circa-2004 file-swapping software systems.

Granted, Apple has a brand that automatically differentiates it amongst the humanode population, but iTunes still has the marketing and dis-tribution costs commensurate with any major online store struggling to make the grade in the commoditizing universe of networked media. And the competition for iTunes is coming in droves.

With iTunes, Apple is still avoiding and underexploiting natural dynamics available in networked media—cost-saving opportunities that might prove critical in building a successful business around digital me-dia distributed digitally. If a consumer is no longer just a consumer, but in fact is a new kind of customer—a humanode with equal opportunity to become producer, distributor, marketer, vendor, *or* consumer—then online music stores built essentially in the image of bricks-and-mortar music stores fall short of what is possible in, and native to, networked media. We *can* build environments to protect intellectual property, or at least preserve revenue streams derived from it, and mitigate undesirable behavior with regards to intellectual property. And we can do it using peer-to-peer enginets.

The downward pressure on per-song prices for downloadable music will be considerable as companies like Microsoft, Amazon, Sony, Wal-Mart, and any of a dozen major retailers or techno-media companies get into the game. Several studies have indicated that the majority of study respondents would pay on the order of $15 per month to use a music file-sharing service. For the same retail cost of a single CD each month, one could trade music over the internet peer-to-peer file-sharing service with impunity. What if the music industry issued, say, ten licenses for what we'll call *trading posts*? Just as the government metes out our wireless spectrum, intellectual-property owners could license *intellectual-property spectrum*—a range of rights to use intellectual property. Of course, the rights holders would be paid for it—perhaps even through an auction, a mechanism that generated billions of dollars in the wireless industry. Each of these trading posts would be responsible for reporting accurate tradelists, much like the play lists radio stations are responsible for reporting to the RIAA. Those tradelists would be matched to monthly revenue for that trading post. Each trading post—which might be set up by existing companies like Napster, Morpheus, Kazaa, or even a peer-to-peer extension of Apples iTunes—would take its cut and the remainder would go to the RIAA, to be distributed to artists and labels pro rata based on the popularity of trades. Think of it: at one time, Napster had 28 million registered users. If only a quarter of those converted to a pay service, Napster would have generated $105 million dollars per month in gross revenue, or more than $1 billion per year. Assume Napster took 30 percent off the top, and you're talking more than $700 million per year to the bottom line of music companies with no associated distribution or marketing costs.

Let's sweeten the pot a bit. Why not actually enlist iTunes, Napster, Kazaa, or Morpheus *subscribers* to move the product? Motivate them to produce, distribute, and market. Take 5 percent of the gross subscription revenue and allocate it for payment to the most active traders (distributors and marketers) at the trading post—a kind of humanode incentive fund. That equates to $50 million per year for the 7 million subscribers of our imaginary example. Track the histogram of trades and correlate it to the incentive fund. The most active traders with the most aggressive and high-quality contribution of production and distribution resources (the quality of the files and amount of disk, processor, and memory on their peer computer) and clever distribution/marketing techniques could make some real cash. There would soon be stories about the people that make a living off of trading posts, not just eBay.

Here's a situation where any humanode, or supernode, can put up one digital copy of a song within a licensed (by a regulating body like the RIAA) trading system. That's the entire cost of distribution and marketing (save the incentive fund allocated from gross sales, not paid up front like today's traditional model), and that distribution and marketing cost is spread across the spectrum of humanode subscribers to any individual trading post, not borne by the trading post owner or intellectual-property rights holder. Any trading outside the licensed trading posts would indeed be illegal, but it would be less difficult to shut down since most honest folks (and most are) will simply pay the subscription. Many of the highly motivated individuals we currently consider pirates would be converted into profit-making allies of music companies.

Intellectual-property spectrum would have a "terms of use" with broad restrictions, given the unpredictable nature of humanode activity. With natural feedback loops built in for consumer-only humanodes to rate producer/distributor/marketer humanodes, trading posts would rapidly iterate into environments that exceed any "free" bootleg service in quality of product and service. But trading posts would also be able to track the naturally occurring behavior, determine the way the wind blows, and quickly offer other appropriate value-added services to humanodes generating incremental revenue.

Let us be frank: piracy will always be a part of any commercial scene. But fighting the battle against piracy solely by enlisting technology for things like copy protection and digital-rights management is a losing proposition. Technology will always defeat technology, and pirates will simply see it as a challenge. It's highly improbable the internet as a whole, and networked media in general, can be retrofitted to handle the *perfect* tracking of intellectual properties and tariffs associated with their usage. The internet's nature is resistant to that kind of attack, and all-encompassing solutions will simply destroy privacy and drive highly motivated pirates further underground. But zoning networked media by issuing limited licenses to engage in certain types of commerce, and regulating the result, is absolutely viable. Marry that with pro-gramming—software code with well-designed content, community, and commerce elements—and usage will flourish inversely proportional to piracy's decline.

We should be reintroducing the concept of fair-use cast in the light of a deeper understanding of networked media.

Emergent Commercial Exchanges

At this point, I feel it appropriate to make note of a particular ilk of enginet. In the context of peer-to-peer systems (like Kazaa) or central-ized exchanges (like eBay), the term "emergent" refers to systems cre-ated to capture and monetize the behavior of buyers and sellers coming together through networked media—but in a way that creates a specific microeconomy within the enginet where free-market dynamics (man-aged or not) can flourish.

Several examples of successful centralized exchanges like eBay, Elance, or dating sites, exist where emergent behavior has rooted. The "value" of product, services, or programming within these commercial exchanges is determined by supply and demand within the enginet, sometimes completely abstracted from "real world" economics. Persistent worlds and massively multiplayer online games take it a step further: they often develop microeconomies where value is completely virtual—their own currency and/or in-game dynamics that solely determine worth of virtual items or services.

At this writing, all peer-to-peer networks have been created with the commerce gene missing, and they have thus far woefully underperformed in monetizing peer-to-peer behavior—virtually or actually. Some, like Kazaa, have clumsily tried to retrofit their P2P platform for commercial adaptation, and they are generating revenue; but as of this writing their approach has served to make their software client a bloated, invasive, and irritating piece of software.

MojoNation came the closest. It was another distributed peer-to-peer platform technology that never became the most popular, but it was unique in a special way that bodes for an enlightened future for P2P communities. The core of the MojoNation technology platform was basically the same as that of Gnutella and others—a small software package called a "broker" (equivalent to Gnutella's servent) that you download and install on your computer. Once you've got the broker, it runs quietly in the background. All you had to do is load the broker in your browser to begin sharing and downloading files on the MojoNation network. Programming that flowed through MojoNation peer-clients was formatted as hundreds or thousands of small, replicated fragments of the original data source spread across the peer-clients in the network. When a peer downloaded data using the MojoNation content distribution technology, the local client pulled the file fragments in parallel from multiple peers; it worked like a swarm of ants cutting up and transporting food to the nest, but in this case the food is reassembled perfectly at the nest into its original form. The MojoNation swarm of peers automatically performed distributed load balancing to get around bottlenecks and gave each peer credit for the work that agent performed on behalf of the swarm.

From the beginning, the creators of MojoNation incorporated a micro-economy into the peer-to-peer system—it was emergent by design. All users on the MojoNation network inherently did business with each other using a kind of currency, unsurprisingly called Mojo, only good within Mojo Nation network. This was a type of micropayment system that ran in the background of the network—a distributed accounting system that kept track of the effort each peer agent had contributed to the network. If a peer within the network was overloaded, the system used pricing to perform distributed load balancing and signal to other agents that another "more mojo'd" peer might be able to deliver the bits more quickly. Brokers that contributed resources during peak usage periods would earn credit within the network and this credit, combined with agent reputations, would be redeemed for any available quality of service improvements when an agent was trying to download content. That is, the more willing you were to give resources when others were in need, the more resources would be made available to you when you were in need. Without some Mojo credit, a peer-broker had to wait in line with everyone else when the network got overloaded. Brokers that had extra Mojo could spend it to move to the front of the line when network demand peaked—by earning Mojo, users get good "karma" within the content distribution system and, potentially, faster service.

Unfortunately, MojoNation is dead, its doors closing for good in early 2002. It made one of the same mortal mistakes of other peer-to-peer networks—not spreading their "mojo" around to intellectual-property holders whose works were materializing and dematerializing all over the network. Their approach to compensating intellectual-property holders was "tips"—relying on the individual humanodes to decide what a digital music or video file was worth to them. But even the most famous of tip-receiving constituencies—bartenders, waiters, and waitresses—historically rely on a base minimum wage, as well. I'd like to believe in the altruism of my neighbor, or that fair values for products or programming can be derived by collective individual transactions where each transaction sets its own idea of fair value. Free-market dynamics might even work in that case if a supply-and-demand dynamic were in effect. But there isn't—there is essentially an infinite supply of digital media, since it is so easy to copy, and there are a finite number of folks interested in buying the essence of that digital media, be it a PDF industry report, an MP3 music file, an MPEG2 movie, a Word document, or a database record.

In the absence of limited supply, there must be some kind of pricing authority. The United States housing market is certainly subject to free-market dynamics, but the Fed still affects that market through manipulation of interest rates. It doesn't set the price of a house, but most certainly influences it. Creators or producers of programming, or by proxy a designated distributor, are the only ones who can set the value of their programming. Raising or lowering value effectively modulates supply, or demand, depending on one's perspective on the transaction. This only works (as a market) if there is a strong feedback loop from the humanodes in place in order to modify pricing if demand changes. Furthermore, in emergent exchanges, more thought must go into the time-varying and context-varying behavior of that pricing. Emergent exchanges must be designed from scratch to allow the nodes (humanodes or supernodes) acting as creator/producer, distributor, or vendor to set business rules and allow them to change, perhaps autonomously, based on market conditions; deterministically, by direct intervention of the pricing authority (the originating humanode or supernode); or heuristically, though some predefined business rules.

The market-based system MojoNation implemented had a flexible set of tools usable for a distributed accounting and credit system running among peers. That was a great start, especially as it applies to my incentive-based suggestions—that is, getting humanodes to do your distribution/marketing/vending work for the creator/producer nodes and compensating them for it in some way. But MojoNation didn't go far enough. The value-tracking system must also be extended to the programming itself, and not just to the allocation and reallocation of network resources. MojoNation spent the time to build in world-class security and privacy, but, as with many clever technology implementations, it may have suffered from technocentritis: a disease that makes technologists build things simply because they can, with little thought for the commercial or moral ripple effect those technologies might have. In a networked world, that kind of disease is debilitating.

Fortunately, it's curable. But in this case the cure resides in networked media programmers deploying the pillars of programming and the basic modes of motivation, and building enginets that are emergent, with a built-in microeconomy that can handle micro- and macrotransactions, and that allows market dynamics to occur within the enginet. Assign the best business rules you can and let the humanodes go, adjusting the business rules and the enginet itself to optimize the "wind" energy. This will allow networked media programmers to monetize the energy of the industrious humanodes behind the noncommercial success of technologies like Napster, Gnutella, MojoNation, and Kazaa and figure out how to monetize them.

Peer-to-peer designers should take a page from massively-multiplayer online games like "EverQuest" and "Lineage," and persistent communities like HabboHotel.com and Trollz.com. These "virtual places" have instilled native emergent economies into their worlds where subscribers can buy and sell virtual items within the world—from suits of armor to dwellings. While some pricing dynamics are influenced by the world-masters, more and more the economics are dictated by pure supply-and-demand dynamics fueled by the subscribers. Increasingly, value earned in the virtual world is redeemable in the real world. This game world dynamic is not much different than what will eventually emerge in the overall telacorpus. Money, after all, is increasingly a virtual construct. We no longer have "real world" metrics like the gold standard to meter currency values. Emergent microeconomies—that is, native economies within networked media programming—should be built into any enginet, whether redeemable or convertible into real-world dollars, pesos, yuan, or not.

The State of Confusion

Linear and interactive mass media depend on a combination of limiting choice and yelling the loudest. Even in a post-cable world where there are ten times the broadcast choices there were a few decades ago, a world with the likes of A&E, History Channel, Discovery, Cartoon Network, and a plethora of specialty channels—even these "narrowcasting" channels require a piece of a finite spectrum for broadcasting, for which a potentially infinite number of players vie. As the amount of programming grows the practical limitation becomes the attention spectrum of a humanode. There's a lot of noise out there from programmers clamoring to attract eyeballs. So how will consumers decide what to watch, listen to, or play? In traditional media, the decision is influenced by who yells the loudest or whispers most cleverly; but networked media offers an alternative.

Put the old mass-media distribution and marketing models in their place. While they certainly have their role in efforts related to brand awareness, they're inefficient ways to get humans to consume—or to produce, market, distribute, or vend. Instead, let us design and organize networked media infrastructures that harness its native dynamics and enable business models that work in the environment. Let's harness those highly independent, individual-minded humanodes using the medium's own dynamics—enginets with emergent commercial-exchange elements built in. Let's organize the economic infrastructure of networked media so you can persuade humanodes to produce, market, distribute, or vend for you, or consume what you've created. Let them exercise a new kind of literacy, one that is emerging naturally and that will require a fundamentally different philosophical approach to programming.

CHAPTER 10

Symphonic Literacy and the Feminine Touch

> *Words are a terrible straitjacket. It's interesting how many prisoners*
> *of that straitjacket resent it being loosened or taken off.*
>
> — STANLEY KUBRICK

On a recent trip to Seville, Spain, I sat one morning at breakfast with a desire only to be left alone to eat and do my crossword in silence. Instead, I was inundated with beeps and toots from the table next to me. At it sat a Spanish couple with two children—a young boy and girl who looked to be about four or five years old. The girl was pestering her father for the use of his mobile phone. The boy already had his mother's and was busily engrossed in a game that was obviously more interesting than his half-eaten breakfast. As the mother's electronic pacifier was capably occupying the son, who was clearly delighted with besting whatever game his parents had seen fit to load on the phone, the daughter had successfully wrested the picture phone from her father and began snapping away. It was obvious she knew how to use it. While my Spanish is by no means fluent, it was good enough to discern that after she'd gathered the photographic evidence she'd desired, she subsequently asked for a bit of guidance from papa in sending the pictures to their grandmother.

These two children didn't know how to read or write, in the traditional sense of literacy, but they were operating what past generations would consider complex machinery to express and amuse themselves with an ease that spoke of sophistication. They were demonstrating a literacy markedly different from that with which *their* parents, I myself, my parents, or my parents' parents grew up.

"This literacy encompasses the full range of capabilities children and adults need if they are going to be full participants in a more participatory media culture," wrote Henry Jenkins, director of the program for comparative media studies at MIT, in his 2003 essay "Media Literacy Begins at Home." "It includes skills in using new media technologies, cultural competencies in understanding how stories are constructed and what they mean, aesthetic vocabularies that heighten their appreciation of diverse forms of expression, and critical frameworks for thinking about the power big media companies exert even in an age of expanding options." Those "cultural competencies" include an expanded comprehension of all three forms of "story" construction—telling, forming and dwelling—and an understanding that media users today are different from past generations.

Marxist Media

Karl Marx believed one of the injustices perpetrated by capitalists was that the workers did not "own the means of production." Over 130 years after the publication of *Das Kapital,* anyone who gains access to a computer can own a means of production—and distribution, if the computer is networked.

Multimedia capabilities are shockingly inexpensive today. Best-of-breed desktop publishing software that matches most of the capabilities of print shops can be acquired for around $800. Photo retouching software good enough for most jobs comes packaged free with digital cameras; if the top-of-the-line package used by the pros is desired, an investment of $600 will nab it. Music scoring and synthesizer software packages good enough for all but the pickiest of composers cost a few hundred dollars. The typical equipment package for a network news crew costs more than $100,000. A pro-amateur package costs around $10,000 (and dropping), providing a technical quality virtually indistinguishable from the former. Virtually anyone who can afford a standard contemporary computer system has the tools to create digital, multimedia works of art, music, and video. And networked media like the internet allow them to share the results with the world.

That doesn't mean programming coming from avocational users will be good. Given a perfect world where everyone has the same access to training and resources, no one really knows how expandable the pool of talent might be. But "talent" means something else entirely in the emerging "big bang" of programming. The key may be more about matching the taste of creators to the taste of consumers, something infinitely easier to accomplish using networked media. One thing is certain: in the computer-equipped segments of the population, access to resources will no longer be the issue.

Creative young people today truly are comfortable with multimedia—that is, with multiple media. They are media literate. These individuals are just as comfortable with the written word as they are with graphics, audio, video, animation, interactive elements, three-dimensional animation, and community- or commerce-based programming. This group is also device literate—comfortable with the use of keyboards, remote controls, mobile phones, and PDAs. These coming generations possess a *symphonic literacy.*

Older, entrenched generations resist this change. Yet frequently they find themselves turning to the youth to "translate" for them the uses of new media and the meaning of their programming (for decades, millions of American parents have turned to their children for help in programming the VCR). Like immigrants to the new country who didn't take the time to learn the local language, they instead rely on their children, the new generation, to effect the family's assimilation.

Four-Year-Old Maestros

Networked media is the kiln for the new literacy, one that allows individuals to break out of their traditional role as consumer. Individuals now have access to a broader palette of media with which to engage, divert, and entertain—tools that were previously available only to the privileged few. Not surprisingly, the young are more comfortable with these new tools than the rest of us.

Jon Medved is one of the principals in Israel Seed Partners, a venture capital company in Jerusalem. He and his neighbors held a block party for Israel's Independence Day. Everyone on the block pitched in to decorate the walled façades in front of each house, and everyone boiled, baked, fried, and roasted all manner of food for the celebration. Back when he first started Israel Seed, Jon had converted his garage into an office, equipping it with several computers. Israel Seed is now ensconced in well-appointed offices, and Jon's four children have co-opted the computers in the garage-office to surf the web, play games, or do their homework. Jon's youngest child, four-year-old Nina, is no exception. During the party, she was immersed in the PC. The sounds and fancy graphic animation jumping on the screen led one to the assumption she was playing a game.

"What game are you playing?" I asked her. "It's not a game," she replied, with more than a hint of four-year-old indignation. "I'm making a movie." She played it for us—a four-minute film made from the *X-Men* MovieMaker program. The characters moved and fought, and there was a sound track—though she complained that it was "broken" and didn't give her enough choices. The film even had a hint of drama and romance. I gave Nina's movie a thumbs-up. Though this little girl didn't even know how to read or write yet, she'd already made a movie that told a story.

Robert Rodriguez, the prolific auteur of hit films like *Spy Kids* and *Desperado,* is a man ahead of his time. On most of his films, he is listed in no less than a dozen roles in the filmmaking process—producer, director, set designer, animator, editor, composer, and several others. He was quoted in the August 2002 issue of *The Onion* stating, "I don't know about the current generation, but all the new generation coming up [are] gonna be multihatted moviemakers, because they're gonna start the way that I did, which was on video, where you're the whole crew." Media technology has become so articulate it transcends specialization. If a filmmaker *can* do it all—that is, if the specialized understanding of a particular technology doesn't get in the way anymore—why shouldn't he/she? Today Rodriguez edits and mixes image and sound in his garage using tools infinitely more available (and affordable) to the average person than what used to be required to create in the medium of film; he predicts that for coming generations, this kind of eclecticism will be the norm.

In 2000, Mike Burns came up with the idea of using "Halo," one of the top-selling games on Microsoft's Xbox game console, as a moviemaking tool. The technique is commonly referred to as "machinima"—the use of video-game engines as a production tool to create linear video animation, an emerging animated-movie technique. He and his filmmaker collaborators create two-to-five minute scripts, record the voices themselves in a closet, and then, like puppeteers, Burns and his pals control on-screen game characters, working to sync their movements to the voice soundtrack. They edit the on-screen images into roughly five-minute videos that have plots, recurring characters, and original soundtracks. By mid-2004, the resultant series—"Red vs. Blue"—had gone from hobby to cult hit, touting 650,000-plus downloads over the internet per episode, rivaling viewing audience sizes for typical cable shows. Their efforts even ended up as a page-one story in the *Wall Street Journal,* which touted the project's writing and novel production techniques. "The literary analog is absurdist drama," Graham Leggat, director of communications at the Lincoln Center Film Society and a video game critic, was quoted saying. "It's truly as sophisticated as Samuel Beckett." Burns and his buddies admittedly grew up playing games—an interactive, storyforming form of consumption—and turned that experience into a clever method for storytelling production, subsequently using the internet to serve their distribution, marketing, and vending aims. They turned a means of consumption into a means of production, and have garnered an audience in the process.

The proliferation of these powerful new multimedia tools has raised an important question: *Is textual literacy important anymore?* Of course—but relatively less so as these tools of multimedia production, communication, and distribution become increasingly articulate. Today children (and adults) have more sophisticated tools for creating compelling text, graphics, animation, 3-D, audio, video, and even databases than the best-equipped media professionals did even fifteen years ago. Historically, juvenile efforts to create a work of art, or a small business like the proverbial lemonade stand, would have limited exposure. Young people today are able to share their fledgling efforts with the entire world; they can reach out to others like themselves—through community features like chat, IM, blogs, et cetera—or easily collaborate on projects over long distances. One of Burns's "Red vs. Blue" collaborators, French composer Nico Audy-Rowland, sends soundtracks for each episode over the internet to the production's "headquarters" in Austin, Texas, from his home in Cambridge, Massachusetts.

Symphonic literacy is a literacy of the C's—content, community, commerce, and code. Naturally, symphonic literacy will take root first among younger groups, who are more open to new behavioral paradigms and attendant technologies than those who reached maturity in earlier eras. Individuals born after 1950 don't know a world without television, just as those born after 1975 don't know a world without the computer.

Individuals born in the 1990s don't know a world without the internet. Recent generations are growing up as comfortable with networked media as previous generations were at ease with the television or the PC. A key difference between members of those older generations and more contemporary generations is that networked media uses tools that empower their users to produce, market, distribute, and vend, as well as consume; we are beginning to express ourselves thusly, through business, education, communication, and recreation.

The networked media generation will want to create, commune, discover, and communicate, and as a consequence will spend more time on the computer than in front of the television. As far back as 2002, the *International Herald Tribune* reported a study by the Pew Internet and American Life Project that found 78 percent of Americans between the ages of twelve and seventeen use the internet. The director of the American Life Project, Lee Rainie, estimates 30 to 40 percent of teenagers would be considered "heavy" users, those who log on for more than five hours per week. And many of these teenagers are not simply using it as a diversion or for leisure time.

At the age of eighteen, Shawn Fanning wrote the code that eventually rocked the music industry and became a household name: Napster. Jeremy McGee started JM Computer Services at age fourteen, and at seventeen created the web-based business TwoToads.com, a child's communication and entertainment site. Aaron Greenspan is the seventeen-year-old president and CEO of Think Computer Corporation, a computer repair business with more than 100 clients. Melissa Sconyers started her web-design business when she turned ten; now sixteen, she contributes to eBiz4Teens.com. By age fourteen, Zach Gage had developed and sold more than fifty computer games.

Another member of the networked media generation, sixteen-year-old Austin Heap, of Powell, Ohio, has been featured in publications like *Wired* and *USA Today*. Austin landed a commission-based partnership with the online music store CDNow and started his own web-based business, PureRadio.net. Austin's elementary school didn't have computers or even typewriters. This entrepreneurial adolescent believes the turning point in his life came when he was "grounded" by his parents at eight years old. As *punishment,* Austin had to read books. When he ran out of storybooks and adventures, he began reading computer manuals. "It was the cut-and-paste thing that entranced me," Austin said. "It was like wow—that's amazing! It disappears from here and reappears there!" As with many kids his age, the elements of networked media became a natural part of his daily life. As a child, he downloaded news on the Oklahoma City bombing from a BBS. As a seventh-grader, he took class notes on a Palm Pilot Professional. Austin admits he can't imagine a world without the networked computer.

In fact, many tech-savvy middle- and high-school students (which is now the majority of students) in the United States say they are increasingly frustrated with the way the internet is—or, more aptly, is not—being used by teachers in the classroom. Another study released by the Pew Project in 2002 found that students are independently using the internet for a variety of educational activities, but do not think their schools take full advantage of the web as a teaching tool. "Outside the classroom and outside any formal instruction, the internet is a key part of [students'] educational instruction," said Rainie. Students use the web as a reference tool, a homework helper, a method of collaboration, a source of advice, and a replacement for books and newspapers, according to the study. Most interviewed said that little of the education-related work they do on the internet is sanctioned by teachers. Students, as much as teachers, want policymakers to address the digital divide, and they want administrators at their schools to provide support to teachers who may not have the training or materials they need to effectively use the web, the study found. Restrictive content filters, usage policies, and time constraints discourage use at school. Most teenagers who participated in the Pew study said they want more internet-related school assignments but want that work to be interesting and engaging.

"We would not consider our children to be literate if they could read and not write. We should similarly not feel that our children have developed basic media literacy if they can consume but not produce media," wrote Henry Jenkins. "Creating media content can range from the traditional, such as writing stories, to the high-tech, such as programming original computer games. Just as reading and writing skills feed on each other, production and consumption skills for other media are also mutually reinforcing." We need to take literacy beyond helping children to become skilled readers and empower them to become storytellers and critics, as well as storyformers, storydwellers, and engineteers. Symphonic literacy, by definition, removes the child from the role of consumer and into the role of multifaceted humanode.

Kids like Nina, Jeremy, Aaron, Zach and Austin are taking full advantage of this opportunity; they will not be satisfied in the limited role of consumer. Nor will they be satisfied with *only* passive, linear, serialized approaches to programming that the word denotes—whether the programming is educational or otherwise. Nor will they be satisfied relying only upon paper, pencil, and the telephone to learn, create, and communicate in education, business, or in their personal lives. Young people are almost effortlessly absorbing the tools and literacy to create compelling and entertaining multimedia programming—whether it is for homework, a "commercial message," a marketing plan, a game, a website, or a sales brief. Symphonically literate, these children are just as likely to move beyond straight storytelling and embrace storyforming or storydwelling—both as experiences for themselves and as programming they create for others. They'll do so because these new forms will feel natural to them. And because they can.

PowerPointing the Way to the Future

The change in literacy isn't confined to members of up-and-coming generations. Everyone has occasion to use some form of storytelling, storyforming, or storydwelling, in their personal or professional lives, and we all have varying talents for creating vibrant stories—whether the "story" is a marketing one-sheet or a fictional game universe.

When the personal computer was introduced in the 1970s, word processing naturally became its most popular feature. The written word is still the primary method most of us use to communicate. By the 1990s, the transformation of the graphic-arts field was also complete. The quality, speed, flexibility, and spotless appearance of digital desktop publishing completely replaced mechanical typesetting and drawing in nearly every art department around the world in less than ten years.

Before 1985, artists who used mechanical pens, design markers, and a T-square were near the bottom of the compensation scale in most companies. Later those who mastered computer graphics and desktop publishing were quickly promoted to the higher ranks, with dramatic salary increases. The artists who did not make the digital transition to the computer were left behind. In his book *Mediamorphosis,* Roger Fidler claims the power and efficacy of these tools tripled graphics in most newspapers, and that the increase in the quality and quantity of visual communications is a direct result of the digitization of media.

But it was in the mid-1980s when Forethought, Inc., a company with two employees, developed a software solution for slide shows and overhead-transparency presentations that eventually became Microsoft PowerPoint. Prior to that time, presentation methods required heavy equipment, darkrooms, and machinists to operate cameras and handle film processing. This method was labor intensive and expensive, which limited the use of high-quality color slides or overhead transparencies to established institutions with larger budgets. PowerPoint, and other programs of that ilk, changed all that, turning the computer into a presentation machine—a business storytelling machine—as well.

A scant few years ago, black and white vu-graphs were still acceptable as a presentation format. Now the minimum expectation in business is for clever, vibrant presentations that use text, graphics, audio, animation, and/or video. Business communicators can use all the "feel good" elements of entertainment storytelling to mesmerize the audience and knock their socks off, again underscoring the fact that all business is show business. Of course, business-presentation software is only as smart and effective as the people employing it. A presentation can be subtle, compelling, and effective, or obnoxious, boring, and disjointed, a determination made through an interaction between author and audience. Remember, there's no accounting for taste. Just look at television.

Magic Transit

Remember the *Magic School Bus* series of children's books by Joanna Cole? The teacher, Ms. Frizzle, and her young students are transported on various learning adventures inside a magic school bus. This fanciful bus could fly, rocket through space, and travel deep within the oceans of the world. Sounds like a PC computer or a game console—with the proper programming running on it.

In the 1940s and 1950s, television was sometimes referred to as the magic box—a means of conveyance into fantasy worlds, history lessons, and other informational journeys. Today, computers and computer-enabled devices like mobile phones are far more capable of offering immersive, multimedia experiences than TV ever could. Computers can transport us into worlds that are articulate renderings of concepts difficult to comprehend with simple words. Any parent sees the difference between their child's interaction with television shows and with DVD programming. The computer takes us one step closer to the commingling of virtual and actual reality.

Certainly, the stand-alone computer is a magical device. But the networked computer is something else altogether. If television offered the user a window, and the computer offered a vehicle, then networked media is offering a rapid-transit system to all parts of the virtual world. The experience networked media offers is a far more personal, interactive, and empowered encounter, without limiting you to "what's on." We have at our fingertips a sort of magic transit, transporting us to points known and unknown.

As more devices become networked together, the box by which we access the network becomes less important than how the humanodes use the network. Viacom conducted a study recently that showed that the average consumer spends 29 hours a day consuming media. These people didn't find some way to add hours to the day; they are multitasking, and they're using multiple devices to do it. The boxes are becoming transparent—not one box in your living room or study, but a multitude of devices in different shapes and sizes, all linked to the same system of networks. This propagation of electronic media devices is forcing an evolution of the human mind and senses. *Homo telanimus* simultaneously listens to the radio and talks on a cellular phone, or cooks dinner and watches television while downloading software. More and more, we absorb bits from this, and send bytes through that, through multiple devices, some of which we carry with us.

The proliferation of devices tied into this über-network has important implications for all industries, and all companies and individuals participating in this networked world. One must become adept at orchestrating programming across multiple media. For instance, a sales force may employ multiple media to communicate a marketing message—the web, video over a wireless network, and fixed media (like DVD), coordinating the multiple media in a way that creates a consistent message and virtuous circle of programming aimed at humanodes, not humans.

Another way to look at symphonic literacy is that it means possessing the ability to orchestrate programming pathways that employ, in varying composition:

- The use of content, community, commerce, and code
- The employment of varied tools of creation (word processing, graphics, animation, digital video editing)
- Multiple media types (paper, CD, DVD, digital files, MPEG video, MIDI, MP3)
- Distribution channels (internet, wireless, television, radio, DVD)
- The limitations and capabilities of multiple devices (PDAs, desktop PCs, mobile phones).

The literacy associated with the programming of all these elements into an articulate and understandable customer experience is complex—symphonic. All this complexity should be invisible to the customers or other intended recipients of this programming; their experience should be entertaining, engaging; they should feel like it's a diversion, rather than work. The end result is a powerful utility—grasping attention, retaining that attention, and satisfying needs. Doing so becomes a challenge for all professions whose job it is to engage and motivate others—from the student doing homework, to a marketer for K-Mart, to a Warner Bros. film producer, to a Union Bank advertising executive. Symphonic literacy is the creative force that will fuel the evolution of networked media. These new creative tools have given the Ninas of the world the ability to design and express themselves through a new form of play. They can tell their own stories for a change, through video, music, or poetry—where and when they wish. Children learn about life through play, and are not only inquisitive, but natural storytellers as well. Networked media gives them a way of exploring, creating, and sharing this experience with others. Their interweaving of the virtual and actual will help create the world of the future and make them better storytellers, storyformers, and storydwellers.

Members of the networked media generation will create their own movies, with their own preferred endings, soundtracks, and characters. They will have their own new definitions for the entertainment experience—and may even find making a movie more fun than watching one.

Filmmaking may become a communal experience, a collaboration conducted through internet communities much the same way a community of programmers helped Linus Torvalds create the open-source Linux operating system. This same group will be equally adept at creating and participating in storytelling or storydwelling experiences, like games of a depth and sweep unfathomable to us today—immersive experiences impossible with today's skill sets and technologies. Symphonically literate children may not be able to give you a verbal definition of a "networked experience." But their understanding of the medium for entertainment, education, or commerce is intuitive, and as they explore networked media, these young people will see possibilities for extending and improving the medium. "Why can't I send this to my friend?" they'll ask. "Why can't I chat here? Why can't I play a game afterwards? Why can't I buy this?" Moreover, how far away would China, Africa, or anywhere else really "feel" to someone who's only communicated via the instantaneous magic of email, or who has spoken to someone there by way of videophone? Would anyone really feel alone in a world saturated with a variety of magic boxes linking anyone to anyone, anytime, or anywhere?

Possessing symphonic literacy versus traditional literacy is as profound a difference as that which exists between a musician only capable of writing a solo piano piece and one who can write for an entire orchestra. What's the common thread between the instruments in a symphony? Rhythm, melody, and harmony. In a symphony, rhythm and melody are the story, threaded through the instruments in harmony, and orchestrated by either the auteur, or a conductor who knows the *story* and is versed in the language of *all the instruments*. The way the industry is organized today is equivalent to a symphony where instruments—business units organized around forms of distribution—are operated by skilled artists who are all attempting to play the same melody, but out of rhythm and out of tune. Why? The problem is that the conductor or auteur of the programming is not the one orchestrating the piece.

How might a company be organized if all forms of media it produced or used were created on the same day? Ironically, most traditional companies are arriving at the right answer from the wrong criteria and in the wrong form. They have the size and scope pieces, but often not the direction and innovation necessary to support the creators of the near-future. One thing is certain: the company wouldn't resemble the patchwork of cultures and business units we see in mass-media companies today. These "Franken-companies" mostly comprise disparate parts sewn together and electrified by the drive for more power, more sales, and a rising stock price. The love for their own creations has blinded the caretakers of these monsters to the waste they perpetuate. Fortunately, as more *individuals* become symphonically literate, enterprises and institutions will eventually follow suit.

To be optimally successful, however, both individuals and institutions will need to tweak their philosophical approaches to reaching an audience, clientele, or customer base—to harnessing the humanodes. They'll need to get in touch with their feminine side.

The Genders of Literacy

Eastern philosophies like Taoism and Buddhism maintain, among other things, that the way to intellectual, spiritual, and physical health is through a synthesis of the feminine and masculine—the yin and yang. But for thousands of years, civilization has been lopsided in favor of the masculine, an imbalance precipitated by the invention of the alphabet, but now going into its final stages as a result of the proliferation of networked media.

The hunter/gatherer era for mankind ended with the emergence of animal husbandry and agrarian culture, estimated at about 10,000 B.C. Before that, the "masculine" hunter values ruled supreme. The agrarian age marked a rise in "feminine" values. Less and less did men invoke the fight/flight response in their search for game; they simply went out to the sty/shed/field, picked an animal, and slaughtered it for dinner. The tending of crops (impregnating the earth with seeds, nurturing them until they grow healthy and strong) and animal husbandry (breeding and nurturing animals) depend entirely on the process of procreation. The Earth had long been considered a feminine power, a belief that continues today through the popular references to Mother Earth and Mother Nature. Primarily agrarian cultures largely threw over the hunter/gatherer animal spirits for an all-inclusive Mother Goddess who represented the "body" of the Earth. For thousands of years, female deities were dominant in the ancient world, since these deities represented nurturing, regeneration, and procreation. Around 3000 B.C., two centers of civilization emerged and flourished in the ancient world—Mesopotamia and subsequently Egypt. It was then that image-inspired *ideograms*—hieroglyphic representations of real-world constructs like animals, heavenly bodies, and geological formations—were replaced by abstractions of sound called *phonograms*. Their language, called cuneiform, quickly evolved to represent both the *image* of a noun and the *sound* of a word. "Necessity, the *mother* of invention," as Leonard Shlain, author of *The Alphabet versus the Goddess,* put it, "forced [them] to create the *father* of all abstractions—phonetic writing," the use and understanding of which modern psychologists and behaviorists associate with masculine, left-brain cognitive function.

The employment of an alphabet turned men and women away from images and animal totems that represented nature and Mother Earth, toward homage to *logos,* gods with no faces—ideas, concepts, thoughts, and values, which they gave life by manifesting them into the physical form of writing. Goddess worship, feminine values, and women's power depend on the ubiquity of the *image*. Monotheistic God worship, masculine values, and men's domination of women are bound to the written *word*. Word and image, like masculine and feminine, are complementary opposites.

Written language spread rapidly to neighboring countries, and literacy led the way to ever greater societal development. Ironically, the earliest Mesopotamian law code on record (around 2350 B.C.) opens with a proscription against polyandry: "The women of former days used to take two husbands, but the women of today (if they attempt to do so) must be stoned"—an interestingly misogynistic tone for a society not long out of its goddess-ruled age.

By 2000 B.C., written language had been around for several centuries. The new literacy pushed aside (in an often violent fashion) the right-brain, emotional, intuitive "image literacy" that existed before. Those that practiced the "old ways" were subjugated under a literacy-perpetuated masculine regime. Ever noticed how lawyers make laws so complex only lawyers can interpret the laws? Multiply that dynamic by many orders of magnitude and you've got it: a male-dominated society that unwittingly used the alphabet to subjugate all of mankind, including females, under the aegis of masculinity.

The spread of the alphabet and increased dependency on abstraction and linear thought processes required by literacy rewired the human brain to favor masculine hemispherical traits. "The perceptions of anyone who learned how to send and receive information by means of regular, sequential, linear rows of abstract symbols were wrenched from a balanced, centrist position toward the dominating masculine side of the human psyche," Shlain asserts. Since men could not wield the *voice* of their god, they settled for wielding the *word* of their god. In men's hands it became the most powerful weapon in history. Ideology is an abstraction—a masculine construct. More people over the years were killed or subjugated over *ideas* than were ever killed over land, possessions or personal disputes. Soldiers have often been compelled to fight for an ideal against peoples with whom they have no personal or family quarrel.

An African proverb states, "*Only when lions have historians will hunters cease being heroes.*" In other words: they who control literacy and literature control history—and, increasingly, the present and future. The broader meaning today would be: he who controls media controls history. And for much of our history, men have dominated media, simply because the predominant media, words on paper or parchment, were more easily mastered by humans with stronger masculine cognitive traits. But those same masculine-born fruits of technology unwittingly sowed the seeds of a feminine resurgence.

The invention of photography and the discovery of electromagnetism combined to bring us film, television, computers, and graphic advertising, all of which are based on images. Increasing reliance on right-brain pattern recognition instead of left-brain linear sequence moved culture further toward equilibrium between the two hemispheres, between masculine and feminine, between word and image.

I must stress that the terms "masculine" and "feminine" are used here in their transcendental sense. Every human is a blend of this dual set of characteristics in varying compositions. "The masculine is sovereignty," St. Germain once said, "the crown upon your soul. Femininity is humility and unconditional love, the heart within the breast of your soul, and together they make the whole soul essence." These traits are applicable to media as well as to human beings.

Tom Wolfe elaborated on Marshall McLuhan's famous assertion, "The medium is the message," in his introductory remarks to the McLuhan video series: "McLuhan's theory rests on a radical premise. He insists that nothing people can use electronic media for—no message that anyone, no matter how powerful or persuasive, can deliver—even begins to compare with what the new media have done to mankind neurologically and temperamentally. They have directly affected the human central nervous system and changed patterns of thought and behavior. In short, they have literally altered human nature." McLuhan observed that media rewire human cognition. This rewiring began in earnest with the invention of the written word and continues today with networked media. Shlain took it a step further, asserting that the written word wired us to favor masculine traits and that the image-intensive and nonlinear media technologies of the nineteenth and twentieth centuries are swinging us back toward the feminine.

McLuhan's "message" is roughly equivalent to what in this book I call "programming," and I agree with his famous axiom, but with a critical difference. Corned beef is corned beef (the programming or the message), but it affects our taste buds a whole lot differently on rye bread (one medium) than on plain white bread (another medium). The medium *and* the message have *equal* impact in reconfiguring human cognition; for linear and interactive mass media to date, McLuhan's tenet could read "the medium is the *masculine* message."

The presentation of written language has consistently taken the form of flat, two-dimensional tablets, parchments, or paper. The physical form of written language was in and of itself fixed, linear, immutable—masculine. Even with the re-emergence of the image—still or moving—we were bound by media technologies with inherently masculine traits. The commercialization of the printing press by Gutenberg in the fifteenth century was an epochal event in the history of masculine dominance, for the first time making printed works a mass medium. The inventions that enabled the rise of the sound and image—electricity (Edison and Westinghouse), radio (Tesla and Marconi), television (Farnsworth and Sarnoff), motion pictures (Muybridge and Edison), phonograph (Edison), and the other basics of modern media—were all created, commercialized, and distributed by men. In some ways, these new image-based media were more masculine than the written word because fewer people could use these more complicated media for creation, expression, and communication. These visual technologies might have delivered another blow to the feminine were it not for the fact these inventions ultimately carried a Trojan horse: imagery, an inherently feminine construct.

The captains of industry and invention who exploited these technologies were all unwitting agents in the rise of the feminine by providing the first mass media in mankind's history whose message was feminine or image-based. The late nineteenth century marked an inflection point for the shift from a *literate* human race back into the *imagerate* human race—a race literate in imagery.

The Feminine Touch

Contrast networked media like the internet with television: television is a masculine, paternal "take-what-I-give-you" medium; whereas the internet is nonlinear, mutable, interactive, and community-oriented, and infinitely deep and mysterious. Networked media like the internet are feminine in nature. Programming each requires a different composition of literacy. Networked media are shifting the balance back toward the feminine, where it should be, where it *must* be for its native programming to be effective and successful.

This evolution is reflective of a shift in the culture from the profoundly masculine to the sublimely feminine—a swing in the balance of power between the different halves of human nature, one that businesses and media programmers will have to heed, consciously or accidentally, to be prosperous in the networked age. The change has nothing to do with political correctness. It's something much broader and authentic. This shift in viewpoint will likely be as profound a human development as the transition from the Middle Ages to the Age of Enlightenment, and may take just as long. We were ready for the internet and its ilk long before they appeared on the scene.

The truth is, networked media can express both masculine and feminine constructs. The advent of these new media is pulling society back to more of a centrist position—a balance of the two sets of characteristics. Institutions would like to relinearize our behavior and relinearize media itself. It is in their nature to do so. They were born from a masculine template. Counseling them on how to modify their organized efforts is no easy task. From the standpoint of programming networked media, effective programming should employ an effective mixture of balance and choice: balance between masculine and feminine traits that always provides users a choice of behavior within the programming itself.

Networked media like the internet are capture (masculine) and nurture (feminine) media, In traditional media, for example, an oligarchy of sorts has controlled the programming. In networked media, oligarchies don't work. Networked media require programmers to listen to and engage humanodes, whether that programmer is a single humanode or a representative of a supernode. Networked media should employ a spectrum of choice from the passive to the active. People can't be *forced* to interact on a periodic or episodic basis—that would be too much like homework, and people will resist complying. New programming should create an experience in which humanodes are required to make a small initial commitment of attention. Often that is accomplished through a passive element, like audio or video that requires a low investment of time and effort to sample. But programming must allow a deeper experience should the humanode choose it, or should a programmer/marketer be successful at drawing them more deeply into the experience through marketing or up-sell.

IKEA is a huge home furnishing and accoutrements store with deep and broad inventory spread out on multiple floors. If you've been to one you know they have a little yellow line or directional arrows that lead the customers through the store, ensuring that they see all the items IKEA's marketing folks want them to see, if they see nothing else. The marketing department has *programmed* the yellow line. But customers can wander from that little yellow line any time they want and find a plethora of other products. They can take IKEA's path, programmed with IKEA's point of view (masculine), or they can create their own path, making their own shopping experience (feminine). Either way, IKEA stands to make money from any purchase. I think IKEA's yellow line is a great analogy for networked media programming. Give the participant a point of view that can be consumed with a low investment of time and effort. But always give the participant the choice to delve deeper into the world of programming—content, community and commerce—created for them, or that you've allowed other humanodes to create within the framework you've constructed.

The rise of feminine-dominant "visual media" during the last century and a half is recalibrating 5,000 years of imbalance. It's no coincidence that the suffragette movement appeared during the rise of photography and film as a media. The development of feminism was interrupted by World War II, but was reawakened by the first generation of women to grow up with television—the women who became the foot soldiers of the feminist movement of the 1960s. Image literacy has been reintroduced into our culture, reawakening a side of our nature that has, by and large, been culturally submerged. Forget about whether TV programming is good or bad; exposure to decades of television images has changed the way we're wired and the way we function. Perhaps the idea of dyslexia—the notion that some people have neural wiring that hinders their development of lexical literacy—shouldn't be considered a handicap. Dyslexics are often more facile with image, audio, or video-based arts and sciences.

Networked media are rapidly evolving to a point where they can deliver television-quality audio and video and imbue programming with the elements of content, community, commerce, and code, giving programmers the ability to provide both point of view and freedom of choice to humanodes. This evolution of media technology will accelerate the rise of imagery and portends a true balance emerging of left-brain/right-brain, passive/active, logical/intuitive, masculine/feminine.

As networked media matures from its technical infancy into adolescence, I believe women will become more than just the dominant users of these media. Women will also likely become the most fluent programmers. It's a fundamental fact that programming for networked media is complex. Tools are emerging, and will continue to emerge, to make it easier; but the fact remains that a different set of skills is required to excel in this regard. Our children are growing up with it naturally. If one wishes to understand the coming generations, and the changes in media preceding, paralleling, and affecting their emergence, one had better seek to master the literacy of a new age.

Even properly embodying all the tenets necessary to program successfully, it's still possible to fail. This is true of any game—learning the rules doesn't guarantee the win. One could come up with an idea for a networked media enterprise, one that brilliantly activates and capitalizes on the power of humanodes, and fail in the long run. For it is a daunting characteristic of the networked media environment that innovative ideas are rapidly commoditized—copied by one's competitors. Just as in any other competitive environment, one must answer this question: All things being equal, all other programming tenets and philosophies having been implemented, how does one differentiate one's programming from other like programming?

CHAPTER 11

Media in Motion

A loud voice cannot compete with a clear voice, even if it's a whisper.
—BARRY NEIL KAUFMAN

The networked media universe is copycat heaven. For commercially oriented programming, this can be problematic.

Even in past, slower-moving eras, bootlegging the ideas of others was common. Thomas Edison turned it into an art. Contrary to legend, he wasn't as much the original thinker as he was the consummate commercial opportunist. Many ideas simply bud simultaneously and spontaneously in multiple minds separated by vast distances. Some even argue that once a thought is manifested, it's in the "ether" and available to anyone else in the world tuned to pick it up. Most of us have had the experience of thinking up something we believe is totally original and saying to ourselves, "Wow, that's a great idea. I should do it." Then you proceed to let that idea slip to the back of a closet in your mind only to see the "invention" appear in the marketplace one, five, ten years later, produced by some enterprising individual who tapped into your ether channel (or so we'd like to believe). Carl Jung would have classified that kind of coincidence as synchronicity.

While access to the lifeblood of invention—capital—is frequently the difference in getting an idea bootstrapped into creation, capital's unavailability is all too often used as an excuse for not doing it. Today, the tools to create applications, products, or services for networked media are all but ubiquitous and becoming even more so. The flipside to that ubiquity is commoditization. Come up with a brilliant and successful service, feature, pricing scheme, or innovation, and you can bet your first round of financing that multiple competitors throughout the networked universe will copy your new concept in a matter of weeks or months. In the absence of robust (read: difficult or impossible to ape) differentiators, programming and pricing tend to become uniform across networked media over time. When Amazon.com proved that people would buy books online, other online booksellers rapidly sprung up offering many of the same features and services. When Barnes & Noble's online store cut its prices, Amazon quickly followed suit.

Furthermore, a person may use Amazon to buy books ten times in a row, but if they get an email from Barnes & Noble that says, "buy one book, get one free," most likely, they'll switch over—at least to take advantage of that one offer. A shopper is much more likely to break the Amazon habit in favor of Barnes & Noble on the internet than they would throw over one bookstore for another in the physical world because it is so much easier to do so. Compounding that price-flattening dynamic are comparison-shopping services. Pricegrabber.com, BizRate.com and RoboShopper.com all offer the ability to search multiple stores across the web in one fell swoop, easily allowing customers to compare prices for a single product or service.

While it may seem that no programming ideas are immune from commoditization—that copycats will endlessly spring up to challenge one's business—there is a short list of programming angles that can't be ripped off (or at least, not very easily). These robust differentiators are customer service, communities of interest, exclusivity, personality, entertainment, marketing, first-in, and last-standing. I do not include price as a differentiator (though it obviously is), since the main focus of this exercise is to find dynamics that buoy prices and margins, not lower them.

Programmers can and should build these differentiators into their networked media programming whenever possible, folding them into the pillars of programming, embedding audience metrics, and incorporating the motive-eight to capitalize on the multidimensional be-bit roles of humanodes.

Customer Service

In this context, customer service refers to a relationship between enterprise-and-enterprise, enterprise-and-humanode, or humanode-and-humanode. A high level of customer service, as we know, engenders a sense of trust and reliability. Consider the following example: Jayne Doe has an ongoing business relationship with a mechanic. The mechanic does good work, and his or her shop is on Jayne's way to work and is generally convenient. Most likely, Jayne will stick with that mechanic even if he or she makes mistakes here and there, or perhaps even if he's a tad more expensive. If Jayne receives a brochure in the mail that says, "$10 off your next lube job" from a competing mechanic, she'll most likely toss it and stick with her regular mechanic. The same applies to Jayne's hair stylist, manicurist, housekeeper, or any other service-intensive business she may use. There is habit and relationship at play here, which provide continuity and comfort. Marketing efforts aimed at getting people to break these relationships and habits can be very expensive. Every business aims to create a high cost of switching, perceived or real, for their customer base.

Returning to our Amazon/Barnes & Noble example, Jayne may jump to Barnes & Noble if there is a compelling reason to do so, such as a special sale. But if her father's birthday is tomorrow and (being a procrastinator) she has only twenty-four hours to get him a gift, Jayne is going to stick with Amazon as the known quantity, assuming she has used the service enough in the first place to know it's reliable. Jayne has a relationship with Amazon based on a level of customer service. She is comfortable that Amazon is going to do the job for her—and make it easy and painless. This sense of ease and reliability is a clear differentiator.

Furthermore, networked media's intrinsic feedback loops allow the service cream-of-the-crop to quickly rise to the top. All shopping comparison sites build in a "rate me" function. Humanodes have the intrinsic ability to provide feedback, giving other humanodes a snapshot sampling of the quality of that programmer's customer service. The same is true of any good enginet—Elance (freelance contractors of myriad skills), eBay (reliability and honesty of buyers and sellers), or Yahoo! Shopping. If anything, networked media's powerful feedback loops make customer service an aspect of networked programming that can be carefully monitored and constantly improved.

The networked media environment provides the capability for one-to-one and many-to-many continuous marketing. In such a fluid environment, maintaining a constant connection to the customer is a better guarantee of lifelong customer loyalty, and the lifelong value of customers becomes far more critical. The technology is available to accomplish these tasks today. The customers can get exactly what they want from a producer, and in turn, the producer can know exactly what version the customer desires—and later should be able to learn how it has been consumed. In many ways, customer service in a networked media environment is about handing power over to the customer.

William Lederer, founder of Art.com and Chairman and CEO of Minotaur Capital Management Partners, a venture capital and portfolio management firm, says his inspiration for the creation of Art.com (now wholly owned by Getty Images) began with listening to customers in an art, print, and frame shop at a local shopping mall. Most malls have one shop that offers a limited selection of lithographs and prints, and an outstanding selection of potential framing options. "I listened to customers," Lederer confessed. Patrons were having a hard time finding what they wanted from the limited selection. There was too much framing and not enough art and prints. Framing took longer than patrons liked and the store hours were inconvenient. Another problem was that the customer had to pay for the product before knowing what the end result would look like. "Put all those [complaints] together and this is one of [those situations] where the [networked media] can do it better."

Customer service should be generalized to support the humanode concept. That is, customer service in networked media must also extend to all five humanode modes—servicing the humanode as producer, distributor, marketer, vendor, and consumer—if the enterprise employs all of those modes in their value proposition to the humanode. In fact, enterprises can enroll humanodes to be customer-service representatives, especially for informational and support services. Building community dynamics like message boards, newsgroups, and instant messaging into programming enables like-minded customers to form knowledge pools capable of helping each other answer all but the most difficult questions. This taps into the natural proclivity of customers to want a hand in defining the product or service that they've chosen to consume—to touch the process end-to-end, from the moment of configuration all the way through to fulfillment and shipment.

Networked media also provides mechanisms to add a nuance to the term—a customer *performing* a service. The *New York Times* reported how Victoria's Secret had inadvertently left security holes in its website that allowed visitors to peek at customers' orders for underwear, camisoles, teddies, and lotions. A customer found the flaw and reported it. Victoria's Secret's initial response was nonplussed and somewhat ungrateful. Instead of thanking the kindly humanode, they reportedly acted somewhat indignantly, asserting that if credit card numbers weren't at risk, it wasn't important that strangers could peek into other customers' buying habits (as well as their names and addresses). The customer ended up taking the issue to the press, which ultimately resulted in the New York Attorney General slapping Victoria's Secret with a $50,000 fine. Here was a humanode essentially acting as an employee, and the company didn't recognize the blessing he'd brought them. It was a form of "customer self-service."

Cisco has been doing just this kind of thing for more than a decade. Patricia Seybold has noted that as far back as 1993, very early in the life of the web, Cisco developed a customer "self-service" website called Cisco Connections Online, which began as technical support in both an actual call center and a virtual website. If Cisco's larger customers couldn't find an answer to a problem in the knowledge-base postings, they would post their own message asking for assistance and wait for help from either a professional Cisco technical-support employee or one of Cisco's other customers—essentially a peer of the inquiring customer. This feature gathered a community (the next differentiator) of certified Cisco technicians that provided added value to their customers in the marketplace. Most technology companies now provide similar offerings.

AmericanExpress.com benefits from having a widely recognized brand name, but the site has not rested on its laurels. In an effort to cultivate a deeper relationship with its customers, AmericanExpress.com employs customer service and communities of interest differentiators through a complex integrated system of all its contact points with customers, in order to know everything about that customer when they call. Information such as the recent purchase of a new car or home signals the phone operator to ask if the customer needs any insurance for their home, or alarm services or other home-oriented products or services. This one-to-one approach to customers increased the site's revenues by 80 percent. By offering more customer service to existing customers, these new companies are not only generating more revenues, but are attempting to instill greater customer loyalty.

Communities of Interest

Human beings—and especially humanodes—are inherently social creatures. We gather around school, church, work, hobbies, clubs, and the like.

Networked media are the first media that actually allow us to commune and connect with each other en masse. This mechanism transcends space and time, and, harnessed properly, creates a powerful differentiator.

One could argue that newspapers or books formed communities of interest around those folks who subscribed to the paper, or read the book. Unfortunately, the printed medium lacks a mechanism for connecting people with shared interests. The connection remains latent, its power untapped. The telegraph was the first medium to build in-media connected communities of interest, but that community was limited to the telegraph operators and amateurs. The telephone put the first community media tools in the hands of the average person. But while the telephone did engender community, it was limited in simultaneous community capability. Clever uses of the telephone emerged that created near-real time community dynamics. The phone bank is a group of people making calls from the same location. A community of sorts, this type of organization is mostly used for polling, sales, and marketing. While a phone bank can scale pretty well in getting information out, or gathering information, this capability pales in comparison to the scalability possible from enrolling humanodes to do it for you. A telephone tree is closer to the mark. A prearranged calling pattern used to get information or an action request to a large number of people quickly, a telephone tree reduces the burden of having one or a few persons call dozens of others. Instead, in an organized and planned order, an initiator calls a handful of people, each of whom calls a handful more, who then call still others until everyone has been reached. (Those of you who are parents with school-aged children may be familiar this technique.)

Networked media offers a magnified and digitally articulate progeny to the telephone tree. Jim Moloshok, chief programmer for Yahoo!'s news, information, and entertainment fare, recently noted, "[networked media] communities are often made up of people that wouldn't be caught dead sitting next to each other on a bus." He went on to consider that New York Yankee fans from different social strata all convene in the same chat rooms, message boards, and instant messaging battles, unconcerned about race, creed, and checking account balances.

In the Cisco example above, community not only expanded the reach of the company, but also provided for round-the-clock technical support. One may be working late one day, stymied by some technical problem. But someone on the other side of the country could very well answer your posting for help or email you a solution. Today, pretty much any company with a customer-support function employs internet-based message boards, blogs, email, or instant messaging that allow their customers access to in-house customer support, or to other customers that may have had similar problems, or to FAQ (Frequently Asked Questions) sections with a compendium of the most oft-occurring problems.

Enabling humanodes to connect and commune with each other around a product, idea, concept, or icon—and offering this experience in an exclusive fashion—adds great value and is a powerful differentiator.

Exclusivity

This is probably the easiest of all differentiators to grasp since it is one of the basic building blocks of capitalism. Exclusive economic control of resources, commodities, intellectual property like patents and trademarks, or products/programming is an extraordinarily powerful differentiator.

Traditional retail models are erroneously applied to networked media. We can generalize a retail outlet as a people-touching enterprise or point-of-sale ("POS") enterprise. Campbell's soup can be found in just about every food retail outlet in America, from 7-Eleven to Safeway. While this makes Campbell's happy, it does nothing to differentiate Safeway from 7-Eleven. Similarly, Amazon, Barnesandnoble.com, Wordsworth.com and dozens of other internet retailers all have essentially the same product slate. Rarely do they have any product to sell exclusively through their store. Online or offline, retail outlets must search for other factors to differentiate themselves, like price, customer service, or convenience (of location, mostly).

In networked media, hours and location are the same for every store on the network. This fact alone chops down the number of differentiating elements available to online stores. Because of the medium's ability to incorporate commerce within the programming itself, "hard goods"—books, electronics, DVDs—are no different from a block of text, a graphic, or a video stream. All are elements of programming. Remember, in networked media, *product is programming*.

Recall that distribution is the act of gaining proximity to the consumer, and it must always be balanced with exclusivity. One doesn't find Campbell's soup in Safeway only; but you can bet Safeway would *like* to have Campbell's soup exclusively, in the same way a television affiliate gets to air *The Apprentice* exclusively in its geographic region, or a neighborhood theater gets to show the installments of *The Lord of the Rings* exclusively. These are typical "syndication" models.

But even syndication models have been bastardized in their application to networked media like the internet. Syndication arose in traditional media as a mode of gaining audience reach in the face of geographic restrictions and barriers—newspapers and broadcasters developed "local market" strategies that gave exclusivity to one affiliate in that market. Exclusivity provided the affiliate with a scarce commodity, ensuring that if there was a demand in their market, a price could be commanded that buoyed value and theoretically kept the affiliate in the black. If two affiliates in the same market had the same product, natural market dynamics would depress the value of the product or programming for both. Market pressure would commoditize that product.

Implementation of syndication models depends a lot on the underlying economic model of the people-touching enterprise. For example, say AtomShockwave were to "syndicate" an animation clip to 100 sites on the internet, each of which is supporting itself with advertising dollars. This arrangement is great for AtomShockwave—for awhile—until those 100 sites figure out they'll all be competing for the same ad dollars and the same demographic to which the animation appeals. In this hypothetical case, syndication drives down CPMs for all the affiliates. AtomShockwave could instead (and does) consolidate the ad sales and sell, in effect, a network, sharing the ad revenue based on respective customer traffic on each affiliate. If the people-touching site is selling the syndicated content (pay-per-view, pay-per-download), the pricing pressure gets heavy under the weight of the "law of commodities"—the tendency for all programming in networked media to become uniform and undifferentiated over time. Extending existing retail distribution models and relationships into networked media is wrong, but arguably it's defensible if conservative, product-based companies don't want to anger their existing bricks-and-mortar retail partners that account for the bulk of their current revenue streams. This acquiescent strategy has its pitfalls, most of which rest on the back of the retailer, or humanode-touching enterprise.

For nascent networked media programming—that which is "new" and requires marketing to gain humanode mindshare—programmers should do all they can to retain control of the revenue economics regardless of how much they've spread their programming across multiple locations throughout the networked media universe. But if the root of the programming already has established itself, there is no reason to spread the same programming over multiple sites across networked media. If Harry Potter news, information, downloads, games, trailers, movie clips, and other programming existed in one place only on the internet, fans would have no trouble finding it.

Similarly, if a product brand has an established following—Nike, Palm, Nokia, Gucci, Manolo Blahnik—there is no reason, other than the politically charged politics around their incumbent bricks-and-mortar relationships, to have product in more than one networked store. If I were a networked media retailer, I'd be bucking for exclusivity of product, or at least windows of exclusivity.

Networked media retailers, IP holders, and programmers of all kinds will design exclusivity into their own product/programming, or will begin demanding exclusive windows for product as soon as they discover that anything that exists exclusively in one place—or whose economics can be controlled—is a differentiator by definition.

Personality

Personality is anything with strong iconic representation. Coca-Cola, Bugs Bunny, Yahoo!, Batman, and Tom Cruise are all iconic representations of something—brand, personality, celebrity. Iconic representations can be trademarked, protected, and used in a focused fashion in any medium, including the internet. Personality, therefore, is a very important and powerful differentiator.

For example, if a personality—let's say Tom Cruise—is chatting on one site on the internet, that's a huge distinction—that's programming, not marketing. Cruise is imparting an exclusivity and uniqueness to the online experience on that site. The site becomes the "official networked media location" for the intellectual property, which could include anything from the rights to a television show, film, games, books, actors, writers, or sports personalities.

Mission: Impossible can (in theory) differentiate itself from countless other *Mission: Impossible* sites by offering a one-hour chat session with

Cruise. The following hour the site can further program a streaming audio or video of a 1970 interview with Peter Graves—the original Jim Phelps from the *Mission: Impossible* television show. Interactive *Mission: Impossible* games can be developed exclusively for the site, as well. Personality can be exploited in many forms in a networked media environment to build value and community. How personality is valued can vary wildly from person to person. One may hate one particular Tom Cruise movie, but love Tom Cruise, or vice versa. The value of personality may be in the eyes of the beholder, but what makes personality so powerful is that (1) it is impossible to copy exactly (there's only one Tom Cruise), and (2) personality is often manifested as something of powerful interest to people, such as an event or shared experience.

AT&T Wireless is the official mobile-phone company to the hit television series *American Idol*. Its wireless network is starkly differentiated from its wireless competitors as fans of the television show can only vote through the AT&T Wireless phone service—to the tune of millions of votes. As reported by Dawn Anfuso, the exclusivity AT&T wrangled from the show jump-started AT&T's text-messaging business. "The vast majority of AT&T Wireless customers have text-capable handsets, but were not using this feature. By incentivising them—via the ability to vote and get *American Idol* content—we were able to significantly increase the number of subscribers who tried texting, which was the primary way for them to participate," says Cory Kallet, senior partner at sales-promotion agency Einson Freeman. The promotion and contest not only succeeded in motivating people to try text-messaging, it met a second goal of driving repeat usage. "More than 2 million users had never sent a text message prior to the kick-off of the program," Kallet says, "and by its completion, more than 5 million emerged as repeat text-messaging voters."

It should come as no surprise that we see an explosive growth in *personality marketing*. Films and television shows rely on it—"from the makers of...," "starring...," "Academy Award winner...," et cetera. Sports "franchise players" are used similarly, becoming a huge draw for fans. Even consumer-products companies specifically manufacture personalities for the express purpose of marketing a product: Snap, Crackle, and Pop; the red dot of Seven Up; the California Raisins; Joe Isuzu; the M&M boys—all are examples of personality marketing. Personality marketing is part brand, part personality, and part character development. A person or character created in a personality-marketing campaign can become an icon unto itself, and inherently become a differentiator.

Entertainment

What is a networked media entertainment experience? Answer: anything into which humanodes immerse themselves during their leisure time—eBay, general shopping, multiplayer games, fantasy sports leagues, surfing, chatting, instant messaging, Kazaa, mobile games, and a zillion other activities. Any experience that captures a humanode's leisure time and attention is entertainment.

Some would argue that personality and entertainment are one in the same, but that is not the case. Personality is iconic; entertainment is immersive. Viggo Mortensen is an icon—a one-of-a-kind celebrity who cannot be duplicated, just as are Tiger Woods, Spider-Man or Yahoo!. All are differentiators. But *Lord of the Rings* is a motion picture people pay to watch in order to have a particularly immersive 120 minute (or so) experience. Similarly, Microsoft's Xbox game platform is a brand, an icon, a personality capable of competitive differentiation; but Xbox's "Halo" game franchise is a world within which humanodes can (and do) dwell for many hours.

Marketing

Marketing is a nonprogrammatic differentiator—in essence, the act of letting the most people and, more importantly, the right people know about product or programming: where and when to find it, and how to consume it.

Networked media like the internet lower the barriers of distribution for all comers. Lowering the distribution barrier inversely affects the need for visibility. One needs higher signal strength (marketing) in the presence of higher noise (mass of choices). Today with 20 million-plus websites out there, how does one raise oneself above the noise? David Israel equates putting up a website with "having your name in the Manhattan phone directory. I think I'm now advertising, so I'll sit around aggressively answering the phone when people might randomly choose to call me."

Two types of marketing become extraordinarily valuable: offline marketing and native networked marketing schemes. Viacom, Time Warner, Disney, and others of their ilk are powerful owners of offline media assets (film, television, radio). These companies now use these offline media assets to market their online properties through commercial spots and by plastering the air waves and products with URLs. Initially, these companies were slow to recognize the power of their offline marketing for driving traffic to their online enterprises. Instead, these companies bought ads from online media companies like Yahoo!, Microsoft, and Real Networks, or gave them programming for free in hopes of promoting their online businesses.

The way these large online companies duped traditional media companies was by duplicating the radio model—that is, free programming in the guise of promotion and marketing. If companies like Disney or Time Warner had required payment for exclusive marketing activities based on their high-profile brands, instead of giving their programming away for free to these online companies—companies with far less audience reach—then Time Warner would have bought AOL instead of the other way around. Yet companies like AOL and Yahoo! had an advantage over the Time Warners of the world within networked media; they were first-in.

First-In

The speed at which technology evolves and markets appear makes the first-mover advantage a potential competitive differentiator. Timing is critical to this differentiator being effective.

A classic case study of the first-mover advantage is Amazon.com versus Barnes & Noble. Amazon was the first company in the online bookstore space and Barnes & Noble spent years trying to catch up—unsuccessfully. The Amazon case has led many to believe that the first-mover advantage is the key to getting a solid head start in any new kind of networked media business. Unfortunately, technology is too volatile and unpredictable, as are the markets and people themselves, for "first-mover" to be a dependable "advantage." There is a first-mover advantage, but it doesn't often last for any great length of time unless one continues to provide an agile platform for innovation. Technology alone is rarely a long-term competitive advantage unless the technology is based on defensible unique patents. Competitors can replicate nearly any innovation—rapidly—leveling the playing field once again.

The success of companies like Amazon.com and eBay is not necessarily attributable to their first-mover advantage, which is ethereal at best, but to their ability to operate effectively within the dynamics of the networked medium to drive their success, and harness the networked energy of humanodes better than their competition. First-mover advantage sometimes doesn't sit well with investors, either; most investors would rather capture an already-existing market rather than create a new one, even though "capturing a market" is a much more expensive proposition. Out of the three titans of the pioneering days of television—Philco, Dumont, and RCA—none have maintained their dominant early positions; all three are either out of business or have been swallowed up by other companies. Without a complementary dynamic, first-in is a short-term differentiator. That complement is the final differentiator: last-standing.

Last-Standing—Mass, Longevity, Scalability, and Profitability

The dot-bomb mercilessly illustrated the last-standing differentiator. One can have great ideas, unique programming, fantastic community potential, and personality up the wazoo, but if one doesn't have enough money to stay in business long enough to be self-sustaining, the jig is up. The first-in/winner-take-all dynamics are still important in networked media, as indeed they can be in fast-moving innovative industries, but having the resources to persevere through rational or irrational market shifts is equally important. "Last-standing" implies tenacity, scalability, and self-sustenance; which ultimately boils down to access to capital and, finally, profitability.

These differentiators are important not only to media companies, but to any individual or enterprise operating in the networked media arena for commercial purposes. All companies must transform themselves to sustain innovation and build a new kind of relationship with a new kind of customer—the humanode.

The Future of Networked Media

Predicting the future is a fool's errand—particularly in the complex and chaotic world of networked media. Still, if weather forecasters aren't vilified for missing the mark once in a while, I'll take the risk in proffering a few forecasts for an equally unpredictable system. Within the next five years:

Symphonic literacy goes on the résumé Some believe, like Brad Davis, formerly of Interval Research, that in the far-flung future we will evolve a kind of visual language, drawing upon a vast database of network-based stock video available to everyone. In the short term, the symphonically literate generation will increasingly incorporate video, audio, and animation into communication that used to be exclusively textual, like memos, emails and résumés. Imagine receiving a résumé that includes samples of the candidate's public speeches, a demo of a product they helped create, a playable mini-game they designed, and a video autobiography.

Peer-to-peer systems go mainstream P2P systems will be used deliberately and successfully by many mainstream companies to replace or augment traditional production, distribution, and marketing techniques, often to alleviate cost or technology limitations involved in moving rich media (such as video) across the internet. P2P will also become the pathway for all kinds of collaborative efforts between anonymous or known individuals—collaborative white-boarding across the network.

It's alive! The proliferation of P2P technologies will advance the field of artificial genetics—artificial life—more quickly than expected. We will see the first incarnations of "living swarms" of pseudosentient software sustain themselves by swimming through the network—the telacorpus—feeding off of whatever computing resources they can find. The primary initial life-forms will be entertainment, but business applications—like virtual door-to-door (or peer-to-peer) sales agents—will soon follow.

P2P press We will see more humanodes creating programming and gathering information that used to be the exclusive domain of supernodes. With cameras now in cell phones, and ubiquitous network access, we will have millions of independent news gatherers in the world, more even than we've seen with the proliferation of camcorders. News stories that used to be underreported for the lack of news personnel on the scene will be covered as never before. (We're already seeing privacy issues crop up as those same microcameras are being used to gather paparazzi-style images.) Similarly, individuals will be able to set up impromptu news radio stations via services like www.Live365.com in the midst of natural disasters like earthquakes or floods. These impromptu services may even be able to coordinate microrelief services.

A problem with authority Networked media programming will become so plentiful that humanodes will begin demanding pedigrees on information. Two things will happen—there will be a boom for branded information sources, and peer-to-peer authority systems will be put in place to authenticate information. The latter is similar to the "ask the audience" feature on the television show *Who Wants to Be a Millionaire,* which employs a sampling dynamic that, given a large enough sample, yields authentic or truthful information. Furthermore, social networking—networks of relatively trusted peers—will evolve to vet news and information. In this respect, the enginets of social networking and blogging will cross-pollinate, changing our conception of what "trusted sources" can be and how they can function.

Product becomes programming Companies engaged in commerce through networked media will offer product exclusively available in their networked media outlets. Virtual stores will become more "programmed," in the traditional sense of the word, with exclusive and custom-made products that will only be available through these individual outlets, rather than through a multitude of different online venues.

At least one technological miracle will emerge Scalable and deployable technologies will arrive that will defy our conceptions of what is possible. I don't know what these breakthroughs will be, but my hunch is they'll be related to compression technology, image and animation synthesis, and free-range agents.

We will see more "brick and click" enterprises Most of these enterprises today, such as Barnes & Noble online, are retrofitted—the click built onto the brick. These efforts have been problematic because of conflicts in supply chains and worries about cannibalization of the parent offline business. In the future, we will see more new companies where "brick" and "click" are co-developed and fully integrated into the original design and vision of the company. We'll also see more companies born "click" extend their business franchises into "brick."

Humanodes will get paid Expect to see a rise in the number of people who supplement their incomes as humanodes. This trend will extend from full-time vocations, such as eBay aficionados who make their entire income from auctions, to avocations—businesses built around humanodes' personal interests that activate and pay them for their efforts as producers, distributors, marketers, and vendors. Many of us will maintain these side businesses in addition to our day jobs, while for others these avocations will blossom into full-time gigs. As a result, more people will be able to have some version of their dream job.

All business becomes show business The distinction between entertainment and nonentertainment companies will continue to blur, as will programming. Even companies with the most mundane of product lines will attempt to project the quality and gestalt of mainstream entertainment in their programming, and the use of media tools will continue to spread through the deepest reaches of the enterprise. Allusions to this last prognostication can be found throughout this book. This trend will not be limited to business. The power to engage with and connect to humans (humanodes) is a much-sought-after skill that extends to teaching, politics, fundraising, babysitting, board meetings, training and just about every human interaction imaginable.

Game and simulation technology will fuel a new type of storydwelling programming The rapid advance of technologies rooted in the electronic games and military-simulation industries will be employed to simulate reality and fool the senses—sight, sound, smell, touch, and even taste. This "perfect storm" of reality synthesis techniques will bring a new kind of literally immersive programming to networked media and television. These true storydwelling experiences will allow real people or actors to "live a fiction" so believably that it will make "reality" television look pedestrian and contrived.

Speaking at the Milken Global Conference in 2001, James Watson—Nobel Prize–winner and co-discoverer of DNA—bemoaned the difficulties that scientists encounter in their efforts to raise funds and gain popular support for their work. "Scientists are conservative...and also boring," Watson concluded. Scientists "don't know how to entertain the world!"

How true. We all need to be more "entertaining"—scientists, businesspeople, teachers, friends, every one of us—utilizing contemporary techniques and endeavoring to embrace a new kind of literacy; but we need to differentiate networked media from the canvases that have come before, and recognize the unique nature of this evolving form of expression and its power as an enabler of individuals alone or en masse.

The tools exist or are improving. The knowledge and literacy is obtainable. A better understanding of networked media dynamics is emerging, putting the power at our fingertips. A new age has dawned.

Index